P9-DDB-985

LEE COUNTY LIBRARY
107 HAWKINS AVE.
SANFORD, N. C. 27330

Mr George Eliot

Mr George Eliot

A Biography of
George Henry Lewes

by

David Williams

LEE COUNTY LIBRARY
107 HAWKINS AVE.
SANFORD, N. C. 27330

FRANKLIN WATTS
NEW YORK   1983

Library of Congress Cataloging in Publication Data

Williams, David, 1909–
  Mr George Eliot: a biography of George Henry Lewes.
  Includes index.
  1. Lewes, George Henry, 1817–1878 – Biography.
2. Eliot, George, 1819–1880 – Biography.   3. Authors,
English – 19th century – Biography.   I. Title.
PR4886.L4Z97   1983   828'.809[B]   83-6740

ISBN 0-531-09813-3

Copyright © 1983 by David Williams. First printed in 1983. All rights reserved. No part of this publication may be reproduced or transmitted in any form or by any means, electronic or mechanical, including photocopy, recording, or any information storage and retrieval system, without permission in writing from the publisher. Printed in Great Britain by St Edmundsbury Press. First published in the United Kingdom in 1983 by Hodder & Stoughton Ltd. First United States publication 1983 by Franklin Watts, Inc., 387 Park Avenue South, New York, NY10016.

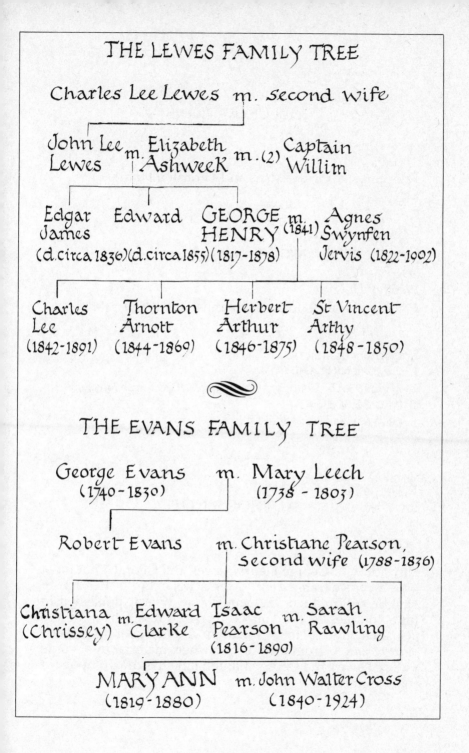

THE LEWES FAMILY TREE

Charles Lee Lewes m. second wife

John Lee Lewes m. Elizabeth Ashweek m.(2) Captain Willim

Edgar James (d. circa 1836)   Edward (d. circa 1855)   GEORGE HENRY (1817-1878) m. (1841) Agnes Swynfen Jervis (1822-1902)

Charles Lee (1842-1891)   Thornton Arnott (1844-1869)   Herbert Arthur (1846-1875)   St Vincent Arthy (1848-1850)

THE EVANS FAMILY TREE

George Evans (1740-1830) m. Mary Leech (1738-1803)

Robert Evans m. Christiane Pearson, second wife (1788-1836)

Christiana (Chrissey) m. Edward Clarke   Isaac Pearson (1816-1890) m. Sarah Rawling

MARY ANN (1819-1880) m. John Walter Cross (1840-1924)

ILLUSTRATIONS

George Lewes with Agnes and Thornton Hunt[1]
Mary Ann[1]
George[2]
John Blackwood[3]
George with the pug[3]
The Priory[4]
Whitley Heights[4]
Marion's inscription on the manuscript of *Adam Bede*[2]

ACKNOWLEDGMENTS
1. The National Portrait Gallery
2. Reproduced by Courtesy of the Trustees of the British Museum
3. Private Collection
4. BBC Hulton Picture Library

AUTHOR'S NOTE

Any study of George Henry Lewes and George Eliot must owe a considerable debt to the scholarship of Gordon S. Haight, who edited *The George Eliot Letters*, published in nine volumes by the Yale University Press. The author is also most grateful to Mr Jonathan G. Ouvry for his permission to quote from any unpublished material by George Henry Lewes and George Eliot that he has drawn upon for this biography.

PRELIMINARY

No biography is true. Every biographer is obliged to seek refuge in guesswork. No potential reader of the life of a man or a woman should be put off by either of these statements.

People are complicated and contradictory – immensely and endlessly so. The creations of the subtlest of novelists are childishly simple and diagrammatic when set against the simplest and most ordinary of real people. Tolstoy's Anna Karenina is a very stripped down lady indeed compared to Karen who operates her checkout till at the supermarket and is swept by inner turmoil many times a day. This doesn't mean that the biographer should abandon hope and turn to fiction. His business is to stick to what facts there are, reconcile conflicting evidence so far as he can, and present a portrait that is recognisably human, recognisably a 'personality'. There's no need for him to stick to the very great and the very famous. Carlyle wrote a life of John Sterling, a Scotsman born in 1806 who came under the influence of Coleridge. He suffered religious doubts which caused him to give up holy orders; he wrote a little, and died at thirty-eight. Carlyle's biography, which remains one of the greatest produced in the nineteenth century, has a ruminative conclusion which begins like this:

All the remains, in palpable shape, of John Sterling's activities in this world are those Two poor Volumes; scattered fragments gathered from the general waste of forgotten ephemera by the piety of a friend: an inconsiderable memorial; not pretending to have achieved greatness; only disclosing, mournfully, to the more observant, that a promise of greatness was there. Like other such lives, like all lives, this is a tragedy; high hopes, noble efforts; under thickening difficulties and impediments, ever-new nobleness of valiant effort; – and

1

LEE COUNTY LIBRARY
107 HAWKINS AVE.
SANFORD, N. C. 27330

the result death, with conquests by no means corresponding. A life which cannot challenge the world's attention; yet which does modestly solicit it, and perhaps on clear study will be found to reward it.

George Henry Lewes achieved very much more than Sterling. He wrote a life of Goethe which remains still the best biography there is in English of the great all-rounder. He was a busy journalist who reached the top of his profession. In the *Leader*, a weekly of which he was co-editor between 1851 and 1854, he wrote a regular piece above the signature 'Vivian' which gives him a claim to be regarded in the history of journalism as the founding father of all columnists. He wrote dramatic criticism of such quality that Bernard Shaw said that he was the only man in the business worth bothering about between himself and Hazlitt. He wrote plays – almost as many as Shaw himself though not of the same quality. Three novels stand to his name, two of which are still readable. In an age when the boundaries between philosophy and science weren't as clearly defined as they are now he wrote lucidly and fluently on both. In 1865 he became the first editor of the *Fortnightly Review* for which he immediately began to write a series of articles later collected and published under the title, *Principles of Success in Literature*. It's a book full of shrewd and practical literary criticism. And it's important to note particularly that word 'success'. Lewes believed passionately in success. If you had ability, if you were prepared to work hard, then success should follow. He was himself always willing to fulfil the conditions and looked forward to the rewards that should come after. He belonged to the type which 150 years on would be described as pushy.

There were many who disliked him on this account. Carlyle and his wife Jane Welsh, who came to know him in the 1840s when he was still only in his twenties, at first thought him ugly and over-eager but changed their opinions. His freshness, vigour and talent to amuse quite won them round and for Carlyle in the 1850s Lewes was 'the Prince of journalists'. The longer people knew him the more disposed they seemed to be to like him. The publisher John Blackwood, who was generous as well as shrewd, lost patience with him once or twice, thinking him greedy; but the friendship easily survived. Lewes had an abruptness of manner in claiming what he deemed to be his due, both in speech and in writing, that could disconcert people.

Simply on the grounds of what he achieved in his own right he is well worth a biography. However, his memory survives principally because for almost twenty-five years he lived in close unwedded harmony with Mary Ann Evans who under the name of George Eliot suddenly began, when on the threshold of middle life, to write novels which so delighted the Victorian public that after Dickens's death in 1870 she was rated the foremost in her profession. The books she wrote after 1870 were reverently received though not perhaps with quite the free enthusiasm which greeted the earlier ones. Anthony Trollope, always disposed to be generous, said in 1874: ' . . . She is sometimes heavy – sometimes abstruse, sometimes almost dull, but always, like an egg, full of meat . . .' The present generation by contrast has no doubts whatever about the quality of George Eliot's later novels. Discussing *Middlemarch* at length in *The Great Tradition*, F. R. Leavis says, amongst much else that is congratulatory, ' . . . It is certainly her strength as a novelist to have a noble and ardent nature – it is a condition of that maturity which makes her so much a greater artist than Flaubert . . .' So there she is, the little Warwickshire country lass, up there amongst the big vogue names.

So is Lewes simply a diligent, supportive nineteenth century man? Is his fame to be comparable simply to that of being the husband of Mrs Beeton? Or, going markedly higher in the scale, a nineteenth century Leonard Woolf? The proposition advanced in what follows – advanced in no cocksure spirit because the warnings sounded in the two opening sentences of this Preliminary should always be borne in mind – is that Lewes deserves recognition and remembrance on very solid grounds indeed: both because of what he did on his own account and also because he rocket-launched up into the stars a tiny, clever provincial lady who lacked self-assurance. Without him Mary Ann – or Marian, as she preferred to be called after she grew up – would have remained Miss Evans, a highly intelligent lady who helped fallible editors to put together their serious minded weeklies and monthlies aimed at the cultured few.

George Eliot wrote no novels before she went to live with Lewes in 1854. Once he was dead she wrote no fiction either. It was Lewes who suggested she write a story. He coached, corrected, discussed, encouraged; he re-wrote, he even wrote – especially when it came to dialogue. The early novels were 'our' novels; he referred to them frequently in this way. His greatest mistake was to advise her to take on the writing of *Romola*, which meant she had to plunge into the life of late fifteenth century Florence. She laboured pathologically at this, with Lewes to help. The book made her much money, but she knew that it wasn't right, and Lewes knew it too. The days after it appeared are the only ones, in a twenty-five year relationship wonderfully full of love, trust and interdependence, when, just possibly, hints of strain appear. After *Romola* Lewes's close association with the writing of the books becomes less marked. '. . . we have only insight in proportion to our sympathy. . .' he remarked, and he believed – rightly in the view of many – that Marian's creative insights flourished best on the Warwickshire ground of her childhood and adolescence. The later books represent her attempt at widening her range. But Lewes, the old professional, knew that for any creative writer the golden rule is: know your range and keep within it.

Why did he join his life with hers? And why did he remain, as he undoubtedly did, unshakeably faithful? Marian was plain. Lewes was small and ugly, but Lewes had a way with him. He was married, and there had been plenty of women before he came to marry the pretty, upper class, unconventional Agnes Swynfen Jervis in 1840. He was amusing. He could sparkle. He never lacked self-confidence. On the face of it you'd think that Lewes, unhappy in his marriage because of Agnes's infidelity (infidelity wasn't taken seriously into account in the Jervis family), would have been looking round for someone pret-

4

tier, younger, and sexually more attractive. But Marian, although she was plain, had that look in the eye which usually goes with strong sexual appetites. Lewes would have responded so that the physical side of the business, so important, would have been taken care of. Was Marian herself a virgin at the time of their first encounter? Impossible to say for certain, but it is probable that John Chapman, the handsome womaniser and shiftless publisher for whom she toiled, had already taken her to bed. Lewes was experienced enough to have been pretty certain about it at their first meeting. And if he was certain that here was no virgin he was the sort of man whose feelings for her would have been quickened rather than dampened by his hunch.

The closeness of their relationship, their tender understanding of each other were unfailing. It's hard to think of a marriage, legal or illegal, that lasted so well and with fewer hiccups. In 1856, at the beginning of their relationship, she told Charles Bray, the Benthamite ribbon manufacturer from Coventry whose influence was strong on her when she was a girl, '. . . in such matters [she was writing about a cheque] I identify myself with Mr Lewes, since there is no *meum* and *tuum* between us . . .' There never was. Of course there were difficulties to be overcome. There was in particular the disapproval of friends in the beginning when faced with their adultery openly and defiantly entered into, and later on public disapproval as well, as soon as she began to be known. This was always a far greater burden for her than for him. He was a man after all and in the 1850s men still made the laws and tended to slant them in their favour. A Victorian man was allowed his sexual freedoms; everyone knew about these but provided there was no brash breaking of the decent silences he could expect acceptance. Lewes's way of life wasn't materially altered when he began to live with Marian. By contrast her situation became dangerously transformed. Once she'd gone down to the docks to join him on the honeymoon journey to Weimar and Berlin she was at his mercy in a total, desperate sort of way which any present day woman in western Europe would find almost impossible to comprehend. If he should leave her now? It was a shuddery

5

question. Her beloved brother Isaac cut her dead for a quarter of a century – until she became a legally married woman in fact; there would have been no Warwickshire haven for her. She would have been a lone lorn creature, a Gummidge without even the saving prefix of Mrs. But Lewes remained faithful right to the end, and what might have been a disaster for her had instead a glorious consummation.

Did Lewes ever feel that he was playing the role of lackey? Did he ever feel that there was substance in George Meredith's gibe about his being a 'mercurial little showman' (with George Eliot for showpiece)? There's no suggestion anywhere, in his words, in his writing or in his actions, that he thought of himself as second fiddler. By the time she'd become famous, after *Adam Bede* and *The Mill on the Floss*, he arranged the famous Sunday afternoons at The Priory, their spacious Regent's Park house, when intellectual London came to pay court to the topmost novelist of the day. But she was his creation and courtship to her was implicit recognition of him. Besides, he felt that compensation was due to her for the ostracised years she'd spent in outer London lodgings whilst he gadded about and brought her back the gossip.

He was a generous man, with wide ranging talents of his own. He was very much of an actor too, a stage Fairy Prince, if you like, with a Cinderella he could work wonders with. It's hard to think of anyone else in English literary history who can lay claim to his special sort of mixed and strange achievement.

1

Red Lion Square, in Bloomsbury, has for long been a favourite meeting place for unorthodox thinkers. Moncure Conway, that serious minded American whose Christianity didn't resemble other people's, ministered at the South Place Chapel, Finsbury from the 1860s, and the Conway Hall, still standing at the north-east corner of the square, is a memorial to him, proclaiming the area, even now, to be a place a-buzz with advanced thinking and a continuing symbol of what has been going on in those parts for upwards of a century and a half.

In the middle of the 1830s a group of youngsters used to meet every Saturday in a pub there. Their number wasn't large – perhaps ten on a good night. Of course there have been thousands of such informal gatherings of very young, or youngish folk, lasting a little while until enthusiasm dried up, ever since the time – not really all that far distant – when ordinary men and women discovered that general sociability was becoming in Britain not only possible but desirable. The French Revolution was what gave the initial push to these socially unstratified meetings. One by one nearly all these Red Lion Square debaters faded away, lived their lives and breathed their last simply as members of an undistinguished and by this time entirely undistinguishable multitude.

The names of three of them though are still remembered – even if only faintly and by accident in two of the cases. There was James Pierrepoint Greaves who developed into 'a mystic very far gone in theosophy'. The Red Lion Square comrades found him funny. 'What do you mean,' someone asked him, 'by speaking of yourself as "phenomenised"?' Greaves had an opaque answer to this. 'I am what I am,' he said, 'and it is out of my Iamity that I am phenomenised.' The rest of them mocked – the temptation after all was great – and Greaves, resentful at being mis-understood, ceased to appear in Red Lion Square on Satur-day evenings. After that he slipped out of sight and has left no mark, no message strong enough to persuade posterity to spare him a thought. And indeed nearly all these young debators of the 1830s faded gradually away from Greaves's fashion and died ordinarily.

The second man, a good deal older than the rest – he already had a wife and two little black eyed children – was Kohn. This is a man who has achieved a quasi-immortality through fiction, because he is the original of Mordecai in *Daniel Deronda*. Kohn was a tradesman, working hard for a small reward as a journeyman watchmaker. Physically there wasn't much to be said for him. His eyes had been weakened through long peering at watch movements; he had bronchitis. But he had dignity as well; and he could think creatively about abstractions. He had read much in the work of Spinoza and seemed even to have understood what he was reading. He possessed, perhaps as a result of this, a serenity of mind which remained unruffled, even though his daily work was comparatively trivial and wholly repetitive. What he'd found out about Spinoza he imparted to the gatherings in Red Lion Square. In particular he instructed a third member of the group – and his is a name which has indeed survived quite lustily and to much pur-pose.

This was George Henry Lewes, at that time a youth of nineteen and studying for the medical profession. This was still only very shakily a profession at all. James Syme (1799–1870), a practical man rather than a theoretician, lectured on surgery at Edinburgh University between 1823 and 1833. As a youth of nineteen he had distinguished himself by inventing a method of waterproofing material, and advances in medical science initially came from this kind of ability. A serious scientific approach to medicine, a recognition of the very high status due to the medical profession generally – these didn't come about until the beginning of the 1840s. Lister, himself a pupil of Syme's at Edinburgh and ten years younger than Lewes, didn't begin on his transforming services to the medical profession until after the mid-century. A century or so earlier barbers had cut off limbs more or less as an occasional grim extension to their essential business of cutting off hair; barbers and surgeons did indeed exist as a unified professional body until 1745. When young Lewes walked the hospitals about 1835–6 his fellow students were artisans rather than academics. Saws and blood soaked aprons were very much part of the apprentice doctor's life. Small wonder that Lewes – strongly imbued though he was with the spirit of scientific investigation all his life long – didn't take kindly to his job. Keats twenty years earlier hadn't either.

The young Lewes gave it up. He could afford, within limits, to choose how he would make his way in life. He didn't belong to the gentry; for him there was no automatic progress from ancient school to ancient university. All the same his background was sufficiently substantial to cause him no difficulties or deprivations of the kind suffered by Dickens.

On his father's side he belonged to the theatre. His grandfather, Charles Lee Lewes (1740–1803), had considerable fame as a comedian. On the first night of Goldsmith's *She Stoops to Conquer* at Covent Garden in 1773 Charles Lee Lewes took the part of young Marlow. By the age of thirty-three he must therefore have got to somewhere near the top of his profession. He even wrote his *Memoirs*, which were edited by his son John Lee in 1805. He talked interestingly enough in these of John Kemble and of his sister Mrs Siddons. He had also readable, if longish, stories to tell of Garrick. It's clear that he was on familiar terms with all of them. He married three times, and it was the second wife, daughter of a Liverpool innkeeper of good standing, who was the mother of John Lee. We have it on the authority of Anthony Trollope that John Lee was very theatrical too. It's safer to put it so than to say that he was an actor. He was Charles Lee's son by his second wife, a woman who brought some property into the family, and the profession called him 'Dandy Lewes'. How much of an actor he was isn't known for certain, but he made no sort of mark as his father had done. But he does seem to have spread his talents more widely. He published a volume of poems in

1811, and a book which he bravely called *National Melodies* in 1817. It isn't likely that these would have been published without having behind them at least a certain measure of financial support from Lewes himself. They aren't the stuff which a publisher leaps at.

What prose writing he did seems to have been limited to the editing of his father's *Memoirs* and to defending the theatrical integrity and repute from an assault made in the 1790s by Alexander Kilham, a Wesleyan, in a tract called 'The Hypocrite detected and exposed . . .' The contestants, both Kilham and Lewes, were published together in Aberdeen in 1794. Lewes's manner here is neither sure footed nor sharp. Something which he vaguely calls 'a correcting desire of estimation' is present in most people, and this 'susceptibility of sham and infamy' gives the stage its efficiency. This claim enables him to assert, though rather mumblingly: 'We should consequently revere the stage and correct ourselves; we should not avoid it as the detector, but as the friendly monitor. If it speaks severe truths, we should condemn our own conduct which gives it the power . . .'

John Lee Lewes, then, was a man of and for the theatre like his father and indeed like his son also. He held a job for some while as manager of the Theatre Royal, Liverpool, and it is to be hoped he was better at managing a single theatre than at defending the whole many layered play acting structure by means of the written word.

He had three sons; George Henry was the youngest and can have had only the faintest memories of his father who died when he was only seven. He had married a Devonshire woman whose maiden name was Ashweek, and he died, not very old, in 1824. The next year the widow took as second husband a retired sea captain named Willim. This man eludes investigation as skilfully as he may once have eluded French privateers. He lived on into the 1860s and, so far as George Henry was concerned, must have stood for the realities of fatherhood much more clearly and commandingly than John Lee. Yet Lewes nowhere makes long reference to him. Francis Espinasse, a not particularly reliable late Victorian literary journalist who nonetheless has at times to be relied on for want of anyone better, wrote a short account of Lewes in a book called *Literary Recollections and Sketches* published in 1893. In this he has an extensive footnote. 'From G. H. Lewes's reference,' says Espinasse (the reference comes from a *Fortnightly Review* article written by Lewes in 1866) '. . . to the social persecution which in youth he suffered from his rejection of accepted creeds, it may be inferred that he and his father were not then on good terms . . .' The presumption must be that Espinasse carelessly wrote 'father' for 'stepfather' since in 1836 John Lee had been more than ten years dead. Captain Willim must therefore have been unsympathetic towards mutinous youth. This is an attitude found commonly in fathers and even more commonly in stepfathers. Captain Willim and his stepson did not get on. All the same Captain Willim must have exerted an influence.

Though Lewes was a Londoner born, he roamed quite remarkably when it came to schooling. When he was about ten he spent, with his brother Edward, about a year attending classes in Nantes. In his *Life of Goethe* he speaks of sneaking off with Edward, without a by-your-leave, to spend occasional Sunday evenings at the theatre. His French always remained outstandingly good; and Margaret Fuller, the American transcendentalist and early champion of women's rights, who met him in London in the 1840s, spoke of him as of 'a French appearing man'. How exactly one becomes 'French appearing' she doesn't say, but the remark isn't one to cause self-congratulation to Frenchmen in general. Lewes, though something of a dandy like his father, was small in stature and exceptionally unprepossessing in his looks.

But why should he, with no discoverable French connections, find himself at the age of ten going to school in Nantes? Captain Willim is the only man to call upon for a tentative answer to this. Nantes after all was and is a place for the building and repair of ships and a seaport too in a small way. Captain Willim may quite reasonably have established some trade connections there when he was in the Indian service, and continued these after he gave up foreign assignments. A long stay in Nantes, round about

11

the year 1827, seems a reasonable enough move for Captain Willim, and, if he was to be there for long, what more natural, in those days when accommodation rarely presented problems, than that he should bring his acquired family with him? The same explanation is by far the likeliest to account for Lewes's period of schooling in St Helier, in Jersey, in the year 1829. When he re-visited the island in the summer of 1857 he was busy with his *Sea-Side Studies* published in the following year. He digressed in this book in order to say:

> The Royal Square seemed to have shrunk to a third of its old dimensions, but with what strange sensations I first re-entered it! The Theatre [the theatre again] had by no means the magical and imposing aspect which it then wore. . . Turning with a retrospective sigh into the Market-Place, I feel the breath of former years rising around me. There is the very corner where we used to 'toss' the pieman for epicurean slices of pudding – a vulgar, but seductive form of juvenile gambling. Close by is the spot where we upset 'Waddy' – adipose comrade, much plagued by his leaner contemporaries – flat into an old woman's egg-basket . . . Among the changes, it was pleasant to find that no longer were criminals publicly whipped through the streets, as I once saw them with shuddering disgust. . .

St Helier's is another small port, and it's likely enough that Captain Willim should have been well known there.

The third place where Lewes was taught requires less guesswork. Frederick Locker Lampson (1821–95), important civil servant and clever versifier, wrote a patchwork book of reminiscences in 1896 which he called *My Confidences*. He says that he was educated in a 'huge, unregenerate school at Dulwich'. This wasn't Edward Alleyn's famous foundation of 1619, but a private place run in Lampson's time by Dr Burney, grandson of the musicologist and nephew of Fanny, Madame d'Arblay. The fees there were high, as much as £100 a year. But Burney had no talent for running a school and even less talent for choosing a competent staff, even though he was supported by the ample charges he made. Having set down his still sour memories of schooldays sixty years past, Lampson adds that G. H. Lewes was also one of Burney's pupils, having left just before his own arrival in 1833. Lewes himself makes no mention, favourable or otherwise, of this bout of education, but Espinasse confirms that he was 'sent to Dr Burney's once famous seminary at Greenwich . . .' Greenwich or Dulwich? There isn't any need to find a difficulty here. Writing of a school sited along the eastern edge of Dulwich, a man as slapdash as Espinasse might settle for Greenwich as a place name much more widely known. And in spite of Lewes's own silence, one fact can certainly be established as a result of his having spent some two or three years there: Captain and Mrs Willim can't have been at all pushed for money. £100 a year was a very substantial sum to have to find in 1830, and, although there's no evidence, it's likely that Edward, Lewes's elder brother, was sent there too. That Lewes left at sixteen and was launched on the world arose almost certainly from his being independent minded and something of a rebel and not from any inability or any unwillingness on the part of Captain and Mrs Willim to settle Dr Burney's bills.

What people do between sixteen and twenty-one is most commonly kept a secret, though 'kept' is perhaps too deliberate a verb. Thoughts and feelings at any rate are extremely strong and extremely disordered and writing them down later on becomes impossible, not because of a willed attempt at concealment but because you simply can't remember. As for actions and occupations – they merge and blur. If you are part of a flock, still being looked after, regimented, then a pattern will have been imposed which will give guidance when you seek out lost time; if you go to a university there may well be friends, publishable later on, who may have their impressions. But Lewes went to no university, and although he wrote fluently on a great variety of subjects he wasn't given to probing deeply or lengthily into his own past. It is true that he wrote a novel or two when he was young and these must reflect personal experience, because a novelist has nothing but personal

13

experience to draw upon, but it is impossible to draw a line in them between personal experience and imagined tale.

Fleetingly he worked as a clerk in a lawyer's office; then there was a spell in the counting house of a 'Russia merchant', and after that he began that walking of the hospitals which proved too gory for him. But more important than any of these were the friendships he made.

About 1837 he came to know the picturesque and notably adventurous Richard Hengist Horne, a man nine years older than he was and one whom a youngster under twenty would almost certainly find exciting. After leaving Sandhurst, Horne had served in the Mexican navy and during the War of Independence had seen action at Vera Cruz and elsewhere. Dangers had crowded in on him – shipwreck, mutiny, fevers and fierce animals. But Horne had survived. Still young, he returned to England and got busy turning himself into a writer. He published a long allegorical poem called *Orion*; in this he dealt at length with the tribulations of the giant hunter of Boeotia who got on the wrong side of Artemis and in consequence got stung to death by scorpions or else, so another legend insists, was altogether more grandly done away with by being turned into a constellation. *Orion* was an altogether too long allegorical poem, published in the decade after Lewes came to know him (1843). Horne published it at his own cost and charged a farthing for it. This was the method he chose – an expensive one – to show his disdain for the British reading public who, then as now, was prepared to spend its money on poets and artists in general only in the rarest and most exceptional cases. Horne was one of those vivid, second rate men – once, though now less often, you used to find numbers of them in the schoolmastering profession – who could kindle the imagination of youth. He certainly helped to kindle Lewes's.

The two must have chattered eagerly to each other because in September 1850 when Lewes, as editor, had recently launched the *Leader* magazine, Horne contributed an article.

These subjects [philosophical and religious ones] my dear Thornton [This was Thornton Leigh Hunt, later to become an important figure in Lewes's story] you and I and Lewes worked at with your father some twelve or thirteen years ago . . . perhaps not altogether in vain, but certainly with no such audience as we now possess, the time was not yet ripe . . .

In youth a gap in age of nine years seems vast. We don't know how the two came to meet, but certainly an eager, intelligent eighteen year old who had left early a school where he can't have been particularly well served, would have found in 'Orion' Horne a great stimulator. And of course the older man, Leigh Hunt himself – Thornton's father – shifty and shiftless and irresponsible in some ways, had shown a vast versatility throughout a life of sharp ups and downs and would have been exciting to listen to. Admittedly Dickens, not usually a particularly rancorous man except where his wife was concerned, pilloried Hunt as Harold Skimpole, but the young Lewes would have seen in him much more than a Skimpole, and Lewes would have been right.

It is again in one of the earlier issues of the *Leader* magazine (July 1851) that we have to look for another glimpse of Lewes as he was somewhere between 1833 and 1837. And this time Lewes speaks for himself. He is reviewing a book by the painter and poet William Bell Scott (1811–90), called *Chorea Sancti Viti*, and subtitled 'Steps in the Journey of Prince Legion', and it was Scott the engraver, not Scott the poet, who was on display. Lewes wrote that the book affected him strangely because it recalled for him 'days of hope, of labour, of intense ambition – days of pure study, youthful hope, and youthful confidence'.

At this point Lewes becomes less vague and more detailed.

Some thirteen years [He is therefore recalling a Lewes aged twenty or twenty-one] were pushed aside, and once more I was sitting beside the grave and high-minded Scott, in his low-roofed study, crammed with books, casts, wood-blocks, sketches and papers . . . He was at that time a wood-engraver by profession, but a poet, a philosopher and artist by ambition . . . I had then the twofold ambition of philosopher and poet. We read together, argued together, told each other all our magnificent schemes, and admired each other with unfeigned sincerity, were sure of each other's success!

Here in fact Lewes very closely resembles a huge number of other eager, clever young chaps all down the ages. He goes on – self-mockingly because as he writes he's an old man of thirty-four:

Among our plans was one to this effect: Scott had conceived a series of designs of the great typical events of life. I was filled with thoughts as he unfolded the scheme to me, and proposed to write a poem illustrative of the designs.

Our fortunes lay apart. I left England and solaced many long winter nights by the composition of my *Life-Journey of Prince Legion*. I have the fragment still and read it not a year ago: it is detestable!

Bell Scott in his preface to the collection confirms that Lewes was eager to write something which should serve as prose accompaniment to the engravings. '. . . Mr G. H. Lewes, who was then also thrusting his oar into unknown waters, proposed . . . to write to them, although I cannot now say whether the subject proved as genial to him as the opera criticism wherein he now disports himself . . .'

It is clear from all this that by the time he was eighteen or nineteen Lewes had made up his mind that clerking wouldn't do for him, accountancy wouldn't do for him, and medicine as practised in his time – although his interest in the biological sciences was still lively and got to be even livelier as the years went by – was also something he couldn't quite face. He had to become a writer. It is a compulsion which has seized many but usually the compulsion fades, swiftly or with painful slowness as it comes

16

to be realised that to write is one thing, to have the product published and paid for is quite another.

A major problem for him was one facing most young would-be writers then as now: how to meet the right kind of people, how to get into the swim. It was less of a problem for Lewes than for many because he was all his life a fluent talker and never suffered from diffidence. Leigh Hunt, indefatigable launcher of periodicals, undismayed witness to the almost invariable brevity of their lives, had in 1835 just gone fifty; he was striving to keep *Leigh Hunt's London Journal* alive, had his money troubles as he almost always did, and was still waiting – he would have to go on waiting for another twelve years – for that civil list pension which would put him on (relatively) Easy Street.

Hunt was a great radical and had been gaoled for two years in 1813 for libelling the Prince Regent. He was also a great man of the theatre and a play, one of his rare successes, called *A Legend of Florence*, would be produced at Covent Garden just five years on in 1840. Having been born in 1784 he was old enough to have seen Charles Lee Lewes on the stage, and this could quite easily have been enough to give Lewes an entrée into the Leigh Hunt circle. Hunt was endlessly sociable and no stickler for age groups. And Lewes even when young was never hesitant about taking the initiative. There is a letter of his, for example, written in 1837, not to Hunt but to this same Scott of the *Prince Legion*.

> 7 Harrington Street,
> Hampstead Road.

Sir –

Leigh Hunt tells me that as 'cordial natures' we ought to know each other. How for that is the case I know not, but this much I do know, that we both agree in heartily loving Shelley [this would be the anti-Willim rebel speaking] are fond of books of poetry, though you are a poet and I am none – and have no doubt there are many other points in which we so far assimilate as to enjoy each other's society, so in spite of its not being *selon les règles* of this most artificial of worlds and might by most people be looked upon as an impertinence (but which I feel assured will not be by you) I take the shortest and easiest way I can think of for our better acquaintance. . . If we like each other we have only reached that liking *per saltum*; if we do not, why, no harm is done, we can 'shrink into our conscious selves' once more. I am a student living a quiet life, but have a great gusto for intellectual acquaintance, with which I am sorry to say, I am not over burdened. If you will overlook this bit of contempt for conventional forms, and are at all inclined to extend the circle of your acquaintance, a line or two will answer all the purpose of the most punctilious and recondite introduction. . .

This is perky and characteristic. Scott, not in quite his first youth, was willing to be sociable although the two had little in common. Scott was reclusive, Lewes outgoing and talkative, eager to read aloud to anyone willing to listen from stuff he'd already composed. Scott had to sit through a drama about Tasso which never came to anything. That Lewes was excited enough about Tasso, though, makes it probable that he already knew plenty of German and that he'd read Goethe's *Torquato Tasso* published nearly fifty years earlier. Scott was certainly impressed by his linguistic range and his conversation which he thought 'exuberant but not very reliable'. When it came to Tasso, Scott ventured to suggest to him that he was perhaps too young to be writing a play about this tormented tragic figure who put too much trust in princes. But Lewes told him, with all the confidence of his nineteen or twenty years, that he knew, perhaps just as well as Tasso, what it meant to live the tempestuous life. He had been 'next to mad with love and its fallacies' he assured Scott; and there's no reason to doubt him. All his life he had an eager questing eye for women and in spite of his ugliness they responded to him.

During those five years between 1833 and 1838, years of trials and errors and extravagances, Lewes was shielded from the harsher knocks of life by having as protection the sufficient if not splendid circumstances of his mother and stepfather. The address on the letter he wrote to Bell – 7 Harrington Street – was the one where his parents lived. The Hampstead Road ran close by and in the 1830s London was beginning to thin out where they stood, and the main road was not far from the start of its climb up to Hampstead and Highgate. There were smarter places in which to live, but this at any rate was a place where he could live for nothing. He wasn't an idler though – not then and not later. In *Problems of Life and Mind*, which came out in five volumes between 1874 and 1879, he tells us that by 1836 he had sketched out – even if he hadn't written – a discourse in which the philosophy of the Scottish school was to be physiologically interpreted. Perhaps at nineteen he wouldn't have known quite what he meant by this, but it betokens liveliness of mind as well as a willingness to try. We know moreover that in 1837 he lectured in Fox's chapel in Finsbury – also on Scottish philosophy. Lewes wasn't, at any age, a man lacking in self-confidence.

In his twenty-first year he went to Germany and earned his keep by giving lessons in German or French. Germany when Lewes arrived there was a loose confederation of about forty states separately ruled in smaller matters but in the main under the thumb of Metternich who, after the murder of Kotzebue – a fluent and defiantly 'unpro-gressive' dramatist – by students in 1819, had been able with the consent of the Tsar Alexander to enforce the 'Carlsbad Decrees' which kept liberalism relatively quiet in the whole area virtually up to 1848. Prussia was by far the strongest single unit in the group, under Frederick William III – a man of sixty-eight by the time Lewes got to Berlin and one who on the whole was sympathetic to Metternich's view that it was better to stick to the devil you knew than to exchange him for another one (called liberalism or prog-ress) whom you didn't know and who might so easily devise entirely different ways of being unpleasant. Lewes's Germany in fact was pretty much the same one as Thack-eray had visited, and written about, in 1830–1. Lewes made Berlin his main place of residence for two years. The formidable, united German Nation-State was still far off.

But there was the *Zollverein*. Motz, Minister of Finance in Prussia after 1825, had skilfully furthered this plan for economic unity. Austria guided by Metternich might cling to the old imperial ways, but Prussia found it easier to become prosperous under the new system, and neighbouring German states found it prudent to join. Four years before Lewes reached Berlin, three of the larger ones, Bavaria, Württemberg and Saxony had come in. There still might be an empire of sorts with headquarters in Vienna, but it was no longer a commercial empire. Goethe had died in 1832. By 1838 there was a strong reaction against him in many German speaking lands, but Berlin on the whole remained strongly for him. Varnhagen von Ense and his wife Rahel Levin* were at the centre of this cult. Lewes studied Goethe and it wasn't long before he was speaking German almost as well as he spoke French. (Bell Scott has rather peevish words to say about Lewes's quick imitativeness which enabled him to shine apparently without much effort – and not merely when it came to the reading and speaking of foreign languages.)

The very bad novel *Ranthorpe* which Lewes wrote when he was twenty-five commemorates, if only summarily, his German years. Lewes is, or at any rate partly is, the young man Percy Ranthorpe who

. . . reviewed the progress of corruption, as it had contaminated his mind, and deadened his feelings – he saw himself ensnared by the arts of a coquette – lived over again the humiliation of his rejected love . . .

[So far it is circulating library stuff and not to be seriously relied upon as autobiography] . . . Well, I shall leave England . . . and . . . the memory of these errors. A new epoch opens. . . Driven from England [Circulating library again] in Germany I shall gain quiet contentment. Self-exiled from his native land, he has now reached the great turning-point of his career . . .

There follow in this novel preachifying, self-encouragement and certainties of a quite familiar kind. You don't

* Varnhagen (1785–1858) was in the Prussian Diplomatic Service and accompanied Hardenberg to the Congress of Vienna in 1814. That year he married the very celebrated Jewish actress Rahel Levin (1771–1833).

have to give up simply because so far things haven't been going exactly right for you. '. . . For shame, ye poets, who have carried within you an exhaustless mine of wealth. Yet knowing one day's poverty, have lifted up your desperate voices to swell the universal cry of pauperism! . . .' Then comes the self-encouragement.

. . . We are mortal men – erring and infirm; there are miseries awaiting us under every form of life; errors beset every profession, and unhappiness darkens the prospect of the most fortunate. Shall we then drag from the hospitals of the world all the squalid sick, and holding up their miseries, exclaim – 'Behold, such is life!' [Lewes's walking of the wards was still disturbingly clear in his mind] – forgetting all the health and strength, the beauty and enjoyment which surrounds us? Because poets have been poor, and have been driven by poverty to irregularities, and sometimes to despair, thus wasting their lives in infamous debaucheries, or in squalid misery – is therefore genius a fatal gift? . . .

Lewes, like plenty of other young men of twenty-one, is sure about the genius, sure that he at least is not going to be easily put down, conscious of irregularities and debaucheries about which, again like others of his age, he is openly horrified and secretly pleased. (There was never anything of the ascetic in Lewes's nature.) There's a good deal more about dissipation later on. '. . . It is a common remark, that the wildest youths turn out the best men. Dissipation, though an evil, is an evil best got through in youth. If there are wild oats to sow, let them be sown early; for bad habits later in life become fixed habits, and the rake at thirty is irreclaimable . . .' Was Lewes a rake at thirty? He wasn't free ranging and entirely mercenary as for example Thackeray's Lord Steyne was represented twenty years earlier, but he was none the less sexually very experienced as we shall see – Mary Ann Evans was always to be strongly attracted to men possessed of the wandering eye: Chapman came before Lewes, but in this respect both men were of the same stamp. Lewes goes on a little later: '. . . There is a

21

critical period in the young man's life, when he may be turned to anything that is good. . . . Of all influences capable of directing him into the right path, none is so powerful as that exercised by women . . .' Captain Willim was no educator of youth in Lewes's eyes.

Apart from Berlin, Lewes spent a few months in Dresden, one of the great cities of Europe until the RAF's shameful treatment in 1945. He delighted in the pomp and magnificence of Veronese as well as in the varied power of Rubens. He wrote a tragedy as ambitious and imaginative young men of his generation tended to do, but nothing much came of it. Then he returned for a final spell to Berlin. (It is possible he returned to England briefly from Dresden, travelling through Vienna and Strasbourg, and then returned to Berlin again in the spring of 1840 for a shortish stay. This would have been in order to sound out the possibilities of enough steady journalistic work in London to ensure a financially safe return. This wouldn't have been a vague, daydream visit. At all times Lewes was a practical, determined man. From the age of seventeen he had been attacking the magazines, and his strong gift for easy sociability had already enabled him to claim acquaintanceship not only with Leigh Hunt and his circle but with Dickens, John Stuart Mill and Bulwer-Lytton.)

What did Berlin and the German visit generally do for him? In the first place it served, and served most usefully, as his university time. When he returned to England in 1840 he was sufficiently well and widely informed to have authority. Not many young men coming down from Oxford or Cambridge in 1840–1 had a width of well digested reading comparable to Lewes's. A. H. Clough*, to be sure, had a knowledge of the thought and art of the ancient world far deeper than anything Lewes was ever to achieve, but in its range and diversity Lewes's intellectual furniture was more impressive than Clough's. He studied and worked

---

* Thomas Arnold's star pupil at Rugby, who came to have doubts about much of Arnold's teaching, but who remains one of the greatest of Victorian poets.

ferociously. Money wasn't plentiful and this kept him from being sidetracked. He earned enough to keep himself by giving English lessons to young ladies of the upper classes, and once clear of the young ladies he settled down to enlarge his own horizons. He had no English companions on hand urging him to come out and play. He was much alone, dreaming of things to come. There's a type of youngster – Lewes was one of them – who enjoys and profits from a spell of this kind. He rambled through the Tiergarten, a wild place then and romantically desolate under winter snow.

The universities of Germany then, as now, have never cultivated separateness on the British pattern. If Tübingen wasn't quite to his taste a student could, without much palaver or paper work, pack his bundle and be off to Göttingen or any other seat of learning which might take his fancy. The Berlin students whom Lewes met would therefore, in some part at least, have been wandering students, not suffering in any way from cliqueishness and eager to form alliances and friendships with anybody who was young and intellectually curious, whatever language he spoke, whatever territory, home or foreign, he came from originally. This meant that Lewes could enjoy what has always been the chief advantage of university life – contact with your equals – without having to bother with matriculation and the Thirty-Nine Articles. It also gave him a pretty good mastery of the German language to set beside his almost complete mastery of French. And the Germany he reached in 1838 was a place bubbling with intellectual life.

On December 10 1835 the German Diet had adopted a resolution suppressing a literary coterie known under the name of 'Young Germany', and five writers were specifically named as being prime movers: Heine, Gutzkow, Wienberg, Laube and Mundt. What they had written, and whatever they might think of writing in the future, was banned. Their works, even their names, could not be mentioned by other writers. It was a violent, even inexplicable, reaction to the work of a group of writers.

Ever since the crushing defeat of Prussian armed forces by

23

Napoleon at Jena and Auerstadt in 1806, a strong rallying reactionary movement had gained influence in Germany. The politicised philosopher Johann Gottlieb Fichte, forty-four years old at the time of the Jena disaster, and at the height of his considerable powers as a philosopher, set to work on his *Addresses to the German Nation – Reden an die deutsche Nation* – which gave fervour and dignity to revivalism. What he said in effect was that it was time for some xenophobia. What folly that the Germans should docilely follow French intellectuals and then allow themselves to be thrashed by French soldiery led by a Corsican. He told the Germans it was time to stop feeling inferior. The Germans had their uniqueness. They had kept their own language; others, the French particularly, had adopted a foreign one. This strong and questionable stuff was elaborated. Fichte thought that man was more formed by speech than speech was formed by man. Abstract speech is put together out of figurative symbolism. This symbolism forces those who use it to think back from the abstract to the symbol itself.

At this point in his thinking Fichte began to soar upwards like Icarus. The French, by virtue of unnatural adoption, had taken over a foreign language with a highly systematised abstract vocabulary. The effect of this was that a Frenchman couldn't think back to the symbol, not, that is, to the original, the ur-symbol. Because the Frenchman is working through a borrowed language his questing mind strikes deadness. Compare, says Fichte, the abundant life of the German's 'Menschenfreundlichkeit' with the chill remoteness of the Frenchman's 'popularité'. And the difference observable here is of the greatest importance. Intellectual movements in Germany are national – if Fichte had been writing 150 years later he would be beginning here to talk about grass roots – whereas in France it is the intellectual aristocracy alone which founds, foments and steers . . .

The gross injustice, not to say absurdity, of much of these arguments scarcely needs to be dwelt upon. But it was potent stuff argued by someone who was dedicated, sincere and endowed with an intelligence of quite exceptional strength and originality. Fichte sowed seeds and men born eighty years after he was dead grew up to see the harvest.

Of course Germans weren't to become Fichte followers to a man. The fierce reaction of the Diet to *Young Germany* in 1835 is proof that hostility to the new nationalism was strong enough and widespread enough to frighten authority. Indeed, when Lewes arrived in Germany, Heine, stricken and immobilised in Paris, was busy composing his *Deutschland*. Germany, Heine was insisting, wasn't the great triumph over Roman civilisation that Fichte wanted to persuade his fellow countrymen that it was. In *Deutschland* he laments the wrong turning he believes his country has taken. He's quite willing to glorify his country and, distant from it, longs to be still living in it. Do you want your native land to be one where poets and thinkers abundantly flourish? Of course you do, and isn't Germany therefore the best of native lands? But Heine wanted a Germany rid of the jingoistic nationalism on Fichte's pattern. For him France represented freedom and so, even though only an exiled paralytic, Paris was a good place to be in. One might compare the eighth of Fichte's *Reden* with the eleventh canto of Heine's *Deutschland*. Fichte talks there of the good omens for a long distance future Germany represented by Herrmann's repulse of the Romans on the Rhine. In the eleventh canto Heine works hard and effectively to show that that great triumph over Roman civilisation hadn't much solid substance except in the mind of Fichte, and *Deutschland* as a whole is a lament on Heine's part over the wrong turning he thinks Germany has taken.

Deutschland wasn't to appear until a year or two after Lewes's departure from Germany, but the anti-Prussian political thinking to which the poem gave expression was very much in the air during Lewes's time in Berlin. Clashes and excitements, both cultural and political, were in the streets, in the cafés, in the arguments between the generations that went on in shuttered homes. There can be no doubt that Lewes profited enormously from his two German years. They were for him the little room in Red Lion Square writ large indeed. They were an effective substitute for university years which had been denied him, probably

25

because his stepfather looked upon university years as a slice of wasted life entered upon just at the very moment when youngsters should be hardening themselves to cope with the tussles of life as it has to be lived. Lewes was by nature a nimble talker and a nimble thinker; Germany increased his readiness and his self-confidence.

He had by now made up his mind to try to establish himself as a man-of-all-work writer and had begun submitting articles to London periodicals. His whole stay abroad lasted for nearly two years, but after the first year he returned to London, making stops in Dresden, Vienna and Strasbourg on his way. Lewes makes his novel hero Ranthorpe live a solitary life in Berlin, but a happy one, 'preparing himself for the great combat with the world' and rambling through 'the wild Tiergarten'. Ranthorpe has a long stay in Dresden on his way back with 'a tragedy in his portfolio', and he feasts long on Dresden's art treasures – the Raphaels, the Titians and the Veroneses. Lewes probably hadn't the means to linger in Dresden as long as that, but it is more than likely that he had plenty of manuscripts in his baggage, even if he didn't have a completed tragedy.

There was a return to Germany in the spring of 1840 – probably because acceptance of contributions didn't come as readily as writing them. But this was to be a much briefer stay. Probably in the summer of that year he managed to land a tutoring job in the family of Swynfen Jervis who lived at Darlaston Hall, Chatcull, in Staffordshire, and who was a member of parliament. This wasn't quite the literary London life he'd promised himself, but it was none the less a job attractive enough to bring him home. And the attraction was the MP's daughter, Agnes, eighteen years old and the person in need of his tutoring talents.

Jervis belonged to a distinguished family. Darlaston Hall was a comfortable, roomy place situated about two miles to the west of Stone, in central Staffordshire. The leading light of the family had been John, born in 1735, later Admiral Sir John Jervis who had, with some help from Nelson, defeated a Spanish fleet of twenty-seven ships off Cape St Vincent in 1797; had been given an earldom as a reward for this and had chosen the title of Earl St Vincent. Agnes was an

intelligent as well as a beautiful pupil, and Lewes, in the space of six months or so, contrived not only to instruct her but to marry her, necessarily with the full consent of her elders, and the ceremony took place in no hole-and-corner parish church but in full and public splendour at St Margaret's Westminster on February 18 1841. The question that has to be asked is: how did this wandering tutor, possessing no educational background in the established, upper class sense, having no recognisable career stretching promisingly ahead of him but instead only an article or two and plans so far unrealised for a brilliant and successful assault on London journalism – how did he manage to land his prize so smartly?

The answers must lie in the self-confident strength of Lewes's personality and perhaps also to some extent in the character of Swynfen Jervis and the mode of life prevailing at Darlaston Hall. Sir Charles Gavan Duffy, one year older than Lewes, and an Irish nationalist who spent his middle years building for himself a most distinguished political career in Australia, returned to England in 1880 and wrote reminiscently about Irish history in the 1840s as well as more gossipy stuff about himself and the people he'd known. In *Conversations with Carlyle* he reports talk between himself, the seer, and the seer's wife Jane Welsh Carlyle, which must have taken place about 1854 – just after the Lewes–Mary Ann Evans scandal had caused a shudder to run through such members of London society as qualified to be called cultured and enlightened. Carlyle had been grumbling about the too erotic content of the novels of George Sand when, as Duffy reports, Mrs Carlyle briskly took him up:

'We had small right,' said the little lady, 'to throw the first stone at George Sand, though she had been caught in the same predicament as the women of old, if we considered what sort of literary ladies might be found in London at present. When one was first told that the strong woman of the *Westminster Review* [Mary Ann Evans, that is to say] had gone off with a man whom we all knew, [Lewes] it was as startling an announcement as if one heard that a

27

woman of your acquaintance had gone off with the strong man at Astley's; but that the partners in the adventure had set up as moralists was a graver surprise. To renounce George Sand as a teacher of morals was right enough, but it was scarcely consistent with making so much of our own George in that capacity. A marvellous teacher of morals, surely, and still more marvellous in the other character, for which nature had not provided her with the outfit supposed to be essential . . .' [Here Duffy interrupts the flow.] 'The gallant . . . was as badly equipped for an Adonis and conquerer of hearts . . .' 'Yes,' Carlyle replied, 'he was certainly the ugliest little fellow you could anywhere meet, but he was lively and pleasant.' In this final adventure, it must be admitted, he had escaped from worse, and might even be said to have ranged himself. He had originally married a bright little woman, daughter of Swynfen Jervis, a disreputable Welsh member; but everyone knew how that adventure had turned out. Miss Evans advised him to quit a household which had broken bounds in every direction. His proceeding was not to be applauded, but it could scarcely be said that he had gone from bad to worse . . .

Duffy had a close knowledge of the political and journalistic scene in London as it was in the early 1840s, but his 'Welsh member' is odd for Swynfen Jervis, who was member for Bridport, so is 'disreputable' wrong too? And if it isn't should the word be applied to the morals of Darlaston Hall as a whole?

Here the balance of probability points to Duffy's being at any rate not far off the mark. Young Lewes was certainly a rebel. He rejected conventional views and conventional morals. He had a roving eye and in spite of being nothing to look at was a busy and successful womaniser. As such Jervis, if Duffy's 'disreputable' is right for him, might well have been willing to admit him as a temporary member of his household where others, especially others with personable young daughters, might have rejected him out of hand. And Agnes herself might well have been eager to go along with her father's principles – or lack of them. Cer-

28

tainly, in the years just ahead she was to show small regard for the sanctity of marriage vows or for the notion of clinging only to one. If Lewes liked variety in his sexual life, so did she – and she may well have taken after her father. But William Bell Scott, who visited the couple soon after the ceremony in St Margaret's, certainly saw nothing disreputable or whorish in Agnes. Indeed he was full of sentimental adulation. A 'child wife,' he thought, and 'one of the loveliest creatures in the world.' And not only was she beautiful, he insisted, but charming too.

However elastic Lewes's views on fidelity in marriage, he was willing to take his duties as provider with the utmost seriousness. He'd trained himself to be a ready writer. Carrying no taint – as he might have thought it – of Oxbridge insularity, he was instead a European and a polyglot. He was also a hard worker and sociable and in no way averse to worming his way in. His range was unusually wide. He had the knack of being pushy without causing irritation or bringing on himself unpopularity. The result was that he began, very quickly, to make good progress in his chosen world of London journalism. If editors checked at what he offered them he was willing to re-write – and do this cheerfully. He told Espinasse, who was a fellow journalist and of his generation, that there 'was scarcely any editor whom he wished to cultivate to whom he could not supply just the article that was wanted'.

And he dealt by no means exclusively in the flimsy and the ephemeral. Periodicals that were serious and solid abounded in the 1840s. Macaulay's review of *Memoirs of the Life of Warren Hastings*, compiled from the original papers by the Rev G. R. Gleig MA appeared in the *Edinburgh Review* for October 1841, and it runs to 137 large pages. Today it could appear quite respectably as a book in its own right. Lewes's gift for exposition enabled him to please the editors of the *Edinburgh*, the *London and Westminster*, the *British and Foreign* and numerous other weighty competitors. In a while Espinasse was able to say, '. . . at a time when of . . . periodicals . . . there were several more than now [1891] he told me, with not unnatural glee, that he had an article in every one of them "except the damned old *Quarterly*".'

Bell Scott's 'one of the loveliest creatures in the world' doesn't seem to have been an unduly exaggerated description of Agnes Swynfen Jervis. People indeed must have marvelled at the whole swift affair because for Lewes to have carried her off represented a remarkable scoop on his part. She was the great-niece of an earl; he married her with her father's full approval; the marriage was at a fashionable church and the ceremony performed by the Rector, Henry Hart Milman in person, and Milman, fifty years of age at the time, already one of the Anglican church's most distinguished scholars and to become Dean of St Paul's eight years' hence, would have devoted neither his church nor his own time to the marrying of nobodies. Her father gave her away and signed the register afterwards. So did Neil Arnott, acquainted with Lewes probably from when he'd been studying medicine, a distinguished physician who attended personally on Queen Victoria, who also invented a water bed and was an expert on ventilation in an age that had great need of it. Leigh Hunt, a man of fifty-seven by then, was also there. A pack of freethinking revolutionaries, Milman must have thought them, but all the same he hallowed a marriage which wasn't to follow the path of orthodoxy for long. Of the elusive Captain Willim there is no word. With no house of their own, Lewes and his young bride lived for a while with his mother at 3 Pembroke Square in Kensington; they must presumably have gone to live with Captain Willim too. And it was in this house that Charles Lee, the first child of the marriage, was born in 1842.

Much has been written about the Phalanstery, the house in Bayswater – Royal Hill House – where an experiment in communal living in accordance with the views of Fourier, French social theorist and reformer, who had died in 1837 and whose book, *Nouveau Monde Industriel et Sociétaire*, had been published in 1829, was being carried out by an enthusiastic, but in the general view entirely unacceptable, little group. This consisted of Thornton Hunt, one of Leigh Hunt's many offspring, and his wife Katherine, John Gliddon (brother of Katherine) who had married Jacinta, another Leigh Hunt sprig, and Samuel Laurence, notable painter and miniaturist, who had married another Gliddon, Katherine's sister Anastasia. Royal Hill House was big and belonged to Arthur Gliddon and his wife, parents of Katherine, John and Anastasia. Fourier believed in Utopia and was prepared to furnish it with nuts and bolts. He thought that the population should be divided into self-sufficient groups numbering between 1600 and 1800 people. The daily round, the common tasks, should be shared and, to get rid of the numbing monotony of life as it tends to be lived, passed round. Men and women should of course live together but without the legal constraints of marriage. If a couple tired of each other then they should change partners without fuss and without disapprobation. If there were children of a first union, that should present no problem because children belonged to the group rather than to the begetters. The stark impracticalities inherent in such notions this group took in its stride. There were two more young female Gliddons on hand to see to the cooking and cleaning. Royal Hill House got along quite well for a while. It is easy to understand why Fourieristic and neo-Fourieristic social ideas should gain popularity with the intelligent young in the 1840s, confronted as they were by the swift growth of industrialisation and the insistent social problems consequent upon this.

Nathaniel Hawthorne, C. A. Dana, Margaret Fuller and other young American intellectuals founded the Brook Farm venture close to Boston in 1841. Much later on Grant Allen, who wrote *The Woman Who Did*, was to launch his 'New Hedonists'. And Lewes and his Agnes sympathised with the ideas of the Hunts and the Gliddons. They were frequently to be seen in their company. But there is no evidence to suggest that they were ever fully pledged inmates of Royal Hill House. Lewes, unlike Thornton Hunt who was his partner in many enterprises, was a diligent man with a chosen career at which he was ready and willing to work.

Eliza Lynn (Mrs Lynn Linton) was almost exactly the same age as Agnes Lewes. She wrote numerous novels which show talent and are still not wholly unread. Ford

31

Madox Ford, a very young man in the early 1890s, recalled her when she was old and put down some of his impressions.

> . . . I was introduced to him [Thomas Hardy] by Mrs Lynn Linton with her paralysing, pebble-blue eyes, behind gleaming spectacles. Mrs Lynn Linton, also a novelist, was a Bad Woman, my dear. One of the Shrieking Sisterhood! And I could never have her glance bent on me from behind those glasses without being terrified at the fear that she might shriek . . . or be bad . . .

In a novel called *Christopher Kirkland* and in an article in *Temple Bar* in 1885 she also put down some pretty waspish recollections of Lewes and the rest of them nearly fifty years before. 'At the time I first knew these people' – this is the prim old lady talking, not the earlier, quasi-revolutionary Bad Woman mockingly referred to in Madox Ford's memoirs – 'they were living in a kind of family communion . . . [They] clubbed together their individually thin resources and made a kind of family Agapemone . . . there were certain Free-lovers mingled with the orthodox rest and of these the most remarkable was that faithful and loving man . . . Thornton Hunt . . .' But, as for Lewes, that was a different matter. In a letter to Herbert Spencer she said she found Lewes 'more antipathetic than any man I have ever known and his love-making purely disgusting . . .'

But for all that, in 1841 Agnes seems to have found nothing to complain of. And as for Lewes, he was preoccupied and hard at it and in no way concerned about what the young Miss Lynn thought of him or of his principles.

2

In 1841 Lewes was in his twenty-fourth year. He was determined to earn a living, and make a name, through writing. He was prepared to write about anything and everything. A book, a play, an article – he considered nothing beyond him, nothing beneath him. His formal education was already a long way behind him and in any case had not amounted to much. To set against that he had managed, like a hard pressed business man in a slump, to diversify. He knew a good deal about medicine and anatomy; he had a good linguistic range – not as curious or as far reaching as had been the case with George Borrow* who had made his assault on literary London, a fierce but calamitous one, seventeen years earlier, but still far beyond the insular average. By now he had French, German, Italian and Spanish, and he once told Francis Espinasse that he read Greek for three hours every day. It's difficult to accept this last claim but none the less to try to accept it is neither foolish nor unreasonable. Lewes liked being flippant, he also liked to startle; but he wasn't a boastful man and he could speak the truth about himself more consistently than most. In addition to this, he could handle abstract concepts and delighted in philosophical speculation. The Germans had helped and stimulated him here. He knew what Hegel had had to say, as well as Fichte. He knew and, in his early days at any rate, supported without reserve the ideas of Auguste Comte as set out in the *Cours de Philosophie Positive* which came out piecemeal in six volumes between 1830 and 1842. He had strong political views. He saw very much eye to eye with George Jacob Holyoake, born in the same year as himself, a man more fiercely radical than his mentor Robert Owen and the last man in Britain to go to prison for professing atheism; and indeed, a little later on after Lewes

---

* Traveller, polyglot, eccentric. Author of two of the most enchanting, unclassifiable Victorian books – *The Bible in Spain* and *Lavengro*.

had become an editor, Holyoake was the man he appointed to be his manager.

From the beginning Lewes aimed his articles at the periodicals, the weeklies, the monthlies, the quarterlies. There were plenty of them. The 1840s were years of vigorous growth in British journalism. Lewes was never a reporter. He was a commentator, an interpreter, a populariser. Anna Kitchel, professor of English at Vassar from 1930, was making a reconnaissance in London in 1929 to help her in her study of Lewes which appeared in America in 1933. She ferreted about in the second hand bookshops of the Charing Cross Road and asked in one of them why it was so hard after eighty-four years to find a copy of Lewes's *Biographical History of Philosophy*. The bookseller had no difficulty at all in supplying her with a reason. 'We can't keep them in stock, madam. The London University students buy them up. You see, madam, they can understand Lewes.' That is a tribute to Lewes's power and, in part at any rate, an explanation of his quick success. He had the expository gift. Amongst the English speaking peoples this is a rarer accomplishment than might be supposed. The French possess it abundantly. We like to say that French television falls below the standard of the British; but listen to a Frenchman explaining something complicated on the French screen, and then listen to an Englishman tackling a similar job at the television centre: the Frenchman will be swift and lucid, the Englishman will hum and ha. Lewes could be lucid and direct in the French way. His year of schooling in Nantes had put its mark on him.

The first article which can with certainty be attributed to him came out in the September 1840 issue of the *Westminster Review*. It is a lively piece about French drama and his recent German interests are much in the forefront of his mind too – he quotes Hegel and is clear enough about where he stands to dissent from the romantic views of A. W. Schlegel. Early in 1842 the *Westminster* accepted another article by him and this one was also on the state of drama. The theatre always mattered a great deal to him: the genes inherited from his father and grandfather are sufficient to explain this. But Lewes was worried by what he rightly saw as the decline of a great dramatic tradition in Britain into drivel. The theatre devoted itself to the provision of frivolous entertainment for the empty headed. And as we look back on the state of the English theatre through the middle decades of the nineteenth century Lewes's concern can be seen to be fully justified. No writer of strong genius seems ever to have addressed himself to the business of writing a play for the stage. Dickens, interested to the point of obsession in plays and play acting, wrote nothing for the stage of any consequence. He was content to spend his vast energy and talent on private theatricals which offered farces like *Two-o'Clock in the Morning* or *Used Up*.

> . . . the drama [Lewes was to write in the *Foreign Quarterly Review*] seems still to be alive, but it is mere amusement. The age is undramatic because the drama has lost its hold on our wants and on our sympathies. The widespread social suffering of the day might furnish subjects . . . but these passions, these wants, find other channels for expression than the stage. The stage is now insignificant compared to the press. Man's higher appetites are satisfied at the library, he goes to the theatre to be entertained. . .

He hopes that someone may soon arrive 'with genius' to alter the present dire situation. 'Then may the drama, assuming altogether a new form, claiming a new office, and exercising a new and powerful influence, become what it was of old and be indeed "Revived".' Lewes wrote too about Goethe as a dramatist and especially about *Faust*. Part One he admired, Part Two, like many others before and since, he wasn't so certain about at all.

This theatrical writing, and particularly what he had to say about Goethe, aroused the interest of John Stuart Mill, eleven years older than Lewes and already distinguished as leader of the Utilitarians. That a young man of twenty-five could so quickly catch the eye of a man of Mill's intellectual stature says much for Lewes's qualities of mind. In a letter written in November 1842 Mill gave him praise but made objections too – a sign that Mill wasn't busying himself simply with empty and facile encouragement.

> I think your article on Goethe decidedly your highest flight yet . . . it recommends itself to my knowledge of him as *truer* than any other writing on the subject I have met with. There are some striking thoughts in it, and although there is considerable Carlylism in the opening pages and something of the *Tranchant* manner which makes people call you by various uncomplimentary names indicative of self-conceit, both of these defects disappear as you go on. . .

Mill, an important man, even by then, in the India Office, was as lofty and austere as his father James Mill had been (he had died in 1836). But the son hadn't quite the father's bloodlessness. James Mill's *Analysis of the Phenomena of the Human Mind* had attached only small importance to people's emotions in its scheme of things. By contrast the son held that a human being intent upon self-development (as every human being deserving of such a title ought to be) should never dismiss feelings as unimportant because it was directly from the feelings that the human imaginative faculty sprang. Mill was writing along these lines in the *London and Westminster Review* between 1838 and 1840. A man in his middle thirties, he was becoming someone who had to be listened to. He was important. Outstandingly able people, like for example the historian George Grote, were associated with him. Lewes had every right to feel pleased and proud at being taken notice of in such quarters. He replied to Mill, at pains to make it clear that he had missed nothing written by him that had ever appeared in print. 'You are certainly a conjurer in finding out my old obscure articles,' wrote Mill in reply. '. . . The "Genius" paper is no favourite with me, especially in its boyish stile which I have since carefully striven to correct. It was written in the height of my Carlylism . . . Carlyle's costume should be left to Carlyle whom alone it becomes . . . As to my "Logic", it has all to be written yet.' And Mill adds an underlined postscript. '*Come soon.*' So, already, it would appear, the thrustful Lewes had made himself personally known to Mill either at India House or in Kensington Square where Mill lived. There is much more in the letter than is quoted here. Mill has obviously taken the young man up and is intent upon giving him guidance and encouragement. He scents a disciple – and Mill was choosy. Even before his marriage Lewes was sending him his articles before submitting them to editors and Mill was responding with close comment, '. . . I have read your Ms which I think very well done & likely when finished and finally revised to be quite suitable for the *Edinburgh.* You have not, however, convinced me that the line between poetry and passionate writing of any kind is best drawn when metre ends and prose begins . . .' Mill goes on to justify his doubts at length before ending with: 'And now without any more on these rather untimely matters let me conclude by wishing you as I do most cordially all possible prosperity and happiness in your new condition, which all I have heard of the lady inclines me to regard as an enviable one . . .'

Agnes, once she had become Mrs Lewes, was eager to foster this relationship of her husband's and to put it on a more fully personal level, but she found it was hard to lure Mill down from his mountain height. 'I am afraid,' he wrote, 'Mrs Lewes will by this time find out that instead of being the *boree* on the subject of an unfinished article I have a strong vocation for being the *borer* in respect of it. By the way, will you kindly make my acknowledgements to her for an invitation I have been favoured with & the *spirit* of which I most cordially accept (I never go to evening parties in the *flesh*) & believe me ever . . .'

Perhaps Mill had heard about the sort of evening parties the young Leweses gave and went to. They doubtless wouldn't have shocked him, but there'd have been nothing in them to attract his cold seriousness. The young Miss Lynn, clever and emancipated though she thought herself, does seem to have been shocked however. It needs to be remembered, though, that she was old when she came to write down, in a novel and an article, her memories of things seen and done long ago. Perhaps by then she was indeed, as Holyoake affirmed, 'suffering from the fatty degeneration of the understanding that comes to the well-fed Liberal'; perhaps the Miss Lynn of the 1840s enjoyed it all the more than the successful novelist of the 1880s, Mrs Lynn Linton, was willing to admit. 'Indecorous' had after all by 1880 become a much more all embracing adjective than it had been in 1840. Take the party she went to given by the Milner Gibsons. Milner Gibson became MP for Manchester in 1841 and later for a short while (1859–60) was President of the Board of Trade. The Milner Gibsons belonged to the liberated ones. He spoke fierily against the Corn Laws, and was radical in thought and deed; any parties given by such a couple would back away from stiffness and formality. The Leweses were there as were Thornton Leigh Hunt and his wife Kate. Thornton, the young woman thought, was more philosophical than Lewes and more free from grossness. Lewes was so ugly, and really quite frighteningly bold. Mrs Milner Gibson was after all the wife of a member of parliament. Was it quite the thing for Lewes to shout across to her, 'Arethusa! Come here!'? And then, when Mrs Milner Gibson very properly took no notice of Lewes's improper imperative, what did Lewes do? Was he abashed? Did he hasten to apologise? He wasn't and didn't. He immediately walked over and sat on the arm of her chair. Lewes simply wanted to be close to her and did whatever was necessary to bring that about. He was always like that: unaffected and aggressive in the nicest way. Miss Lynn was also much put out – or at any rate Mrs Lynn Linton said she had been – by the way the gentleman sang. 'Samuel Hall' was a favourite, a ditty that remained current amongst undergraduates in changing rooms and on bump supper nights right down to the 1930s. 'Oh! His name was Samuel Hall/*And* he only had one ball/Damn his eyes! Blast his soul! Bloody hell!' The words don't now seem as outrageous as all that, but Miss Lynn from Keswick wasn't amused.

It's evident though that Mill didn't steer altogether clear of Lewes's pretty Agnes. From the following bit of weighty joviality he seems to have given the couple bachelor entertainment (Mill himself didn't marry till 1851): 'I will make no more crusty tea for the incarnate solecism if she calls me a w—— but I will not write the atrocious word. No one is *that* but from a consciousness of being hated by women and deserving to be so . . .' 'Incarnate solecism' is a bit opaque, but Mill is presumably referring to Agnes, and in bringing in 'solecism' he's reminding the pair of them that a crusty old bachelor doesn't mind a young woman calling him a whoremonger. When Lewes had been in correspondence with George Sand (there was to be more than one female George in Lewes's life), he sent the reply on for Mill to see, and Mill answered:

I return Sand's letter which it was very pleasant to have an opportunity of reading. I have no right or claim to send any message to her but I should be very willing she should know that there are other warm admirers of her writings and of herself even in this canting land – among whom I am neither the only nor the best . . . I am by no means biassed in favour of the article [one of Lewes's] by its compliment to myself, which rather tells the other way, for I have a dislike of seeing my own ugly name in print. Tell the lady, with my best wishes, that I am getting very hungry. Yours (in the dual number) . . . After receiving your last note I re-open this to add my warmest congratulations.

It is strange to find Mill whom one thinks of as a man who was all mind and no body, busy at the time on his *Logic*, editing the *London and Westminster Review*, expressing himself so warmly in favour of the uninhibited Sand who lay down naked on a bed, and invited Prosper Mérimée, an experienced roué but at that moment quite taken aback, to do what he could for her and was genuinely disappointed when the author of *Carmen* failed through surprise to come up to scratch. It's less surprising to find that Mill had not taken long to yield to the attractive warmth of the young Agnes and was prepared to invite himself archly to a meal however much he disliked evening parties. This note must have been written at the end of November 1842 because the postscript refers to the birth of the Lewes's first child, Charles Lee, on November 24 1842.

Articles for the reviews were expected, all through the nineteenth century, to be long and solid. The *Edinburgh Review* for October 1841, for example, contained a notice, by Macaulay, of an edition of the memoirs of Warren Hastings (Governor of Bengal, 1772–84) compiled by the Reverend G. R. Gleig. Macaulay's contribution runs to about 48,000 words – by today's standards a shortish book on its own account. Lewes stretched his quick mind and retentive memory to the utmost in providing articles for these reviews (there were two in the *Edinburgh* itself during 1843, on 'Dramatic Reform' and on 'The Classification of Theatres').

In addition he was at work on *The Biographical History of Philosophy*, a commission from the publisher Charles Knight, born in 1791, the son of a Windsor bookseller, who went to London in 1822 and was one of the first to realise – many were to come along later – that industrialisation and the consequent rapid coming together of large numbers of people in urban groups were bound to give rise to a hunger for self-improvement and self-education. Knight began a venture which he called Knight's Weekly Volume Series. Each book cost a shilling and Lewes's *Biographical History* made up four of the series. Knight was delighted with what Lewes produced. The hungry mouths looked up and were fed. Lewes's four books, each one quite small, were bought. And the uninstructed masses weren't the only ones to be pleased. The work took a lasting hold and the cultured few nodded approval. Frederick Harrison, pundit and Positivist, who was only fourteen when the *Biographical History* came out in 1845, could say of it a very long time after that it had, 'influenced the thought of the present generation almost more than any single book except Mr Mill's *Logic*', and Beatrice Webb, looking back on her life in her autobiographical book called *My Apprenticeship* published in 1926, speaks of Lewes's work as being of help when as a young woman she was trying to discover where exactly she herself stood on abstract matters.

Lewes's secret was that he always managed, whatever

subject he was tackling, never to be wholly abstract. Lewes's philosophers weren't merely walking systems and theories. They had all of them lived lives and he was careful to describe these with all the considerable vivacity of which he was capable. He himself is no philosopher. He's quite candid about this, indeed it becomes gradually clear that for philosophy in its fullest abstract sense, for systems which float high in the air with no tethering cable reaching down to the solid earth, he hasn't really much sympathy. Metaphysics is a clever man's plaything; there's no need for the ordinary person to approach it with any special awe or reverence. First causes? Last things? Here the metaphysician will do well not to be too venturesome. He should stick to his own particular bit of garden because if he goes outside he may find himself sinking in a quagmire as unplumbable as Bottom's dream. Only the scientist, by observing scrupulously, by being patient, by being content to go forward only in very tiny steps, may some time in the far future arrive at what may with any confidence be called conclusions. In other words Lewes falls into line behind Auguste Comte whom he greatly admires; the hard headed modern man should accept the Comtist position as the only one really tenable. Lewes is brisk and confident about all this – and it was probably only his acceptance of Comte's aggressive certainties that enabled him to tackle the enormous task which Knight proposed. He puts his own position quite crisply in the preface he wrote for the 1846 edition of his book. The last paragraph of this runs: 'Some objection may, perhaps, be made to the amount of criticism mingled with the exposition. In this, though sinning against the office of Historian, I have been prompted by the one steady purpose which gives this work its unity, viz: That of showing by Argument, what History shows by Facts.'

The biographies of his philosophers which Lewes prefixes to his study of their intellectual antics are thumbnail and readable:

Francis Bacon was born on the 22nd January, 1561. Mr Basil Montagu, the laborious and affectionate (we had almost said idolatrous) biographer of Bacon, wishes us to

41

believe that the family was ancient and illustrious; and favours us with some flourishes about Bacon retiring to 'the halls of his ancestors'. This is somewhat different from the story of Bacon's grandfather having kept the sheep of the Abbot of Bury . . .

[Kant] lived to a great age and never once quitted the snows of murky Königsberg.

Early in the seventeenth century, on a fair evening of summer, a little Jewish boy was playing with his sisters on the Burgwal of Amsterdam, close to the Portuguese synagogue . . . Amsterdam was noisy with the creaking of cordage, the bawling of sailors, the busy trafficking of traders . . . the whole scene was vivid with the greatness and the littleness of commerce. Heedless of all this turmoil . . . untouched by any of those strange questionings which a restless spirit cannot answer, but which it refuses to have answered by others – heedless of everything but his game, that little boy played merrily with his sisters. That boy was Benedict Spinoza . . .

This isn't much more than quick journalistic patter, if you like. But all the same you feel that an eager young man is writing and that he's prepared to take a little trouble to awaken your interest.

Lewes isn't at all overawed even by Hegel.

We may, [says this young man] by way of anticipation, observe that Hegel's notion of God becoming conscious of himself in Philosophy, and thereby attaining his highest development, is founded on the above process. [i.e. the process whereby two negatives make a positive or two minuses a plus] God as pure being can only pass into reality through a negation; in Philosophy he negatives this negation, and thus becomes a *positive* affirmation. As a display of perverse ingenuity, stolidly convinced of its entire seriousness and importance – as an example of unhesitating confidence in the validity of verbal distinctions – the philosophy of Hegel has perhaps never been equalled. As Dr Ott epigrammatically remarks, 'Ici l'absurdité se pose comme méthode fondamentale.' Twenty volumes 8vo – twenty serious volumes attest the seriousness with which this method was pursued.

As he grew older Lewes came to see that it wasn't perhaps wise to be quite as larky about Hegel as he had been as a young man. And he was able to make modifications and enlargements of the original text because the *Biographical History* was a large and lasting success with the public. Edition after edition was called for all through the middle years of the century, and by the time he came to write his last preface to it, in December 1870, the book had been largely rewritten.

I had long felt that . . . Leibniz and Hegel were very inadequately presented . . . In the edition now issued my readers of twenty years ago will hardly recognise the *Biographical History of Philosophy*, so considerable have been the alterations and enlargements. They will see, indeed, the spirit and the purpose still unchanged; but this will be like recognising in an iron-grey citizen the feature of the third-form boy. I adhered to the Positive Philosophy in 1845, and I adhere to it still. But . . . much that was conviction then has ceased to be conviction now: my estimates of men and theories have altered in the course of the years . . .

So he still fights under the Comtist-Positivist flag, but reading the amended, iron grey man one sees that even Comte isn't by now quite the answer to everything.

The book is written for a market and lays claim to no original profundities. All the same it is a remarkable achievement for a young man still in his twenties – more especially when it's remembered that the *History* was only a part, even a small part, of what the newly married man, with babies coming along, produced between 1841 and 1846. The amount of reading which his book must have required is staggering. When had he found time for it all? The answer to this lies almost certainly in his two German years – his privately conducted university time. He must have been lonely there – no enduring friendships appear to have been struck – and money must have been tight. He read with the intensity and voracity which only intelligent youngsters at the end of their teens can manage. When Knight signed him up Lewes must have known that he'd gone over much of the ground already. Without that certainty he couldn't possibly have undertaken it. The book is forthright and lively; it has the *'tranchant* manner' which Mill had so much admired in one of his *Review* articles on Goethe.

How many exactly of these articles he had published between 1841 and 1846 can't be known because it was a time when anonymity was much in vogue and by-lines hadn't the importance they've since acquired, but twenty-one substantial essays we can be certain of: seven in the *British and Foreign Review* (on Hegel's aesthetics, the character and works of Goethe, French metaphysics, the state of historical science in France, the state of criticism in France, Alfieri, and the three Fausts – of Goethe, Marlowe and Calderón); two in the *Edinburgh* (on dramatic reform and the classification of theatres, and on Lessing); four in the *Foreign and Quarterly Review* (English history and character on the French stage, the Spanish drama – Lope de Vega and Calderón, on A. W. Schlegel, and the rise and fall of European drama); one in the *New Quarterly Review* on Jean Paul Richter; seven in the *Westminster Review* (on French drama – his first published piece in September 1840, on Shelley, authors and managers – the regeneration of the drama, on recent tragedies, on English criticism and anonymous writing, on Spinoza's life and works, and charges against Niebuhr). It's a formidable list. He hops about over western Europe (France, Germany, Italy, Spain) and everywhere appears at home and informed. Philosophy, science, dramatic criticism, general literary criticism – Lewes is a confident, buccaneering polymath.

How many Englishmen, writing in 1844, could have discussed the treatment of the Faust-figure by three different writers of genius in three different languages? George Borrow? Well, perhaps, but George was always such a narrowly linguistic man and what he might have produced would have been one sided and lame. Edward

FitzGerald? On Marlowe and Calderón he could have done as well as Lewes, and probably better, but German wasn't much in his line. 'Another shot have I made,' FitzGerald told Lowell in 1878, 'at *Faust* in Bayard Taylor's version: but I do not even get on with him as with Hayward [This was Abraham Hayward, fourteen years older than Lewes, who wrote busily and well for the magazines and who produced in 1833 a prose version of Goethe's *Faust* Part One] hampered as he [Taylor] is with his allegiance to original metres etc. His Notes I was interested in: but I shall die ungoethed, I doubt, so far as poetry goes . . .' It's hard to think of anybody else sufficiently well equipped linguistically to have made any showing comparable with Lewes's on an ambitious subject such as this. And yet here is a young man of twenty-seven, with no Trinity College, Cambridge, behind him, indeed with no college anywhere behind him but only Dr Burney's 'Huge, unregenerate school at Dulwich' – and that only for a couple of years before his leaving at the age of sixteen – settling swiftly to tackle it, although he had a big and difficult book on the go as well. Added to this there was a novel, *Ranthorpe*, being scribbled down at what must have been breakneck speed (it shows signs of a man working with not one minute to lose, with a young wife to see to who is pregnant for the second time), and there had to be party going (so that he could get to know editors who might hire him), and roystering and singing with the Thornton Hunts and the Samuel Laurences. And yet under the burden of it all George Lewes and his Agnes were blithe and happy. Carlyle remembered long afterwards how 'they used to come down of an evening to us through the lanes from Kensington, and were as merry as two birds.'

Lewes couldn't command the same space for his articles as Macaulay, but nevertheless they were very substantial pieces indeed. One, for example, called *The Philosophy of Art: Hegel's Aesthetic*, came out quite early. It was probably only the second piece of his to get into print, appearing in the *British and Foreign Review* in the autumn of 1842. It runs to about 14,000 words, and about twenty-five years later Lewes reprinted it as a tailpiece of another of his books, *The Principles of Success in Literature*, which had first appeared, by instalments, in the opening numbers of the *Fortnightly Review*, and gave it a new title, *The Inner Life of Art*. He's much more reverent and sympathetic towards Hegel here than in the *Biographical History*. He begins by rebuking his fellow countrymen for not taking art seriously enough, for being too preoccupied with the state of the market. How wise by contrast is German philosophy which theorises elaborately about Art, considering it to be 'something far transcending any commerce yet invented'.

Lewes then goes on to ask the old, old question: What is poetry? and comes to his answer pretty smartly. There are two parts to it. First, poetry is 'the beautiful phasis' (appearance, one might say, or, perhaps, realisation) 'of a religious idea', and, further than this, poetry must be 'the metrical utterance of emotion'. Both of these definitions respectfully conform to Hegelian notions. The metrical part of his definition is developed first, and the proposition is well argued along lines by now very familiar if in some ways – though not in all – outmoded. The 'religious idea' part of his theory is the more interesting. We must, he thinks, 'regard every Idea' (in the Hegelian sense) 'as partaking essentially of the religious character, which is the formula of any truth leading to new contemplations of the infinite, or to new forms in our social relations . . .' He seems to be feeling his way a bit here, but he battles on: 'Thus liberty, equality and humanity (the threefold form of this century's mission) are not, so to speak, "doctrinal points" in the formalised religion of the epoch; but in as much as they express (in the final analysis) the object and faith of the crusade in which all Europe is now sensibly or insensibly engaged, and as they have to complete a great social end, so may they be considered as eminently religious. . . .'

Here Lewes proclaims his humanist, egalitarian faith – 'this century's mission' as he calls it – and it's one which he keeps faith with all his life through. Of course he's anxious that his readers should be clear about his use of 'religious' and 'religion': let no one suppose he's thinking specifically about Christianity. He has a footnote which defines his position exactly: '. . . By religion here we do not mean the Christian religion only, but every religion of which we have

46

knowledge. We are here neither confounding nor separating the true from the false, but simply stating to what all equally pretend . . .' And he comes gradually round to Shelley, his poet of poets, whose work gives perfect expression to the holy trinity of concepts which he's been proclaiming – that liberty, equality and humanity for which, in the famous passage from the 'Defence of Poetry', the embattled poets themselves are the unacknowledged legislators. Lewes accepts that he isn't a poet himself, but he and his like have also an important role to play in the century which is theirs.

> This, then, being a critical, conscious age, its artists must be critical to fulfil its demands; and aesthetics we take to be one of the means of elevating it out of the 'slough of despond', although it must likewise be emancipated from 'Commerce' and be placed on its own high pedestal, with real priests at its altars and real faith in its worshippers; – so long as the 'commerce of sweet sounds' is the jingling of guineas, little can be hoped for . . .

The closer you look at this young man Lewes as he depicts himself in these early writings, as he sketches out a quite consistent attitude of mind, the more you are reminded of the young H. G. Wells, born half a century later. Lewes is a prose man – so is Wells. Lewes talks at length about poetry (as we've seen), and Shelley's, out of all the great poetic names belonging to the generation before his own, is the one he finds the greatest, the most likely to endure because he of them all can sustain most readily the role of poet-as-prophet. Though when he quotes from Shelley it is from the prose writer of the *Defence* –

> . . . [A poet] not only beholds intensely the present as it is, and discovers those laws according to which present things ought to be ordered, but he beholds the future in the present, and his thoughts are the germs of the flower, and the fruit of latest time . . . The most unfailing herald, companion, and follower of the awakening of a great

people to work a beneficial change in opinion or institution . . .

It's writing of this kind, not specifically the writing of a poet
at all, which kindles in Lewes the fires of his Shelley-
partisanship. And how exactly his enthusiasm mirrors
Wells's. 'People in themselves are all right,' Lewes seems to
be saying. 'It's simply the system that's wrong.' He wanted
above all to put the system right ('to work a beneficial
change in opinion or institution' was Shelley's way of
putting it), and once that had been done we'd all be safe
aboard a swift intercity train bound for the New Jerusalem.
Wells's humanistic probings into the future follow similar
thought patterns – until right at the end of his long life by
which time he'd seen all his blueprints for a good time lying
out in the cold rain of reality, shapeless, crumpled and
indecipherable, and, with all to do again, turned his back
on the wretched world in order to write (1945) the half
hysterical *Mind at the End of its Tether*.
For Lewes the motives for disillusionment never
became compulsive. To the very end it was possible for
him – even if with an increasing number of reservations –
to stick with Auguste Comte who preached that social
phenomena should be subjected to scientific observation
and who insisted comfortably that social science would
study the conditions, facts, and inter-relations of society
and subject these to the laws of order and to the laws of
progress . . . It sounded all right at the time and no one
should mock Lewes for his allegiance without first taking
into account the facts of the years through which he lived
and the pressures that were on him, as they were on
anyone who lived and thought – Carlyle, Clough, Mill,
Matthew Arnold and armies of others besides – through
the middle years of the nineteenth century. George Saints-
bury, the stout old Tory who wrote a *History of Criticism* in
three volumes between 1900 and 1904, remembered Lewes
well, though by then he was more than twenty years dead,
and had this to say of him: 'Much may be forgiven to a man
born in the first quarter of the nineteenth century, when he
uses the words "progress", "success", and the like: but not

everything.' And he said of him also, with the sort of shrewdness that can only come from hindsight, that he was a man who carried 'the stamp of the Exhibition of 1851 . . . upon him.'

His boundless industry during those first years of his married life wasn't exhausted even by a history of philosophy and by getting on for a million words of periodical journalism. He also wrote, in 1841 or 1842, a play called *The Noble Heart*. It was put together, one would guess, without much pause for reflection. He had been reading widely in the Elizabethan dramatists as well as Spanish playwrights like Lope de Vega and Calderón (these last two were the subject of an article he published in the *Foreign Quarterly Review* in 1843 and of a book which came out three years afterwards). Lewes gave his characters Spanish names – Don Guzman, Leon, Juanna – but there's no life, no substance, in any of them. Don Guzman, no youngster, is in love with Juanna who comes from the lower orders of society. Faced with a proposal of marriage from the eminent one the girl agrees: What else in the circumstances can the poor thing do? But on the day of the wedding Don Guzman's son Leon makes an untimely, unexpected reappearance. He's back from the wars, and he's back to claim Juanna because the two have been committed to each other secretly – this would have caused no start of surprise in any audience at all experienced – since well before his call-up. Don Guzman yields to the claims of youth, puts all fleshly urges behind him, goes off to enclose himself in a desert place in order to ponder on last things and his viaticum. End. Any plot summary can be made to sound silly if the writer intends it so; but Lewes's play deserves no more sympathetic treatment. It is hasty, derivative, full of rodomontade and nowhere truly imagined. It gives the impression of having been composed in brief snatched moments between nursing the baby and thinking over what next to say about Spinoza.

Lewes had to wait a good while before anyone could be persuaded to put it on, but it was performed at last, in April 1849 in Manchester, where Geraldine Jewsbury – Manchester's woman novelist number two (after Mrs Gaskell) –

saw it and thought highly enough of it to write in the *Examiner and Times* that here was a play which would stay permanently in the repertory. In February 1850 it was produced in London at the Olympic Theatre. In Manchester Lewes had taken the part of Don Guzman himself – the theatre was in his blood and there remains much to say about his connection with it – but in London two notable actors, G. V. Brooke and E. L. Davenport were in the main parts. The audience gave the piece an enthusiastic reception and even at the end asked to see the author – a request not often made in 1850. But the printed critics thought it tedious. There was too much commentary and not enough thought-in-action. The piece was withdrawn after eight performances, but one failure, after years of waiting, wasn't enough to cure Lewes of his itch to write for the stage. The unpretentious works which he was to write under the pseudonym of Slingsby Lawrence still lay ahead.

Ranthorpe, too, a three volume novel in its original form, was written in 1842. And like the Spanish drama it found no ready buyer. Chapman and Hall eventually published it in 1847, but only in a considerably shortened form. Lewes makes this clear in his short preface: '. . . when I state that the one volume now presented to the public was originally three, the critic will easily understand how certain faults of construction, and sins against *l'art de conter*, arose from so great a change in the structure and proportions of the whole . . .' And it soon becomes obvious to any reader prepared to stick with it that drastic, neck-or-nothing cuts have been made in the text. The book is jerky and breathless, closely detailed at one moment, taking flying leaps the next. Some melodramatic action – a murder, an execution – is dreamt up and draped round, not Lewes's autobiography exactly but all the same round something not far removed from personal history. At the beginning Percy Ranthorpe is nineteen, a hard-up clerk nursing ambitions to be a poet but getting no encouragement from an unsympathetic father. 'Mr Ranthorpe had a very special contempt for poets, and never lost an opportunity of expressing it before his son. He himself had been all his life a speculator; and because he had pursued the chimera of making his fortune, he considered himself eminently a *practical* man. A life of unsuccess had failed to teach him . . .' Do we here get a glimpse of the elusive Captain Willim? To suppose so would be to make a guess, but a guess with the balance of probability on hand to support it.

Percy leaves home and his job in order to become a writer. He also leaves behind his love, the orphaned Isola Churchill whose father had been Ranthorpe Senior's one time partner. He finds no acceptance for his poems unless he's prepared to pay to have them published. Only the single one, 'The Poet's Heart', accepted while he was still a lawyer's clerk – the one therefore which supplies the final stiffening of his determination to leave home and risk his future – stands to his name. He's met Wynton, another neglected genius 'old enough to be Percy's father', but the sad circumstances of the Wynton home fail to put him off. 'The room into which he was shown made a deep impression on him. Its poverty was hideously distinct; small and low, it had no carpet, the coals were contained in a kitchen shovel in one corner, and the only fire-iron was a poker worn to a mere rod. Cowering over a miserable fire sat Wynton's wife, a woman evidently born and bred a lady, and who seemed meekly to bear her fate . . .' It's possible here to catch a glimpse of Mr and Mrs Leigh Hunt, life's battles still for them far from being over. The picture is overweighted on the sombre side, admittedly: Hunt's disasters, though real and frequent, never quite dropped to the level of Lewes's Wynton. His poker never got quite so thin. But all the same Lewes, very close indeed to Hunt's son Thornton at the time of the writing of *Ranthorpe*, must have had some thought of Hunt in his mind as he was writing this. Hunt was a next door neighbour of Carlyle in Cheyne Walk for some years from 1833. Carlyle was busy lecturing and busy also getting on in the world when he put this in his journal on May 15 1838:

One must submit; one must struggle and sing . . . Hunt's criticism no longer friendly; not so in spirit, though still in letter; a shade of spleen in it; very natural, flattering even. He finds me grown to be a something now. His whole

51

way of life is at death-variance with mine. In the *Examiner* he expresses himself afflicted with my eulogy of *thrift*, and two days ago he had *multa gemens* to borrow two sovereigns of me. It is an unreasonable existence ganz und gar. Happily I have next to nothing to do with Hunt . . .

Next door but next to nothing. What a disagreeable person Carlyle had become in middle life. For Lewes-Ranthorpe, however, Wynton-Hunt was an opener of gates. Ranthorpe takes lodgings near him and manages to live on eightpence or ninepence a day, and Wynton's 'prospects shortly brightened a little. Wynton had got an engagement on a weekly newspaper of good repute, and hoped to be able to introduce Percy to the editor, and so manage to find a place for him also . . .'

Wynton does just that, and Ranthorpe is in. He talks, eats and socialises with the writing crowd, finds himself accepted, and 'every Sunday morning the paper lay upon his breakfast table, and made him feel that he was "somebody", as he cut the leaves and eagerly read over his own contributions.' Then Ranthorpe's father dies and leaves him a little money. So, with Isola's backing, Ranthorpe leaves his paper in order to devote himself to his tragedy. At this point we arrive at the end of Book One of *Ranthorpe*. Is it worth going on? Tempting perhaps to say No to this, because Lewes, so far at least, has shown no aptitude for controlling the pace of a novel. He is constantly breaking off in order to weary the reader with generalising, moralising discourses. These are entirely predictable and serve only to leave the story bobbing idly up and down in the doldrums. (Lewes hasn't at all Thackeray's trick of endowing authorial asides with enough vigour and characterfulness to give them an important, even vital share in the conduct of the story as a whole.)

But Charlotte Brönte, writing to Lewes as author to author (*Jane Eyre* came out in 1847 – the same year as *Ranthorpe*), has clearly found quite a lot to respond to in a first novel written by someone almost exactly her own age. 'I did not know such books were written now. It is very

52

different to any of the popular works of fiction; it fills the mind with fresh knowledge. Your experience and your convictions are made the reader's; and to an author, at least, they have a value and an interest quite unusual.' Charlotte Brönte's opinion has never been the received one but it has the natural ring of genius, not much aware of precedent and practice, picking up an echo from far below the surface.

Lewes hasn't sorted out the differing aims and objects of a contributor to the *Westminster Review* and of a writer of fiction. But he can write sharp dialogue and he can handle a scene. The evening at the theatre, for example, when Ranthorpe's tragedy gets its first – and last – performance, is done with vigour and has the verisimilitude that comes from hard knowledge.

Lewes dedicated his novel

TO HER
who has lightened the burden of an anxious life
this work is dedicated by
HER HUSBAND

In 1847 therefore all was still well between George Lewes and Agnes Jervis.

They were an emancipated couple. Agnes wasn't by any means content simply to bear his children (they had three sons by then). She was a good linguist, in French and Spanish particularly, she kept her eye on what journalism was doing abroad, made translations of material which she thought might have a London interest. Lewes, with the easy uninhibited friendliness which was natural to him, swiftly got to know most of the people of any account in his – and her – chosen field and was able to place her work as well as fend for himself. In 1844 they moved from Mrs Lewes senior's house in Pembroke Square to 2 Campden Hill Terrace, also in Kensington and not far away. Thornton Arnott, their second son, was born there, and there Thackeray drew them in their domesticity. Agnes is at the piano, George stands beside her, hand in trouser pocket. His mouth is open and he's in full voice. He loved to be a performer. Thornton Leigh Hunt stands a pace behind, his thumbs in the armholes of his waistcoat; he isn't singing himself but he's obviously having a happy time.

Two years later they moved a few paces away to Bedford Gardens, where they stayed until they parted in 1855. All along it was a very independent minded marriage, a partnership of equals which was determined that the world should be made clearly aware that it was a partnership of equals. Lewes went off when he felt like it. So did she.*

Lewes made several journeys abroad and these lasted a considerable time. Obviously since he was writing his *Biographical History of Philosophy* it was essential that he should be in close touch with what European writers, the French and Germans particularly, were thinking about matters relevant to his large theme. He had at least two meetings with Comte. The first was probably in 1843 when Comte, aged forty-five, had just separated from his wife, and Lewes with his easy, winning ways, made a good impression. 'A loyal and interesting youth,' Comte assured Hill in a letter. The second meeting was in 1846 and this time Lewes found Comte deeply cast down because the day before Clotilde de Vaux, the love of his middle age, had died. He was a tetchy and quarrelsome man but friendly, at that moment anyway, to the English, to Mill especially, who had persuaded Grote, Molesworth and Raikes Currie between them to support the French philosopher not with high sympathetic sentiments but with hard cash to the tune of £240 per annum. Comte would have been grateful too – if gratitude was ever in his life a sincerely felt emotion – to Lewes for what he said of him in the *Biographical History*. Lewes as a critic was never a man to gloss over what he felt to be faults, and he could see faults in Comte, but, to make

* It needs to be remembered that struggling though they were they could still manage two servants, Martha Baker who was concerned primarily with the children, and Annie Bauce who was there to shoulder the common tasks. (It's hard for us to realise now what a vast difference the virtual disappearance of domestic service as a means of earning a living has made to the ordering and patterns of life.)

up, he also saw immense importance in Comte's work and proclaimed it.

Anxious as to we are that Comte's philosophy should occupy the serious attention of everyone who aspires to the title of philosopher, we must nevertheless declare that Comte's works are not calculated to be popular. Six stout volumes are enough to make the student pause ere he begin; and the length of the journey is not lightened by any graces of style. The truth must be told: Comte is a wordy writer; but he is not obscure, coins no terminology to bewilder the reader, repeats what he says in various ways, so as to ensure intelligibility at the expense of some *ennui* . . . Modern philosophy opens with a method – Bacon; and ends with a method – Comte; and in each case this method leads to positive science, and sets metaphysics aside . . .

Comte ought to have been pleased.

It was Mill, already enjoying a European reputation, who provided Lewes with the introductions necessary for these visits. Victor Cousin, incubating his *Du Vrai, Du Beau et Du Bien*, a tedious book not now much thought of but in its day greatly esteemed, was one more of the people he met in Paris. De Tocqueville, a great Anglophile and much beloved of the Whig Party, was another, and far greater, notable whom Lewes got to know through Mill. In 1845 he was in Berlin reviving memories and visiting – or more probably re-visiting Varnhagen von Ense, the elderly diplomat husband of Rahel. Hers had been (she died in 1833) the principal salon for the intelligentsia at the head of the German Romantic movement – Schelling, Tieck, Bettina von Arnim and the rest. After her death Varnhagen kept it on and it had been through him that the young Lewes had come to know – or at any rate to nod respectfully towards – this band of innovators who belonged to his father's generation rather than to his own. What Agnes did during these European excursions we don't exactly know; but it's safe to assume that she saw much of Thornton Hunt and his wife Katherine Gliddon when, in 1845, they went to join the

Phalanstery, the Bayswater venture in communal living in the house belonging to Katherine's father Arthur Gliddon.

Yet we still aren't at the end of Lewes's whirlwind of activity over the first lustrum of the 1840s. All his life he was closely bound up with theatre. He read enthusiastically in the dramatic literature of the past – Spanish, French, Italian and German as well as English; he went to see plays, abysmally bad though most of them were in the England of the 1840s; he wrote critical notices of what he saw; he even took over where his father had left off, and acted himself.

In 1846, whilst he was still waiting to find a publisher for *Ranthorpe*, he published *The Spanish Drama, Lope de Vega and Calderón*, based on material already contributed to the magazines, notably the *Foreign Quarterly Review*. Somehow, somewhere Lewes had acquired a full and sufficient knowledge of Spanish and had found time to read Lope de Vega. This sounds harmless enough – until you remember that Lope wrote almost as many plays by himself as did the rest of the dramatists of western Europe all banded together. There are about one thousand five hundred credited to him – and even that staggering figure doesn't include shorter pieces and the *autos sacramentales*. Calderón was responsible for a mere one-to-two hundred; but the two between them offered a daunting mountain of subject matter to a ferociously busy man in his twenties. All the same, Lewes contrived never to drag his feet under the weight of his burden and what he says of Lope is as readable as it is perceptive. He may not have read every one of the fifteen hundred, but he got the sense.

If you go to him [Lope] with critical spectacles dogmatically bestriding your nose, you will be ill-contented. If you expect to find a Shakespeare, a Molière or a Schiller, you may save yourself the trouble. But there is an endless charm in Lope – his gaiety. His unflagging animal spirits playful irony, and careless gaiety, keep your mind in a constant smile, which gently curls about the lips. There are tragical scenes in his plays and touches of real pathos, which go right to the quivering heart; but they do not abound. Gaiety is the element in which he habitually lives . . .

There's more in *El Mejor Alcalde del Rey* and in *Fuente Ovejuna* than is covered in what Lewes says here, but Lewes is on the right lines and what he says is agreeably and readably said. And what he has to say about Calderón's much admired *La Vida es Sueño*, is greatly to the point. It's a play, he thinks, that is 'neither more nor less than a very interesting romantic caprice of an ingenious fancy – a play which, in point of treatment, is not more elevated than the cloak-and-sword comedies, although in point of subject it belongs to the region of romance.'

In the *Westminster Review* for January 1842 he had much to say about the state of the drama in his own country. He called the article 'Authors and Managers, the Regeneration of the Drama'. Lewes uses Tomlins's book (1840) called *The Past and Present State of Dramatic Art and Literature addressed to Authors, Actors and Managers* as a peg on which to hang his comments and proposals. He saw, as did Tomlins, that the state of the English theatre, as it stood at that time, was grievous indeed. Writers who had something to say, who had imagination, couldn't be bothered with it. All forms of competition were hampered by the system of 'patent houses': during the winter months two theatres, and two alone – Covent Garden and Drury Lane – had the right to put on plays. For the length of the summer season the Haymarket Theatre took over. But the monopoly exercised by these three theatres extended only to plays which communicated exclusively through the medium of the word spoken – either prose or poetry. By reason of this quirky rigidity, 'mixture plays', or melodramas, began to be put on in what were called 'minors' – places of entertainment where ragbag offerings tempted the audiences – and audiences were ready and waiting to be entertained because industrialisation was swelling the towns with a population which clamoured to be diverted in its brief periods of leisure. Farce and tragedy, songs and jigs – everything came on the one ticket.

Lewes saw the evils besetting the world of the theatre,

recognised the poverty of inspiration, and was prepared to suggest remedies. He thought a system of specialist theatres might be made to work. Obviously the monopolistic patent theatre system would have to go. The new theatres, each catering for its own particular kind of audience, would win over the cooperation of genuine writing talent and in time the heavy hand of the actor-manager would cease to be strong enough to ward off young talent from outside the profession. But these new young writers, Lewes insists, must recognise that writing for the stage is a difficult art and time has to be spent in learning it. Then, in these new houses, which must be small and dedicated, not barnlike, drama in England may stand a chance of coming alive again. As it is, theatres have degenerated into places providing simply ephemeral amusement. '. . . the ages of Pericles and Elizabeth were dramatic because great dramatists rendered them thus . . . at no very distant date some man will arrive . . . keen enough to perceive the wants of his age . . . Then may the drama . . . claiming a new office and exercising a new and powerful influence, become what it was of old . . .' However wide of the mark his own piece, *The Noble Heart*, may be, Lewes was right to be indignant and concerned about the theatre of Vincent Crummles as he saw it existing all around him when he was a young man. The *Westminster Review* article was followed by two more in the *Edinburgh Review* in July and October 1843. 'Dramatic Reform' was the title now, and 'Classification of the Theatres'. And all his life he was to show, in the words of the dramatic critic William Archer, 'a passion for the theatre at once enlightened and enlightening'.

In the early months of 1849 came another long spell away from London and his family. He received an invitation to deliver a course of lectures in Manchester and Liverpool. Through February he delivered six lectures at the Liverpool Mechanics' Institute. For these he drew on his *Biographical History of Philosophy* and repeated them at the Athenaeum in Manchester during March and April, and it was here too that he appeared professionally as an actor. The year before he'd taken the part of Sir Hugh Evans in Dickens's amateur production (very lavish, near professional in quality) of *The*

Merry Wives of Windsor. Dickens, in his thirties and with energies more inexhaustible than Lewes's, if that can be imagined, was always looking for some excuse which would give him the opportunity of acting. The shaky state of Leigh Hunt's finances was perennially there asking to be relieved, and so Dickens toured to help him; the bankrupt playwright Sheridan Knowles was another opportune lame duck whom Dickens planned to put into circulation again by putting him in charge of the Shakespeare house in Stratford which the town had decided to buy provided an endowment could be raised to refurbish and maintain the property. The amateurs had given performances in Birmingham, Leamington, Manchester and Liverpool during the summer of 1848; whether Lewes took his poorish Welsh accent around with them all the way isn't certain, but he was Sir Hugh Evans for much of the time at least.

The acting part he undertook with a professional cast was in *The Merchant of Venice*, put on at the Theatre Royal Manchester on March 10. Lewes was Shylock. The papers said: 'This evening Mr G. H. Lewes, the popular author, will make his début in *The Merchant of Venice*, one of the plays selected by Her Majesty at Windsor Castle.' Lewes made Shylock sympathetic – an interpretation the theatre going public of the middle century weren't used to. People agreed that he played the role as no one else they could think of had played it, and, Yes, certainly, when you came to think of it, Shylock was a man who had suffered wrongs and was justified in wanting to see them righted; yet, Lewes, with all his fluency, his self-confidence, his experience in facing the public, his acting blood, still lacked the indefinable quality which could use all these attributes in combination on a stage in an acted play. 'His best friends,' wrote Espinasse, who saw him perform at the Theatre Royal, 'were obliged to admit that Nature had not intended him to be an actor . . .'

Perhaps it was simply his physical smallness: the large spaces of the theatre made him seem waiflike and ineffective. In a salon, or a drawing room, or a club, or even in places that were rowdy but intimate like Evans's Singing Room or the Cyder Cellars or Thackeray's Back Kitchen,

Lewes could always make his mark, even dominate, but the stage, though he loved it, somehow always diminished him.

Lewes's confidence in himself through those early years of his marriage is unbounded. He must have persuaded himself that he could successfully combine the professions of journalist, serious author, popular novelist, and actor not only in the plays of others but in his own as well. As for lecturing – perhaps he might make use of all his talents at once when he came to the lectern. Geraldine Jewsbury took an interest in him: he wasn't much to look at but he had plenty to say. She wrote to her London friend Jane Welsh Carlyle about him that February,

> Lewes is still lecturing here . . . He takes extremely well to the people here and they seem to like him. He and — are become very good friends. I like him so much better than I thought I should in London when I saw him; he really is a good fellow . . .

And after a fortnight more she was even more enthusiastic.

> Lewes is making a prodigious sensation down here, only his moustachios have hurt people's sense of propriety and nothing but the report of his wife and an unascertained amount of family could have stood against them. People here are morbid about moustachios. He might have brought a harem with less scandal. Still, he is a great favourite in spite of them . . . I like him extremely. I think there is a great deal of kindness at the bottom, and there is a geniality I enjoy amazingly . . .

'The report of his wife and an unascertained amount of family' is a bit arch – even a bit opaque. What she meant of course – and someone as clever as Jane Carlyle would have grasped the point immediately – was that in spite of looking so raffish, Lewes by all accounts had a loving wife to give the lie to any charge of lack of respectability, and three children as well.

Only a short while after this, he appeared again in *The*

60

Noble Heart. The piece opened on the 16th April, preceded by an announcement on the 14th in the *Manchester Guardian* (only a weekly at that time): 'On Monday will be produced a New Tragedy (never acted) entitled *The Noble Heart.* Mr G. H. Lewes, the author, will sustain the principal character.' As we've seen it wasn't of course new, but eight years old. Still Lewes failed to conjure any response either out of press or patrons, and his last appearance as an actor, again as Shylock, was at Edinburgh in November 1849. In 1851 he wrote of acting, calling it, 'an art in which I have a personal ambition', but it was an ambition which remained unrealised.

Espinasse, who was working as a journalist in Manchester during the time of Lewes's visit, saw a good deal of him while he was there. The picture we get of the young Lewes over this comparatively short period is much more detailed than anything else we have of him up to the middle 1840s. Espinasse's article on Lewes in his *Literary Recollections* is thirty pages long, and no fewer than seven of these are devoted to the couple of months or so he spent in Manchester in 1849. The effect of this is to make him seem even more frantically busy than usual over this period – busier even than during his normal Kensington days. This impression may well be false, but all the same it's certainly true that he did much, and initiated more, whilst he was there. In particular he made useful friends. Vaughan, Principal of the Lancashire Independent College, lived in Manchester and also edited the *British Quarterly Review* to which Lewes had already contributed. After getting to know him, Lewes managed to sell him two more quick articles, on Macaulay and on Disraeli, both of which appeared in 1849. He also met at the Jewsbury parties Stavros Dilberoglue, a young Greek business man established and working in Manchester. Dilberoglue had strong communist leanings and probably knew Engels, not far away in Liverpool. Dilberoglue was to have a considerable influence on Lewes's novel writing. Indeed Lewes was so impressed by him that he gave him an important part to play in his novel of the early 1850s, *The Apprenticeship of Life.*

Between *Ranthorpe* and *The Apprenticeship* Lewes had

found time, amongst all the other things, for a second novel which he called *Rose, Blanche and Violet*. This dates probably from 1847, that is, from the time when *Ranthorpe* was accepted for publication. Lewes rushed hard at it as he did at everything in those days. The interpolated moralisings are still a burden on the reader but they don't drag on the skirts of the narrative quite as persistently as in *Ranthorpe*.

In the prologue Captain Heath, a smart yount military chap, is calling on Meredith Vyner whose youngish wife has just died. Vyner lives in Wytton Hall in Devonshire by the sea. He is feeble, indolent, rich and Lewes presents him to us briskly.

> There was something remarkable though not engaging in his appearance. He looked like a dirty bishop. In his pale puffy face there was an ecclesiastical mildness, which assorted well with a large forehead and weak chin, though it brought into stronger contrast the pugnacity of a short blunt nose, the nostrils of which were somewhat elevated and garnished with long black hairs. A physiognomist would at once have pronounced him obstinate, but weak; loud in the assertion of his intentions, vacillating in their execution. His large person was curiously encased in invariable black; a tailcoat with enormous skirts . . . People laughed at Meredith Vyner for his dirty nails and his love of Horace . . . but they respected him for his integrity and goodness, and for his great, though ill assorted erudition. In a word, he was laughed at, but there was no malice in the laughter.

It isn't the way characters are pushed on to the stage in the novels of the 1980s. Mrs Carlyle wrote harshly of it. 'Execrable', she thought. '. . . I could not have suspected even the Ape of writing anything so silly . . . I . . . should . . . have laid it aside in the first half volume if I had not felt a pitying interest in the man [pitying perhaps because she felt sympathy with a man struggling with such vigour to make a career and a living for himself – though there's no suggestion that at any time Lewes was fiercely hard-up in the Dickensian Hungerford Stairs sense] that makes me read on in the hope of coming to something a little better . . .'

Perhaps Jane Welsh is being a bit toffee-nosed here. She did read on. That's the important thing. And you don't read on unless your author has given you legitimate hope that there is going to be something better. And when the author has told you on page six that one of his characters looks like a dirty bishop, then you feel inclined to push on – without any fake nonsense about feeling sorry for him. Vyner marries again, so quite soon Lewes has on his hands four important women characters, the three daughters by his first wife, Rose, Blanche and Violet, and the second wife herself. There are important other women characters too. And here Lewes shows a subtle understanding of motive and feeling. He wasn't, and never would be, a cicisbeo – although there were later to be those prepared to call him so – but he always loved and understood women. He could make them love him – even Jane Welsh Carlyle came round in the end and spoke of 'poor dear Lewes' and of 'the Prince of Journalists'.

Like *Ranthorpe*, *Rose, Blanche and Violet* suffers from an overplus of authorial comment. Lewes is for ever being prompted to write little essays devoted to general meditations on what the characters have been doing or saying or suffering. He can even be moved to break off in order to say: 'Upon what slight foundations sometimes hang the most important events!' There's plenty of liveliness though, especially in the dialogue. It is the work of a hard pressed, busy, plentifully gifted writer who hasn't yet settled in his own mind what exactly he wants to do with the abilities he knows he has.

All through that first visit to Manchester he and Agnes kept up a busy correspondence. 'During one of his visits to my own domicile,' says Espinasse, '. . . Lewes gave us most sympathetically – for with all his faults he was then an affectionate husband and always an affectionate father – nursery stories of his children, sent him from London by his wife, who, he said, wrote to him unfailingly every day.' Was Agnes at this time being attentive only to deceive? It is unlikely. Candour and freedom had been characteristic of

63

the couple's relationship right from the beginning. If Agnes Lewes and Thornton Hunt had decided by then that it would be a good idea to go to bed together Agnes would have immediately told her George that that was how it was.

Later that same year Lewes was in Manchester again, not this time to lecture but to make preparations for something much more ambitious. It was the right time, Lewes felt – and Thornton Hunt was of the same opinion – to introduce more competition into the field of weekly journalism. As daily papers *The Times* and the *Morning Chronicle* were by then strongly established. At the same time the heavy quarterly artillery boomed. What Lewes and Hunt had in mind was a new weekly which should provide a platform for radical, leftist views. Lewes came north at the end of 1849 in search of backers.

3

Lewes did well as a fund raiser in the north. A rich German who owned a calico printing works close to Manchester and who was liberal in his sympathies dug into well filled pockets. At W. E. Forster's house at Rawdon he came in touch with others sharing the German's views and something of his wealth. In particular a very old and extremely well heeled clergyman, the Rev Edmund Larken pitched in with a large sum of money. Old enough to be able to remember as a youth the excessive blood lettings of the French Revolution, he was a most improbable supporter of troublesome innovation of any kind. Yet a supporter he was. He had helped to translate George Sand into English; he published his sermons and in one of them gave an outline of Fourier's horrifying notions about social reorganisation. The stance of the projected *Leader*, as described to him by Lewes, seemed necessary and right for the times in which this ancient man found himself living. Plans for the new paper, as a result of Lewes's mission, could now go forward. Geraldine Jewsbury was his warm ally throughout his campaign. On January 1 1850 she wrote to Jane Welsh Carlyle, adding at the end, 'What do you think of his paper? I am glad it is afloat.' On March 30 1850 the first number of the *Leader* appeared. Thornton Hunt specialised on the political side, Lewes on th literary. The general supervision they shared. They were joint editors.

By now they were sharers on a much more personal side as well. The *Leader* was born on March 30; Edmund Alfred Lewes was born two weeks later. A happy conjunction you might say. But little Edmund Alfred was a Hunt, not a Lewes. In 1849, that year when her husband had been so multifariously busy not only in London but in Manchester as well, Agnes had also been busy having an affair with his closest associate – perhaps even one might risk saying his closest friend. Lewes took his cuckolding by Thornton Hunt buoyantly. After all nothing had happened that went contrary to his advanced principles. In the June 15 issue of the *Leader*, doubtless aware that the news was going round that little Edmund Alfred was the product of alternative fathering, Lewes wrote of his family and spoke of 'four boys and a human Rose in the shape of their mother'. This was affectionate, loyal – and true. Four boys. Chivalrous of him not to stick with three; perhaps this was because those to some extent in the know might have asked: What were they doing about little Edmund Alfred?

Mrs Carlyle, hawklike always, had felt that things weren't perhaps quite right much earlier that year.

> Little Lewes came the other night with his little wife, [she wrote to her cousin Jeanie] . . . speaking gratefully of you all – but it is Julia Paulet who has taken his soul captive! He raves about her 'dark, luxurious eyes' and 'smooth, firm flesh'! His wife asked 'How did he know? Had he been feeling it?' In fact his wife seems rather *contemptuous* of his raptures about all the women he has fallen in love with on his journey [referring to Lewes's northern expedition] which is the best way of taking the thing – when one can. I used to think these Leweses a perfect pair of lovebirds always cuddling together on the same perch – to speak figuratively – but the female lovebird appears to have hopped off to some distance and to be now taking a somewhat critical view of her shaggy little mate.

Here Mrs Carlyle is saying in fact that Lewes was a womaniser so that on the purely personal side, quite apart from the abstract, notional, libertarian theories they were both wedded to, Agnes could feel herself perfectly justified in going to bed with Thornton. How did he know about Julia Paulet's smooth firm flesh? This is Agnes's question, and she feels and shows contempt; the natural woman pushes the theoretical one out of the way and holds the stage. Eliza Lynn, who wrote about it all long afterwards, who nourished embittered feelings about men and whose impartiality isn't to be relied upon, was also as we've seen pro-Thornton and anti-Lewes. In *Christopher Kirklan* which is autobiographical she wrote:

Among others [she is talking of the early 1840s] I fell in with that notorious group of Free Lovers. . . But though those who floated on the crest of the wave [Lewes and George Eliot] . . . had the more genius and the better luck, he who made personal shipwreck [Thornton Hunt] and from whose permitted trespass the whole thing started, had the nobler nature, the most faithful heart, the more constant mind, and was in every way the braver and the truer man. He whom society set itself to honour . . . partly because of his own brilliance and facility, was less solid than specious. The other [Thornton] whom all men, not knowing him, reviled, was a moral hero. The former betrayed his own principles when he made capital out of his 'desecrated hearth', and bewildered society by setting forth ingenious stories of impossible ceremonies which had made his informal union in a certain sense sacramental, so that he might fill his rooms with 'names', and make his Sundays days of illustrious reception. The latter accepted his position without explanation or complaint, and was faithful to his flag, indifferent to selfish gain or social loss . . . It must never be forgotten too that he who afterwards passed as the fond husband, betrayed by the trusted friend, was, in the days when I first knew them all, the most pronounced Free Lover of the group, and openly took for himself the liberty he expressly sanctioned for his wife. As little as he could go into the Divorce Court for his personal relief, because of that condonation and his own unclean hands, so little did he deserve the sympathy of society for the transfer which afterwards he put forward as his own justification and that friend's condemnation. . .

This is strong, harsh stuff about a man six or seven years dead when she wrote it. Was Eliza Lynn right completely? Was she right at all? She is right in thinking, along with Mrs

67

Carlyle, that Agnes was very far from being the first, or the last, woman for Lewes. He was an ugly, whiskery little jockey of a man who liked women and had the knack – a tremendous physique and dazzling good looks has little to do with it – of making women want him and yield to him. She's grotesquely wrong about the informal union and about impossible ceremonies. By plighting your troth in St Margaret's Westminster you are making as low an obeisance to the proprieties as is humanly possible. 'Moral heroism' aren't words that instantly spring to mind when thinking of Thornton Hunt, who was as charming and as shiftless and as unreliable as his father. She is right though about the 'permitted trespass'. Between the Hunts and the Leweses there were no cover-ups. If you felt yourself physically attracted to another man and he to you, then you told your husband how it was and went to bed with him. And for the husbands of course the same irregularities applied. Lewes gave the young Edmund Alfred his name and that was the end of the matter. He and Hunt were preoccupied by the stresses and excitements accompanying the launching of a new paper. Perhaps Agnes, with babies all round her, was beginning to feel that there was perhaps too much preoccupation. In Agnes Swynfen Jervis a certain babyish prettiness went startlingly along with a strong mind and a strong will.

Thornton Hunt was seven years older than Lewes. As a child he had had a chance to familiarise himself with prisons and prison annexes much in the way Dickens was to be institutionalised – if quite briefly – a little later. His father had been given two years for libelling the Prince Regent, though what Leigh Hunt had printed – 'this Adonis in loveliness, a corpulent gentleman of fifty' – doesn't sound as blistering as all that. But then, Leigh Hunt was never the luckiest of men. In 1821 Shelley, recognising in Leigh Hunt a loyal assistant rebel, invited him to Italy. His ample journalistic experience would be useful to Shelley and Byron in their launching of their subversive quarterly the *Liberal*. Hunt accepted the invitation, set off for Italy with his numerous family, and a rough journey they had of it. They didn't reach Leghorn until June 1822. Shelley sailed across the Bay of Spezia to greet his henchman. Between them, and with Byron on hand as well, they would make authority quake and do great things for freedom. But after only a few days Shelley went sailing again and was drowned. After the body had been washed up at Viareggio on July 19 it was Leigh Hunt, with Byron and Trelawny, who witnessed the burning. But with Shelley gone, Byron and Hunt found that they couldn't work well together and after four issues the *Liberal* failed to come out. Struggles and a belated, defeated return to England followed for the Hunts. Thornton's boyhood had more than its fair share of high tragedy and harsh mishap.

Refusing to be put off by his father's misadventures, Thornton was determined to be like him and become a journalist. And also like his father he would be a man of the left and the scourge of the Tories. He had longer experience than Lewes – on the *Spectator* and, as early as 1837, on the *Constitutional*. For the first year at least he was editor-in-chief of the *Leader* and saw to it, Lewes approving, that the *Radical* got the fullest possible publicity for what they were doing and saying. W. J. Linton worked with them on the paper. Linton, a fierce Republican, who married the disapproving Eliza Lynn in 1858, was a wood engraver of repute as well as a writer, and wanted to align the paper unconditionally with the European Republicans; his rebellious anti-establishmentarianism was gradually to become too much for Thornton and his co-editor.

Indeed, round about the mid-century there begins to be perceptible a certain cooling off in Lewes's radical ardour. He had accepted – once – that there should be nothing to complain of in being made a *mari complaisant*, but the point came when he had had enough of being liberated. Thornton continued to satisfy the sexual demands both of Kate Gliddon and Agnes Jervis, and on October 21 1851 Agnes produced a sister, Rose Agnes, to team up alongside Edmund Alfred. Again Lewes accepted that the infant's surname should be his, but felt that one performance in the role of cuckold was enough. He separated himself from his 'four boys and a human Rose in the shape of their mother'.

He and Thornton continued to work together on the

69

Leader and the paper, ideologically running in junior partnership with the *Westminster*, continued to be supported by the liberal elements of the intelligentsia until 1855, when the *Saturday Review*, in which J. R. Green* and FitzJames Stephen† played the same liberal tunes but with an authority and an unction – unction counted for so much in the mid-century – which Hunt and Lewes couldn't quite match, gradually bumbled it out of business.

Lewes found consolation in the friendship of the valetudinarian philosopher Herbert Spencer‡ – not a man, one would have thought, perfectly suited to rally anybody lying spreadeagled amidst the ruins of a marriage – but that apparently was how it was. Towards the end of the decade Lewes noted in his diary: 'I owe him [Spencer] a debt of gratitude. My acquaintance with him was the brightest ray in a very dreary, *wasted* period of my life. I had given up all ambition whatever, lived from hand to mouth and thought the evil of each day sufficient.' He even began to have his doubts about Comte. In August 1851 the *Leader* reviewed Comte's *Système de Politique Positive*:

> We do not hesitate to declare our belief that this second portion of his system will be many, many degrees below the first portion, and that he will find but few adherents to the forms of his new religion. In the very nature of things this part of the task must be open to more cavil; he has to construct a science of society, and commits what we cannot but regard as an enormous blunder in attempting to regulate the *details* of the future. He here falls into the trap of all Socialist System-builders.

We can't be absolutely certain that this review is actually the work of Lewes, but in any event it would have had to pass

---

* 1837–83. English historian. Author in particular of the deservedly still read *Short History of the English People*.

† Sir James FitzJames Stephen (1829–94). Distinguished lawyer and general writer. Brother of Sir Leslie Stephen and uncle of Virginia Woolf.

‡ 1820–1903. Philosopher. Over the course of a long life he attempted a synthesis of abstract philosophy and natural science.

his scrutiny. It sounds like the work of a man disillusioned with any notion of the perfectibility of man and with the beneficent possibilities of systems, Comtist, Fourierist or other.

Yet in spite of the dreariness and waste which he talks of as belonging to this time, his work in the *Leader* is varied and sprightly enough. He began a feature called 'Open Council' and this – familiar enough now in weeklies under the title 'Letters to the Editor' – was new and welcome in 1850. W. E. Forster put forward his view that unemployment was an evil that should not in any circumstances be tolerated. This was startling, coming when it did. People wrote to point out that there was a difference between socialism and communism but found the distinction as difficult to draw then as do their descendants 130 years on. De Quincey, respected and elderly, thought it 'distinguished by its ability, by its hardihood of speculation, by its comprehensive candour, but, in my eyes, still more advantageously distinguished by its deep sincerity'.

Lewes was concerned in the main with what today would be called the 'back half' of the paper. He wrote about books and plays as currently on offer, and he wrote a general, notebook type column in which sharpness and sprightliness were aimed at and weightiness for the time being laid aside. In addition, soon after the paper's début, he began to serialise in it his third novel *The Apprenticeship of Life*. All this amounted to a very large amount of stuff indeed for a still youngish, matrimonially harassed man to keep going steadily all at the same time. The novel he probably had in part already by him. It was to be in three parts: 'The Initiation of Faith', 'The Initiation of Love' and 'The Initiation of Work'. No Part Three ever appeared. Did he suppress it or did he grow tired of the venture and never write it at all? Lewes was too self-confident a man for the idea of suppressing anything he'd written ever to cross his mind. The probability is that the first two parts lay already to hand and that he became too busy, too preoccupied with other projects, ever to complete the third. All the same, what we have of *The Apprenticeship* is enough for it to be rated higher than either *Ranthorpe* or *Rose Blanche*. He has clearly been reading Goethe's *Wilhelm Meister* – and indeed may well have already made a start on what was to be the best of all his books, the *Life of Goethe*. In this third novel Lewes is still much too fond of inserting essay-commentaries on the action. The communist-Christianity of the Manchester expatriate Dilberoglue plays a part; Lewes calls him Frangipolo. Armand is the name Lewes gives to himself, and as in the first part Armand moves away from doubt towards Christian faith, contrary to the swing of the times, under the influence of his Greek friend. Armand's family of unbelievers will have nothing to do with him after this (Lewes is here probably constructing a mirror image of the relations between himself and his stepfather), and Armand goes off to Paris (instead of Berlin) at the beginning of the second, and better, part of the novel. The sexual duelling between Armand and Hortense is subtle and convincing. A good writer as well as a man by now thoroughly experienced in such affairs is clearly at work. Political plottings (we are moving up towards the shake-up of 1830) supply genuine excitement, and Armand exchanges Hortense for another woman. 'All progressive natures are inconstant, hence the notorious inconstancy of poets and artists.' Was he thinking of Thornton Hunt or of himself? Of both probably, but the large general statement is something we could have done without.

He held strong views about education and expressed them frequently in the paper. His own scrappy schooling, his self-sustained study of modern languages and cultures rather than the Latin and Greek still all pervading in English schools and universities, encouraged him to be strong for change. He was quite willing to recognise that Latin and Greek had their place but they shouldn't be allowed to sit like a broody hen over the whole nest. You could train a mind on French and German just as well. More effective and more important than either discipline was science, and it is at this point that Herbert Spencer makes a second appearance. Carlyle, always too eager to cut people down to less than size, considered Spencer an 'immeasurable ass', and indeed he has been much mocked. His high seriousness was so intense and all pervading as to amount almost to an affliction, but not many nineteenth century intellectuals of this country possessed stronger intelligences than he. Darwin's evolutionary theories of 1859 were in some measure anticipated nine years earlier by Spencer, but his weakness was that he lacked the strength of mind to accept loose ends and gaps. For him a theory had always to be buttoned up. 'Survival of the fittest' is one of his phrases and it was to be he more than anyone who would turn Lewes's quick restless mind towards scientific investigation. They met in 1850, right at the beginning of Lewes's time on the *Leader*, and became friends. It was an odd friendship because in most ways no two men could have had less in common. Lewes was joky, sociable, a sexual adventurer; Spencer was painfully prim and always morbidly concerned about his own health and safety. But they both had enquiring minds and a willingness to work hard. For both of them education had been something won by their own efforts. No public school had thrashed the classics into them. Oxbridge had had no hand in finishing them off.

Spencer contributed a series of articles to the *Leader* which he called *The Haythorne Papers* – unsigned of course which was normal for the time, but Spencer wouldn't in any event have wished to be openly associated with a paper like the *Leader* because of its socialist leanings. In these papers Spencer was developing Lamarck's evolutionary studies and Lewes's own later work on these lines – he was a populariser, it must be remembered and not, except perhaps marginally, an original academic researcher – follows the Lamarckian-Spencerian line pretty closely.

Whilst Spencer and others were giving weight to the *Leader*'s pages Lewes himself turned to sprightly, wide roving pieces which after a while he began to write under the 'Vivian' pseudonym. He also turned to book reviewing, including a review of Wordsworth's *Prelude* in August 1850. He was always bravely – perhaps foolhardily might be better – willing to tackle anything, but when he wrote about poets he was always a man wandering in the dark. Neither his intelligence nor his imagination were of the kind which could lead him to any true and valid comprehension of 'the consecration and the poet's dream', and what he has to say of the *Prelude* is inept to the point of being embarrassing. Tennyson the Laureate and public poet also suffers at his hands, perhaps to some degree more deservedly. If we are to have public poetry at all, it's hard to think of anyone who's worked the mine more effectively and movingly than Tennyson in the Duke of Wellington Ode, but Lewes dismisses this as 'an intrinsically poor performance' which displays his gift for cheekiness at its most breathtaking. When he is dealing with prose he comes out much better. To say that Thackeray's style is a 'flowing garment' is to make a comment as apt as it is true.

The 'Vivian' column began life on May 4 1850 and Lewes's dramatic criticism, where on the whole he showed himself happiest as a journalist, was another article on its own. But three separate pieces a week soon proved too much even for Lewes's energy, and Vivian and dramatic criticism as well as lighthearted topicalities soon appeared above the same signature. Lewes, actor by descent and actor more or less manqué in his own person, has much to say in his *Leader* theatre articles of the English theatre of his time. Bernard Shaw thought highly of him as a dramatic critic, so did William Archer. Matthew Arnold considered that dramatic criticism was the strongest of his many literary lines.

Towards the end of his life, in 1875, he revived and added to his theatrical writings of this period in a collection which he called *On Actors and the Art of Acting*. He disliked the bloody extravagances of the minor Elizabethans; he thought there should be more 'realism' in the contemporary theatre, and his assessments of leading actors of the time – Charles Mathews and his wife 'Madame Vestris' in particular – were shrewd and candid. They came from a man who knew what he was talking about, who had acting in his blood. A London dramatic critic of the 1850s hadn't much to write about except actors: the dramatists were uniformly imitative and undistinguished. But for all that Lewes was perhaps happier in a theatre stall than anywhere else on earth. In the issue for November 22 1851 he wrote in his paper: 'Re-opening! What a beautiful word!

74

How full of hope and joyful promise!' Then he tells his readers that 'new plays are to be produced by Jerrold, Marston, Lovell, Slous and Boucicault . . .' (Boucicault was only twenty-nine years old at the time and just beginning, so Lewes can't be blamed for getting his name wrong. W. B. Jerrold, son of Douglas, was even younger, having been born in 1826. The play of his, *Cool as a Cucumber*, was produced first in 1851 and is the forgotten little thing which, amongst others, prompts Lewes, on very slender grounds, to be 'full of hope and joyful promise'.)

Just before this he spoke of his 'bachelor condition' (he had parted by now from his Rose) which meant that he had 'nothing to do in the evening when all the theatres were closed'. Indeed he had by then, busy and bothered as he was, joined the ranks of the dramatists himself. These plays of his – upwards of a score – are of small account. Indeed they can scarcely count as his at all, being for the most part adaptations from the French, and they were done for Mathews and his wife who put them on at the Lyceum. *La Joie fait Peur* became *Sunshine through the Clouds*; *Mercadet*, by Balzac no less, kept its French title but with an English additive – *The Game of Speculation* (which would lead us to guess Balzac without even the mention of his name). A while later Hollingshead, another theatrical man, had the notion of using this Balzac piece at the Gaiety Theatre, but then he learnt, as he says in his autobiography *My Lifetime*: '. . . Mr George Henry Lewes Slingsby Lawrence [Slingsby Lawrence was how Lewes the adaptor-dramatist concealed himself] had cut the ground from under us with his forty-eight hours' adaptation, his phonographic echo of Balzac . . .' Edmund Yates who had that resounding row with Thackeray at the Garrick* thought *Mercadet* the best of all the Mathews's successful ventures at the Lyceum, but Lewes himself was under no illusions about the value of his

* A journalist, Yates wrote a piece for *Town Talk* mildly criticising Thackeray for modifying his stance according to his audience. Yates based this on a conversation at the Garrick of which he and Thackeray were members. This was in 1858. Thackeray was furious at this, claiming that here was a breach of club privacy. Yates had to resign, though Dickens supported him, and bad relations between Thackeray and Dickens were never healed.

contributions to the literature of the Victorian stage. As 'Vivian' he could take a stick and beat himself in his own paper – and did so. In May 1853 another Slingsby Lawrence adaptation was presented at the Lyceum and, as Vivian, Lewes was ready for it with his hatchet.

> Slingsby Lawrence – lucky dog! – has, I am told, made another 'hit' at the Lyceum in the three-act comic drama *The Lawyers*. You must not expect to have my opinion thereon! When at Easter he inflicted us with nine acts of elaborate failure [this was his *A Strange History* at the Haymarket] I 'cut him up' with the impartiality one 'owes to one's friends'. He did not see the friendliness of my candour, and there has been a coolness between us ever since. If I were to praise him now, I should be accused of 'interested motives' – a desire to reinstate my fallen position. My best plan is to stay away altogether . . .

Of course everybody, or almost everybody, who read the *Leader* knew who Slingsby Lawrence was, and this, like many other references in similar tone to his work as a dramatist observed from a mock *tertium quid* position, should be taken as perfectly genuine self-criticism. Lewes never suffered from false modesty, and if he wrote pot boiling stuff for the Mathewses at the Lyceum, was perfectly willing to recognise it for what it was. Even so, his work as a dramatist can't be wholly dismissed. Of *The Lawyers*, for example, *The Times* had this to say. 'We would almost give the adapter, Mr Slingsby Lawrence, the credit of an original production. *The Lawyers* is a thoroughly English piece, the dialogue is written with English vigour and the abuses of the Bar are satirised with a perfect feeling for the professional peculiarities of this country . . .' And *The Times* critic went on to show that he knew the French original put on at the Gymnase and that Lewes was doing more than simply demonstrating that he could put French very readily into stage speakable English. 'The adapter has altered the plot of the Gymnase piece in several essential particulars, as will be seen when we state that the character which is so well acted by Mrs Charles Mathews and is so important to the general effect has no existence in the French original.' All the same, it is as a dramatic critic rather than as a writer for the stage itself that Lewes shines most brightly. He worked roughly a four year stint as dramatic critic for his paper, and when one bears in mind the generally exceptional poverty of the material he was dealing with throughout that time, it's astonishing how lively, readable and intelligent his commentaries are. Was he perhaps too generous in his praise? Well, he believed that it was only by being overkind in some measure to what precious little hints of promise there were – and he had a quick and sure eye for these – that the country's theatrical standards stood any chance of rising. Shaw, Wilde and Pinero were only just born or on the point of being born when Lewes's regular weekly dramatic criticisms came to an end, but Lewes paved the way and Shaw, looking back over the journalistic first-nighters between himself and Hazlitt, picked confidently on Lewes as the one most worthy of attention.

Herbert Spencer was no theatregoer. He would have been afraid of catching cold or even, the times being how they were, some far more desperate infection. Yet however vast the difference in temperament, the two men had become friends very quickly after their first meeting early in 1850. Spencer stimulated Lewes's interest in scientific observation and experiment; Lewes, with the *Biographical History of Philosophy* fresh in his head, was able to fill in for Spencer gaps in abstract speculation. (At seventeen this boy from Derby had started work as an engineer with the London and Birmingham Railway. In the 'higher' sense, he was virtually self-taught and Lewes's quick, accurate appraisals of men as thinking reeds were of the utmost value to him.) Spencer, so solid and yet so timid, took pleasure in the company of one who appeared so easy, free, confident and amusing. 'As a companion,' he said, 'Lewes was extremely attractive. Interested in, and well informed upon, a variety of subjects, full of anecdotes and an admirable mimic; it was impossible to be dull in his company.' It's astonishing how much unanimity there is, amongst all those weighty people, on this matter of Lewes's charm and

77

verve, his ability to suit his talk and manner to the company he happened to be keeping at any particular moment, and to have been able to arouse such responsiveness in a man as dour, as unplayful and as aloof as Spencer is the strongest proof one can offer of the wide ranging strength of his personal appeal.

This ebullience of his becomes more surprising over the years of the mid-century. The years 1850–4 and, quite despairingly after October 1851 when Agnes bore her second child by Thornton Hunt, were times of dire personal difficulty for Lewes, working as he was with an unrelenting fury of energy to keep his paper fed and, in its inevitably modest way, prosperous. Perhaps he found Spencer's cold imperviousness to the usual human emotions and the pretty usual human mess in some way comforting and reassuring. They talked at length together, about abstractions for the most part, and accompanied each other on those vast Victorian walks which went such a long way towards counter balancing the effects (dire on poor Thackeray) of those vast Victorian meals. Yet he never so much as hinted to Spencer that his Agnes was sleeping with Thornton Hunt, his co-editor, and this points clearly to what was always another strong trait in Lewes's character. He was one of those men who in conversation wanted always to please, to be engaging. And he had the gift – it's a fairly rare one and a precious one too if you have anything of the careerist in you and want to push upwards quickly – of knowing instinctively what the particular person he was talking to would like to hear. And Lewes would tell him just that. By the same token he knew what subjects to avoid. Spencer, quite for certain, wasn't the sort of man who would enjoy hearing about cuckoldry, and in the huge autobiography he published in 1904, a quarter of a century after Lewes was dead, he had no knowledge at the beginning of their friendship of the marital tempests this biographical philosopher was sailing through. How admirably thoughtful of Lewes to keep his cool, so the aged, hypochondriacal philosopher thought, and paid him tribute. '. . . But alike then and afterwards I was impressed by his forgiving temper and generosity. Whatever else may be thought, it is undeniable that he discharged the responsibilities which devolved upon him with great conscientiousness, and at much cost in self-sacrifice, notwithstanding circumstances which many men would have made a plea for repudiating them . . .' Spencer is here consciously taking the line of counsel for the defence. And this of course is understandable. Herbert Spencer was about to take an improbable, yet none the less central, part in establishing what was to become, with only a year or two of delay, the most famous, the most talked about liaison amoureuse of Victorian England.

4

Mary Ann Evans arrived in London from Rosehill, Charles and Cara Bray's substantial house about a mile away from the centre of Coventry, in January 1851. Her solid, God fearing, competent estates–managing father, Robert Evans, had died in May 1849. He wasn't stunningly rich, but all the same there were comfortable portions for all the members of his family. Mary Ann received £2,000 in trust together with household goods to the value of £100. She had nursed him devotedly for the last five months of his life but she lacked, he thought, the seriousmindedness proper in his daughter and couldn't be regarded as his favourite.

A fortnight after her father's death she set off, with the Brays, her friends since 1841, for a tour of the continent. She was low in spirit, as well as physically weakened, by her long attendance on her father. Charles Bray, who had married Caroline (Cara) Hennell in 1836, was a ribbon manufacturer; Cara's family too were in the same trade, and ribbon making, in the 1830s and 40s, was a profitable business. The Brays were very comfortably off indeed. Bray, having trouble around this time with the doctrine of the Trinity, had ceased to profess Christianity before his marriage and had found refuge in the science of phrenology as expounded by George Combe.* Bray and his Cara were in a position to maintain their considerable unorthodoxy

---

* 1788–1847. Wealthy writer on sociology and, above all, phrenology. He wrote too on education and urged reform of the prison system. He had a considerable influence on thinking people and was far from being an imposter; his views on education in particular were taken up and spread widely. His *Elements of Phrenology* (1824) persuaded many very intelligent people that study of the contours of the skull would yield much guidance about the character of the patient. His own character had much to interest the student: at whiles a debauchee and then a contrasting spell of high moral principles in the conduct of his personal life.

quite boldly. When they married Bray was enjoying the reassuringly solid income of £1,200 a year.

The party spent two days in Paris before moving on to Lyons by rail and coach. From there they took to the river in the usual way as far as Avignon. Turning eastwards to Nice, they rounded the Alps by the coast road and then went northwards again to Switzerland and Vevey. After a brief stop here Bray took Mary Ann to Geneva, left her in the large Pension Plongeon and started back to the English midlands. In October she removed in order to stay with M. et Mme D'Albert-Durade in the Rue des Chanoines. The couple were middle aged, musical, and, she was assured, had 'beaucoup d'esprit'. She paid them 150 francs a month, had breakfast in her own room but dined with them. She stayed there till mid-March 1850, when M. D'Albert escorted her all the way back to London. The sledge trip over the Alps wasn't something a young woman only just past thirty was to be expected to undertake on her own. She stayed briefly in London and then returned to the Brays at Rosehill. D'Albert stayed on in London and was in England for two months visiting her briefly at Rosehill. She took him to see Kenilworth Castle. She wrote to him to her life's end and they addressed each other as 'tu'. In taking the long and arduous journey to London – for no payment because Mary Ann's capital was in trust and she had only £90 a year of income – and in lingering so long in a foreign land D'Albert showed devotion. Was there something of an affair between them? Probably not. But with Mary Ann Evans at just turned thirty it is unwise to be too positive on the point.

How was she now to plan her future? The question was a troublesome one. The Brays were welcoming. Phrenologically and theologically she and they were at one. Yet clearly it wouldn't do to think of herself as a permanent resident at Rosehill. She had already shown signs of outstanding ability. In January 1844, when just twenty-six, she had embarked on the formidable task of translating Strauss's *Leben Iesu* into English, moreover, it was indirectly through Cara, or rather through Cara's brother, Charles Hennell, that this commission had come her way.

81

Charles, sickly and tuberculous, married Elizabeth Rebecca Brabant in November 1843. He had, as early as 1838, brought out *An Inquiry concerning the Origin of Christianity*, a work quite out of line with the solid orthodoxy of Mary Ann's father but which influenced her own thinking considerably. Not long after his far from outrageous work appeared Charles was visited by a medical man from Devizes, a Dr R. H. Brabant, who felt he must see Hennell because he (Brabant) was also engaged upon a similar kind of work (but unfinished) which was large in scope and was intended to cast doubt upon the supernaturalism inherent in Christianity. Brabant invited him to Devizes, and there Hennell met his daughter Rebecca, Rufa as she was known, who only a few days later received a proposal of marriage from him. Rufa was, even then, in the early stages of putting the intractable David Friedrich Strauss into English. The doctor was against the marriage to begin with, as well he might have been seeing that Charles Hennell had a killing disease on him, and no further movement towards a marriage was made for upwards of a year. Then, holidaying with some of his many sisters, Hennell met Rufa again, and in the autumn of 1843 they were married. This was a Unitarian affair conducted in London at the Finsbury Chapel and Mary Ann was a bridesmaid.

After the wedding Brabant, much taken with Mary Ann, invited her back to Devizes, his notion apparently being that having just lost one daughter he might acquire another who would do just as well, or perhaps even better. Characteristically, Mary Ann was delighted by the idea. For her always any man was better than no man – even if that man was a semi-fraudulent old person of sixty-two. 'Ever writing and re-writing' was how the vinegary Eliza Lynn saw him, 'correcting and destroying, he never got farther than the introductory chapter of a book which he intended to be epoch-making.'

Dr Brabant was a married man and his wife was blind. Dr Brabant was also lavishly attentive to Mary Ann. Mary Ann was put into the best of humours by this; Mrs Brabant, blind though she was, became quickly aware of what was going on and had a sister in the house to do battle for her.

Although I told you that the Devizes air was good for me, [Mary Ann told Cara] I have been anything but well since I came, and after reading German for two hours to the Dr. I have often felt so faint as to be obliged to lie on the sofa till walking time . . . We are going to dine . . . this evening . . . Dr Brabant spoils me for everyone else and the Trennung from such a companion will be very painful . . .

Earlier in the same letter she shows true understanding of herself when she says, accepting that Devizes, with all its *schwärmerei*, and herself would soon have to be parted, '. . . I shall miss my lessons from the arch-phrenologist! Never mind, I shall miss, too, being told that I have some very bad propensities and that my moral and animal regions are unfortunately balanced . . .' None of this is perhaps to be taken too seriously. As a letter writer, Mary Ann, both early and late, was capable of being archly playful in a manner that is hard to bear. But there's no doubt that she liked Dr Brabant immensely, and if blind Mrs Brabant became upset about it – well, there was nothing much that Mary Ann felt in the mood to do about that. 'Beautifully sincere, conscientious and benevolent and every thing besides that one would have one's friends to be. He is just come to invite me to walk as a reward for the good character I am giving him . . .' Blind Mrs Brabant had probably long since given up trying to do anything much about the doctor, but if only she could have aimed it straight how much she must have longed to take her stick to this intellectual, but frisky, young lady. Early in December however Mrs Brabant did manage to see her off and Mary Ann returned to Foleshill and her ailing father.

But in the first month of 1844 Rufa Brabant found tackling David Friedrich Strauss and marriage both at once a bit too much for her; so her *Life of Jesus* was handed over to Mary Ann. This was mainly through the good offices of Sara Hennell who had had much to do with the undertaking originally and was to remain until the middle 1850s Mary Ann's closest friend. Sara gave the details when, at the end of her life, she wrote a memoir of her brother Charles which was privately printed in the year of her death.

> The work . . . went on till their marriage, [Charles and Rufa's] and then it was passed over into hands that were in every way competent for it: those of our friend Miss Evans, who lived at Foleshill, adjoining Coventry. I still, though quite unnecessarily, continued my supervision, and I found in it a real pleasure from its showing me with what delicacy the meaning was being made to transfuse itself . . .

She finished the Strauss translation at last in April 1846 and it came out that June, published by John Chapman but having no note as to the identity of the translator. During these years, and indeed right up to 1849 when her father died, she also sent pieces to the *Coventry Herald* which was conveniently edited by Charles Bray. One of her contributions to the paper was a review of J. A. Froude's *Nemesis of Faith*, and Froude, who had by this time read the anonymously translated Strauss, was discerning enough to recognise the same hand in the Strauss translation and in the review of his own book. Froude wrote to Chapman to find out the name of this reviewer. Cara Hennell wrote to her sister to say: 'Poor girl, I am so pleased she should have this little episode in her dull life . . .'

In a very small way, therefore, Mary Ann had begun to see the beginnings of a possible career ahead of her when she returned to England after her eight months of Genevan recuperation. She had also, immediately after finishing the *Leben Iesu*, started work on the immensely more difficult *Tractatus* of Spinoza – a strange coincidence, this, since it was in May 1843 that the to-her-unknown Lewes published his *Westminster Review* article on Spinoza. It wasn't Lewes that set her off: she'd begun before his article appeared, but what he wrote may well have encouraged her.

Then, in October 1850, career prospects for Marian – this was how she was now signing herself – became suddenly clearer. Indeed they became bright and exciting. John Chapman arrived from London at Rosehill. He came with Robert Mackay, a well heeled middle aged bachelor Wykehamist whose book *The Progress of the Intellect, as Exemplified in the Religious Development of the Greeks and Hebrews*, least catchpenny of titles, Chapman had recently published. Chapman had persuaded the *Westminster Review* to take an article on Mackay's work, and wanted Marian to write it. She did this and made a long, solid, capable job of it. The article appeared in the review in January 1851. John Chapman was twenty-nine at this time, a tall and handsome fellow with a wife fourteen years older than he was, a physically unattractive lady who had in compensation brought to the marriage sufficient capital to enable Chapman to adventure into the risky business of independent publishing. He lived at 142 Strand, very large premises which allowed him to conduct his business on the ground floor and then, on the floors above accommodate himself and his family and also run, with Mrs Chapman presiding, a brisk boarding house business as well.

When her article was finished, Marian – didn't she trust the post? – took it up herself to 142 Strand and stayed there a fortnight. Chapman after all was a most attractive fellow just a couple of years younger than herself, a practised womaniser, and a much more exciting personality altogether than Dr Brabant of Devizes. The Chapmans had three children, two – aged six and five – lived at home; the youngest, who was a deaf mute, had been kindly taken over by Mrs Chapman's brother who lived in Nottingham. In addition, not an impermanent boarder but part of the household, was Elisabeth Tilley. She was pretty, about the same age as Chapman, and helped his wife with the boarding business and with the children. She also slept with Chapman when the mood took him, or her, or both of them together. Did Marian take in this complicated situation during that fortnight in November 1850? Almost certainly she did: she was prodigiously intelligent and her beady little eyes missed little. Sometimes on Friday nights Chapman held parties for his authors. At one of these Marian met Eliza Lynn, whose somewhat indelicate stage novel *Realities* Chapman was shortly to publish despite marked disapproval on the part of Mrs Chapman. Eliza, three years younger than Marian, was effusive in welcoming a newcomer. Marian was 'such a loveable person,' Eliza said. If the young Miss Lynn, bespectacled as she was, could make her way alone in literary London, Marian felt certain that she could and was determined to try. She went back to stay with her sister Chrissey (Mrs Edward Clarke) at Meriden over Christmas, but by January 8 she was back at 142 Strand, an inmate, an independent freelance. Chapman met her at Euston and noted in his diary that she was friendly but formal. Probably Miss Tilley had warned her in advance that for the sake of good relations all round she should hold him off.

The first plunge brought no literary success and in place of it strong and immediate emotional thunderstorms. There the four of them were: Chapman with his hazardous publishing ventures; Susanna the neglected wife in her forties whose capital and labour kept the whole venture afloat and who rightly felt that she was getting no sort of a bargain for her money; Elisabeth Tilley who felt that her claims on Chapman were at any rate stronger than those of this Warwickshire miss who was failing to make any significant progress in the literary world save in the subordinate role of translator. Marian met ex-curates who had lost their faith, like Thomas Wilson who was about to lose his job as Professor of English at the new Bedford College for women. She tried for work on the reviews but without success.

> There is really no time to do anything here, [she told Cara] I am a poor never-having-time-to-clean-myself potter's wessel. Mr Hickson [then proprietor of the *Westminster*] . . . writes that he shall not have room for it [a review she had written] and that the subject will not suit on this occasion, so you see I am obliged to be idle and I like it best.

Did she 'like it best' because she was having an affair with Chapman? Was it simply a matter of hand holding and sighs and tears, or did she go to bed with him? There can be no certain answer to this question. All that can be said is that Chapman was handsome, promiscuous and a liar and that Mary Ann's sexuality was always insistent and powerful. Chapman kept a diary, but the pages for mid-February 1851 have been torn out. This doesn't of course in itself prove anything beyond the fact that between the three women and the one man in 142 Strand strong emotions all round were being excited that month and crackling high tension filled the air. What is certain is that by the beginning of March, Susanna Chapman and Elisabeth Tilley had decided between them that if one woman couldn't stand mistress of the field at 142 then at any rate two contenders would be better than three and that Mary Ann had best pack her bags and be off back to the midlands. T. P. O'Connor, late Victorian parliamentarian, journalist and gossip, remembered chatting with Chapman as they walked along the Strand in the 1890s. As they passed this by now elderly Don Juan's premises of long ago Chapman 'gave my arm an eloquent squeeze, and whispered, "You know, she was very fond of me!"' Would Chapman have bothered to say this so long afterwards, when all passion was spent, when George Eliot the famous had been dead over a decade and was beginning to slide down from her pinnacle, unless she'd been his mistress? It's certainly hard to believe that he would – but Chapman was a vainglorious man.

Back in Rosehill Mary Ann sent stiff little business letters to Chapman; but then in April Chapman struck lucky. A wealthy freethinker called Edward Lombe offered to back his unorthodox publishing with substantial money, and Chapman took over the *Westminster Review* from Hickson. The immediate and urgent question was how to run the paper, because Chapman's strong point was always charm rather than brains. Francis Newman, his missionary journeys on behalf of the Plymouth Brethren long behind him and now a sturdy unbeliever, offered to help him; so did phrenologist Combe. But Chapman saw himself in the role of editor and liked the look of what he saw. Fleeting doubts about his intellectual capacity to fill such a job did occur to him though, and the thought of Mary Ann, hard working, intelligent and, he was sure, adoring, came into his mind.

Charles Bray, probably not aware of any tangled webs, suggested to him that he should visit Rosehill, and at the end of May Chapman went, as might be expected making light of the fury of two deserted women in the Strand.

Predictably Chapman talked her into coming back. She 'put herself in my hands prepared to accept any arrangement I may make either for her return to the Strand or to any house in London I may think suitable in October . . .' He says also that during this visit he wrote the greater part of the Prospectus for the *Westminster* now soon to appear under new leadership, and 'gave it [the Prospectus] to M. to finish.' One's guess would be that M. would have been given quite a lot to finish. Whether he offered her a salary he doesn't say. Perhaps he thought that free board and lodging would be quite adequate remuneration for services rendered. At any rate on September 29 Mary Ann/ Marian was back in her old room in the Strand. Susanna Chapman and Elisabeth Tilley took no pleasure in her return but Chapman had waved his wand of irresistibility over them.

Marian was immediately in the literary swim. Contributors had to be selected and talked to. Chapman, all for sociability, gave parties. And it is here that Herbert Spencer returns to the story. Both he and Lewes – the ever busy Lewes – were contributors to Chapman's *Westminster*, and a week or so after taking up her job with the review, on October 6 1851, Lewes, Spencer and Marian all happened to find themselves in Jeffs' bookshop in the Burlington Arcade and Spencer made the introduction. No immediate spark was kindled. She thought Lewes an unimpressive little chap with an ugly face. Spencer on the other hand, if no sexual magnet, had clearly a strong intelligence and was close at hand. He worked as sub-editor on the *Economist* and its offices were immediately across the way from Chapman's place in the Strand. Spencer was only thirty-one. 'Propinquity does it,' as no less a person than Mary Arnold (Mrs Humphry Ward) was later to remark.

Much has been written – notably by Spencer himself and also by Mrs Sidney Webb – about what was possibly, and possibly not, a love affair between Marian Evans and

Herbert Spencer. The terrace of Somerset House was only a stone's throw from the offices of both of them, and Chapman, possessing a key, had access to it. In 1851 the embankment had not been built so that the terrace afforded clear access to the river and provided therefore an agreeable, if sometimes whiffy, place for promenades. Ford Madox Ford has a story, and if it is untruthful then all one can do is point out that the source of it is no less a person than the Secretary to the Inland Revenue.

My uncle William Rossetti Mr James [Henry James] considered to be an unbelievable bore. He had once heard the Secretary to the Inland Revenue recount how he had seen George Eliot proposed to by Herbert Spencer on the leads of the terrace at Somerset House . . . The Inland Revenue headquarters is housed in that building and the philosopher and the novelist were permitted by the authorities [Ford doesn't seem to have known about Chapman's key] there to walk as a special privilege. 'You would think,' Mr James exclaimed, with indignation, his dark eyes really flashing, 'that a man would make something out of a story like *that*. But the way he told it was like this,' and heightening and thinning his tones into a sort of querulous official organ, Mr James quoted: 'I have as a matter of fact frequently meditated on the motives which induced the Lady's refusal of one so distinguished; and after mature consideration I have arrived at the conclusion that although Mr Spencer with correctness went down upon one knee and grasped the Lady's hand he completely omitted the ceremony of removing his high hat, a proceeding which her sense of the occasion might have demanded . . .' Is that the way to tell *that* story?

Well, amongst the Rossettis, so beset by aberrations and *nervosité*, William Michael is undoubtedly the solid and reliable one. Henry James may well have been not far off the truth in considering him a bore, but William Michael wasn't the sort of man to make up a story. Perhaps the Secretary to the Inland Revenue was pulling Mr Rossetti's leg? But that again isn't the sort of frivolousness one associates with a mid-nineteenth century Secretary to the Inland Revenue. Would Henry James have invented the whole thing in order to give weight to his point about the boringness of William Michael Rossetti? This isn't likely either because the James that Fordie knew was the immensely avuncular, pernickety Lamb House James and not the friskier, youthful immigrant of 1870. So perhaps in the end one is driven to the conclusion that here is Fordie exercising his abundant talent to amuse.

What evidence there is would suggest that the likelier one of the pair to go down on one knee on the leads of Somerset House, high hat or no high hat, would have been Marian Evans. She wanted a man and the ascetic, Spencerian reserve might well have had its attractions for her, coming fresh as she did from Chapman and his Tarquin's ravishing stride. And beyond doubt he felt drawn to her. She was a woman of outstanding intellect, someone on the plane of Harriet Martineau or even on a higher plane still – and, unlike Harriet Martineau, there wasn't one ounce of masculinity in her. She was dependent. She wanted an escort. His journalistic job was a help because it was a source of free tickets. 'My free admission for two,' he says, 'to the theatres and to the Royal Italian Opera, were, during these early months of 1852, much more used than they otherwise would have been, because I had frequently – indeed nearly always – the pleasure of her companionship . . .' But Marian wasn't beautiful. She had nice eyes some said, but she wasn't beautiful, and she knew she wasn't beautiful and when she examined herself in the mirror, which she often did, the fact was there and it distressed her. Hard to believe though it may be, this lack of physical attraction seems to have counted for a great deal with Herbert Spencer. Writing as an ancient celibate in the early 1900s he announced with staggering smugness, 'Physical beauty is a *sine qua non* with me; as was once unhappily proved where the intellectual traits were of the highest.'

Whatever happened above Somerset House a firm understanding between them had been reached by the end of April 1852. 'We have agreed,' Marian wrote to the Brays, 'that we are not in love with each other, and that there is no reason why we should not have as much of each other's company as we like.' Whether Herbert Spencer would have gone along with the wording of that first sentence of hers is much open to question. 'He has told me that he is not in love with me,' would probably have been the likelier version so far as he was concerned, and as for what the Secretary to the Inland Revenue saw or didn't see on the leads of Somerset House, that must be left as a subject for debate between the five of them – the Secretary, Herbert Spencer, Henry James, William Michael Rossetti, and Fordie – in one of the more exclusive Senior Common Rooms in Paradise.

All that summer of 1852 Spencer continued to take her out in a cautious kind of way – to the opera at Covent Garden for example – if the man-woman relationship was ruled out: 'he is a good, delightful creature and I always feel better for being with him . . .' She laboured hard for Chapman in the Strand, suffered headaches – 'My room here has the light one might expect midway up a chimney,' she told Combe, 'with a little blaze of fire below, and a little glimmer of sky above . . .' She came more and more to see that Chapman was a fraud and that the effective conduct of the *Westminster Review* rested upon her shoulders and hers alone – the unregarded plain spinster with a passionate heart and a powerful intellect. Her sister Chrissey's husband, Edward Clarke, became suddenly and seriously ill in the mysterious Victorian way and died in a matter of hours, leaving six children, the eldest not yet fifteen. Marian hurried to Meriden that Christmas (1852); her sister would be left with about £100 a year, little indeed even then to cope with the numerous responsibilities devolving upon her. Isaac, the eldest brother and now head of the family, grudgingly agreed that he might be able to do something, if only a little, to help, and in January Marian went back to London persuaded that slaving as Chapman's dogsbody was the least unpromising way in which she might be able to help.

The winter of 1852–3 was indeed a time of trouble for both Marian and Lewes and, after that introduction the year before, they began, as Spencer cooled, to see more of each other. Lewes was beginning to see that the absolute rigidity of marriage vows as proclaimed in the Book of Common Prayer, and publicly uttered though inwardly mocked by himself and Agnes in St Margaret's Westminster not so many years before, might after all have something to be said for it beyond the sinewy perfection of Cranmer's prose expression. He told Marian, we don't know exactly when, of Agnes's continued liaison with his *Leader* colleague Thornton Hunt: Was he, George Henry Lewes, to consent to act as legal father to a growing number of bastards fathered on his wife by his partner? And if he were to refuse so to consent, how was he to shape his life in the future? By condoning the relationship at the beginning and accepting the first fruits of the Thornton-Agnes fornications as his, he'd put himself out of court for ever as an appellant for divorce. He told Marian all this; she took pleasure in her role of intimate confidante. It was a role she always enjoyed. She went about with him. As 'Vivian' in the *Leader* he got tickets for everything. Soon she knew all about the troubles besetting him: a polyandrous wife who persisted in producing children he hadn't fathered but who none the less got intermixed with the genuine articles. Sexual freedom was still acceptable in theory, but he became more and more exasperatedly conscious of the practical difficulties and tensions this freedom could lead to. Perhaps the rigid prohibitions of orthodoxy – thou shalt not do this, thou shalt not do that – stemmed from an awareness of the harsh dilemmas which sensible sounding humanistic theorists were laying up for themselves once they started acting out their principles. By November he was calling often at 142 Strand, and not necessarily always on business. 'When I had sat down again,' she noted in November, '. . . rap at the door – Mr Lewes, who, of course, sits talking till the second bell rings . . .' And by the following March, 'We had a pleasant evening last Wednesday. Lewes, as always, genial and amusing. He has quite won my liking in spite of myself.' The 'in spite of myself' is interesting. It must mean that in spite of emancipated ideas Marian still couldn't quite discount the fact that a married man was a married man. Dr

Brabant was a married man, so was Chapman, so now was Lewes, although a sorely tried one. Why was it always the ones who had already made solemn promises to others who rapped at her door and stayed chatting for so much longer than the proprieties could possibly consider appropriate?

They were both of them working hard, Lewes bursting out all over the place in a way she couldn't manage. As Slingsby Lawrence he was adapting plays for Mathews, he was preparing for separate publication a series of articles he'd done for the *Leader* under the title of *Comte's Philosophy of the Sciences*, and then there was the boulevardier, theatre loving Lewes who wrote his weekly 'Vivian' piece for the paper. Marian enjoyed going round with Vivian. That April she said: 'I am taking doses of agreeable follies . . . Last night, I went to the French Theatre, and tonight I am going to the opera to hear *William Tell*. People are very good to me. Mr Lewes is especially kind and attentive and has quite won my regard, after having had a good deal of vituperation. Like a few other people in the world, he is much better than he seems. A man of heart and conscience wearing a mask of flippancy . . .' The vituperation must have been verbal. It must have happened during the earlier of those long chats in her workroom in the Strand when he told her first how he felt about his Rose having been plucked by Thornton. But by the summer of 1853 there was never in her mind any thought of vituperation. She quite understood. And it was nice to go backstage on the arm of Vivian and watch the actors and actresses – wild, unintellectual creatures – taking their grease paint off. In return she gave him a hand when he was pressed with his philosophical articles. When it came to dealing with Comte, or even with the vastly more profound and elusive Spinoza, Marian could handle the problem as well as he – perhaps even better.

Later in the summer she took six weeks off and took lodgings in St Leonard's. The weather was kind and the 'genial air – so different from what I have had for a year before – make me feel as happy and stupid as a well-conditioned cow . . .' There's no certain evidence that

93

Lewes went down to see her there, but they were very close by then, and he probably did. Unlike his friend Herbert Spencer, Lewes was no ditherer where women were concerned. If by that time, the late summer of 1853, he'd decided that Marian was a woman he wanted – and it's pretty certain that he had – he'd have been most unlikely to have seen wisdom in a six weeks' total suspension of companionship. More probable would have been a return to the seaside to take her a crunchy contemplative stroll over the shingle and thence back to her lodgings. And there his natural aptitude in the conducting of an affair together with his considerable experience would have told him how best to proceed.

Certainly one decision was come to during that seaside stay: she would no longer stay unsalaried working for Chapman at 142 Strand. The paper was having a *succès d'estime* but wasn't proving profitable; Marian needed money because now there was widowed Chrissey and her six children to be helped. Propping up the incompetent Chapman with her outstanding abilities wasn't likely to advance her materially. Lewes would have told her as much. She continued for the time being to keep a directing hand on the *Westminster Review*, but from October she went to work from a new address, 21 Cambridge Street, Hyde Park Square, a boarding house run by a landlady who could cook.

Here she could live a private life unobserved by Chapman and his two watchful ladies. Here Lewes could call and stay for as long as he liked. Here quite certainly, if not at St Leonard's earlier, they became lovers. 'I have gained . . . a great deal physically by my change,' she told the Brays, and they were free to take that adverb any way they liked.

In November she told Chapman that the labour involved in doing his work for him in addition to her own was proving a load heavier than she wanted to bear. She knew that Chapman's money difficulties were getting more pressing with every month that passed. It was she who had the disagreeable job of coping with overmatter. Chapman would commission material from people who often enough were well worth giving space to – Spencer perhaps, or

Froude or Huxley – and as a result Marian would be faced with an abundance of copy far exceeding the *Westminster*'s frail ability to digest. But who was she to serve a rejection slip on a commissioned author? And sometimes she would find herself having to deal not only with a commissioned author but with a man who had put money of his own into the re-launching of the paper after the takeover from Hickson. Phrenologist Combe for example, who supplied an impossibly long piece about prison reform and naturally expected to see himself in print. Chapman's solution to this awkward problem was a simple one. He told Marian to thin the thing down. But of course what Combe's piece wanted was major surgery. Sheet upon sheet would have to be ripped out and then it would fall to Marian to put an emaciated Humpty-Dumpty Combe together again in some sort of shape that the public might find acceptable. It was a good deal to ask of an associate editor, and Chapman blithely asked it. She wrote appealingly to Combe himself. 'If I were sole editor I would take the responsibility on myself; but being a woman and something less than half an editor, I do not see how the step you propose [of printing Prison Reform in extenso] could be taken with the naturalness and bienséance that could alone favour any good result.' Chapman, however, demanding but also wheedling, managed to put off her intention to quit. Perhaps his wheedling was helped along by her own money difficulties, and by the fact that as a translator from the difficult German, she had already committed herself to Chapman to provide a follow-up to the Strauss translation. Chapman furthermore had commissioned an original work from her, to be called *The Idea of a Future Life*, and it was natural that by this time – after all she was thirty-five – she should want to see herself launched as a writer on her own account.

Then also in the spring of 1854 Lewes's headaches, his general lack of physical robustness, the worries brought on by his domestic infelicity, combined to force him to lay aside for a while the huge variety of writing stints he had taken upon himself. Marian willingly helped out with some of the work he might otherwise have had to let slide. On April 18 she wrote to Cara:

. . . I am rather overdone with the week's work and the prospect of what is to come next. Poor Lewes is ill and is ordered not to put pen to paper for a month, so I have something to do for him in addition to my own work which is rather pressing. He is gone to Arthur Helps in Hampshire for ten days, and I really hope that this total cessation from work in obedience to a peremptory order will end in making him better than he has been for the last year . . . No opera and no fun for me for the next month! . . .

Clearly Marian had taken him on. She writes about him in a wifely – almost maternal – way. For a year and more Marian has been watching over him, taking the troubles of his wasted life upon herself, and now that he has for the time at least worked himself to a standstill she is willing to shoulder some of his editorial and authorial burdens as well, even though she has for the time to forgo the visits to the theatre on the arm of Vivian. Indeed the Vivian column didn't reappear in the paper until May 20, and even when it did return the internal evidence would suggest that Marian has been at work doing her best to imitate Lewes's airy man-about-townish touch.

Ten days with Helps didn't cure him. His headaches and toothaches, the ringing in his ears went disturbingly on. A trip to Paris failed to alleviate and at Bray's suggestion he submitted himself to the drastic remedies of Dr Balbirnie, a medical man taken very seriously at this time. Ten years earlier he had brought out a book called *The Philosophy of the Water-cure*. He practised at Malvern. He made his patients go about wrapped in wet sheets and even if they didn't squeak and gibber they certainly must have had cause. Consumption and scrofula, he claimed, yielded to his therapies, and certainly Victorians in large numbers believed him. Numerous hotels called 'Hydros' lingered on round the coasts of these islands until well into this century, Dr Balbirnie being their only begetter. And Dr Balbirnie also, it appears, managed to chase the headaches out of Lewes's overworked cranium. When he got back from Malvern he wrote a *Leader* article in his Vivian role about the water-cure and gave the doctor a handsome testimonial. When hospitable Hampshire and rackety Paris had brought no oblivion, he says, ' – at this moment a visit from my friend Dr Balbirnie, which ended in a visit *to* him, came as hydropathic salvation . . . Dr Balbirnie is a man of science, and enough of a man of letters to sympathise with and understand the ills to which literary flesh is heir. He persuaded me to come and try Malvern.'

And Dr Balbirnie seems to have managed to do more for him than for some. When he got back in July Marian and he had become firm in their intention to come out into the open immediately about their liaison. In the second week of that month her Feuerbach translation appeared. She had had enough of Chapman and his excessive demands and his constant financial crises. She was tired. Like Lewes she suffered from many, many headaches. Lewes urged that the thing to do now was to go away together, to somewhere abroad, Germany for preference. He couldn't divorce Agnes, still with Thornton Hunt, because of that generous, mistaken impulse which had led him to acknowledge as his own the first fruits of Agnes's and Thornton's bedding down together. And living together as man and wife would be easier abroad. At home the Victorian rules inevitably meant that they'd have to suffer boycott and reprobation.

It's strange perhaps that a couple as freethinking and as unfettered as Marian and Lewes should have allowed themselves to be frightened by this. They knew perfectly well, as did everyone in their circle, that such public attitudes were nothing but a gigantic sham. The Brays, the Chapmans, the Brabants, the Hunts, the Gliddons, the Samuel Laurences – for the men, and for some of the women, promiscuity was an accepted norm. And if we were to extend the circle wider we have only to think of Charles Dickens, Wilkie Collins and Augustus Egg on the rampage in Paris in the 1850s to have further proof that the tightening of Victorian lips into a thin disapproving line at sexual frolics was a wholly Tartuffian exercise. Yet there it was. Whilst themselves having no qualms of any kind about their action they both recognised that – for a time at least and for the benefit of the public at large – it was officially morally reprehensible.

On June 28 Marian went to the Lyceum to see the Slingsby Lawrence piece called *Sunshine Through the Clouds*. Lewes had adapted this from Madame de Girardin's *La Joie fait Peur* – both of them titles wholly apt to the situation they both of them found themselves in. Marian thought it 'Wonderfully original and beautiful [a piece which] makes one cry rather too much for pleasure'. Then on July 10 she wrote a tidying-up letter to Sara Hennell. 'I am going to pack up the Hebrew Grammar, the Apocryphal Gospels, and your pretty Titian, to be sent to you. Shall I dispatch them by rail or deposit them with Mr Chapman to be asked for by Mr Bray when he comes to town? I shall soon send you a goodbye, for I am preparing to go to "Labassecour".' In other words she didn't want even Sara to know exactly where she was off to. Charlotte Brontë's *Villette* had come out the year before and in it she calls Belgium 'Labassecour'. Sara would have read *Villette* so would she conclude that Belgium was to be her destination? Sara was free to conclude whatever she chose. Nine days later she wrote again to Sara and the Brays. 'Dear Friends – all three, I have only time to say good bye . . . Poste Restante Weimar. . .' Next day they were off.

5

It became a famous partnership, and it lasted all their lives. Thackeray died on Christmas Eve, 1863; Dickens died in June 1870. Once they were gone Marian Lewes as she signed herself was promoted by general consent to the position of principal English novelist. Lewes? Well, the role of Lewes in all this is as puzzling as it is interesting.

In 1854 Lewes was a far weightier figure than Marian. He had established a considerable reputation for himself amongst the intelligentsia of Victorian England. He was radical, Benthamite, reformist. He stood alone as a guide to philosophy and philosophers all down the centuries; he championed and interpreted the innovative philosophers of his own age; as 'Vivian' he played an entirely different literary role: as columnist he kept his finger on the pulse of current affairs but kept his touch light; as a dramatic critic he never lost his enthusiasm, never adjusted his judgments to suit the needs of a period when the English stage, rich enough in performers, was dismally short of dramatists of quality. He wrote busily for the stage himself, even though he was content for the most part to go to Paris for the original play and then work on a pretty root-and-branch adaptation of this. Novels? Well, at any rate he had written some as a very young man, and although they wouldn't now stand up to reissue they do contain lively scenes and sharp dialogue. At the time of his great decision he was working during odd moments on a biography of Goethe which is still read.

So why, once the steamer the *Ravensbourne* had started to thrust its way down the Thames and thence out towards Antwerp, did Lewes, quite slowly and bit by bit of course, begin the process of building up his beady eyed little partner into a monumental prophetess figure who was to dominate the London literary world of the 1870s and early

80s? Or did he have nothing much at all to do with it? Was he satisfied simply to be agent, financial adviser and publicity man? Was it just that by 1854–5 Marian Evans, Warwickshire's second volcanic genius, was ripe to erupt?

These aren't easy questions. When she sailed up the Scheldt in the first light of that fine summer morning in 1854, Marian was within four months of completing her thirty-fifth year. Victorian life expectancy would have put her well into her second half. At the age she was at that moment Emily Brontë had been four and a half years dead, Charlotte had written *The Professor, Jane Eyre* and *Shirley*; Marian had learnt how to put a paper together, had translated Strauss, and had written something notably tedious of her own about Feuerbach. Mrs Gaskell, admittedly, was another late developer, but then she had married at twenty-two and had borne children, and she was to put it on record later that in her view prime time was time devoted to her children and not to novel writing. During that long, honeymoon, spent for the most part in Weimar and Berlin, Marian plunged into no novel, no short story. She translated, she wrote a review for the *Leader* on Sir Benjamin Brodie's *Psychological Inquiries*, but her creative imagination still lay strangely quiescent. Lewes by contrast, although physically still far from well, was very busy. He was half way through his biography of Goethe when they set off together, but decided, once they reached Weimar, to scrap what he had done and start afresh. His book had been based mainly on Goethe's own *Dichtung und Wahrheit*, but he was able to gather plentiful fresh facts about his hero in Weimar and was able to talk to many people with personal memories of the great man who had been dead a mere twenty-two years when he arrived with his serious, hard reading lady.

And yet this lady, so mysteriously slow to get started, was quite quickly to establish a great reputation as a novelist. When she died in December 1880 her position as England's number one novelist was unassailed and apparently unassailable. After 1880, though, there did set in a slow decline in esteem. When Leslie Stephen wrote a short book about her life and work which was published in

1902, he noted at the end that, her '. . . works . . . have not, at the present day, quite so high a position as was assigned to them by contemporary enthusiasm . . .' And he thought that this might perhaps be due 'to the partial misdirection of her powers in the later period'. This was the period of *Middlemarch*, *Felix Holt* and *Daniel Deronda*. There's no doubt that Stephen was reflecting the views commonly held about her near the turn of the century. In the Edwardian decade she was thought to be ponderous, over solemn. Meredith was the man to admire. And indeed, right up to 1945, she remained under something of a cloud.

Then, in 1948, came F. R. Leavis, choosy picker of winners, to the rescue. Leavis was a man who delighted in placing his favourites in a thinly populated Valhalla. Joseph Conrad was in it. So was D. H. Lawrence. And George Eliot. One can imagine them nodding distantly to each other up there where the space was large and the population sparse. And as for Leslie Stephen and his 'misdirection of her powers in the later period', what nonsense that was. *Middlemarch* was the crowning glory of English novel writing – could there possibly be a novel in the language to set beside it? Author of *The Great Tradition*, editor of the radical literary magazine *Scrutiny* (1932–53), Leavis as a teacher was immensely influential, and it's thanks to him that George Eliot's name now stands very high indeed. Perhaps there's an adjustment still to be made to her exalted critical rating.

Of course, no one with any sense is going to argue that there isn't a very great deal to admire in the fiction she wrote. *The Mill on the Floss* and *Adam Bede* are splendid novels; *Silas Marner* has delicacy and charm. But *Middlemarch*, *Felix Holt* and *Daniel Deronda* – wasn't Stephen perfectly right to see in them a misdirection of powers? And how far was she dependent on Lewes? Would she ever have managed to complete a novel without him? It's important to attempt a reply to this question. The picture drawn by Cross, her first legal husband who came forward, young and willing, to bridge the two years' gap between Lewes's death and her own, is of Lewes as the reverential drudge agent, the devoted go-between who brought closer together the stately world of Victorian letters and the shy, solitary genius working away at all those books. It's difficult to accept this, but it's equally difficult to disprove because Lewes himself showed no inclination to put himself forward in any more glorious role. Yet it was he who got her started. It was he who thought she might have a novel in her, or at any rate short stories for the magazines, and suggested, after their return to England in 1855, that she have a try. Money after all wasn't plentiful, and influential people were shaking their heads over them for doing in public what they themselves, very many of them, were doing in decent privacy. It was in September 1856, well on into her thirty-seventh year, that she began on *Amos Barton*, the first novella of the three which were to make up her first published fiction, *Scenes from Clerical Life*. *Adam Bede*, her first full length novel wasn't published till February 1 1859, and after that Lewes noted delightedly in his diary: '*Our* [my italics] books are selling at a glorious rate.'

Why should he say 'our'? Was it simply the natural word to spring to his mind when thinking of an all embracing union and partnership? This seems improbable. That year he was busy preparing papers to read to the British Association, to meet in Aberdeen, on 'Muscular Sense, and Sensory Motor Nerves': he never calls them 'our papers'. Marian left the science to him. Did he leave the fiction to her?

It's true that *The Mill on the Floss* and *Adam Bede*, to instance her first two big successes, are vastly better novels than any of Lewes's three. But his, it should be remembered, were written at a great rate when he was very young. They were very shaky stuff, and Mrs Carlyle had laughed at them. But they'd taught him much about technique. Furthermore, with a score or so of adapted plays helping, they'd taught him even more about the art of writing dialogue. In *Adam Bede* Marian introduces the character of Mrs Poyser, the mistress of Hall Farm. She is a lady extremely good at holding her own – in her cosy Victorian way a very liberated woman indeed. She is sharp, shrewd, wholly disinclined to female nineteenth-century submissiveness in any form, and, above all, she's funny. 'I allays

102

said I'd never marry a man as had got no brains; for where's the use of a woman having brains of her own if she's tackled to a geck as everybody's a-laughing at? She might as well dress herself fine to sit back'ards on a donkey.' This is good salty stuff. Marian proved herself very quickly to be an immensely able and wide ranging imaginative writer. All the same, Mrs Poyser's talk, once you leave the Warwickshire earthiness out of it, smacks much more of Lewes than it does of his common-law wife. After all, what evidence is there, apart from talk such as this, that Marian had a sense of humour? In the nine volumes of her letters there's a good deal of what might be termed archness and a good deal more of subtlety and penetrative insight; an outstandingly intelligent woman lies behind them. But a woman capable of being funny in the Poyserian way? Hardly. Lewes by contrast was well known, in the very far from thick headed company he kept, for his ability to be lively, amusing and funny. He had written dialogue for a long string of plays. Marian had written no dialogue at all.

Towards the end of the German honeymoon, when they were in Berlin, Marian showed Lewes the opening – how tentative, how brief we don't know – of a novel she'd planned some while ago. He didn't encourage her to go on but he did think that it showed that, somewhere, there might be a novel, or at any rate a short story or two in her. But certainly Lewes wouldn't have pushed her during the German sojourn. For a Victorian woman in her middle thirties Marian had done a famous deed and after the excitement of that dash to the *Ravensbourne* she was suffering reactions. Disapproval of what she had done was coming close to home, coming strong, and coming also, sometimes, from surprising quarters. Why should that almost liberated lady Harriet Martineau* see fit to frown? Marian got pettish over that and wrote to Chapman in October 1854

---

* 1802–76. A hard working writer, preaching feminism and agnosticism. She believed in Mesmerism, too, translated Comte's *Cours de Philosophie Positive*, wrote novels, but achieved fame with her *Illustrations of Political Economy* (1877). She was talented, formidable and deaf. Her *Autobiography* (1877) is notable.

from Weimar: 'She is sure to caricature any information for the amusement of the next person to whom she turns her ear trumpet. *Au reste* the thing is done and it is useless to dwell on it . . .' 'The thing is done' – at that moment of writing she sounds as if she was regretting it. Isaac, her beloved elder brother, disapproving for a long time of her retreat from religious orthodoxy, was quite outraged by this elopement with a married man. The break with Isaac depressed her. He was moreover the executor of their father's will and the trustee funds due to her from that will – not vast in amount but sufficient none the less to be important – had to pass through his hands. Isaac was in a strong position: he could not only disapprove of her unorthodoxy and then later of her shameless sexual impropriety, he could also show that disapproval by holding tightly to the purse strings and make it as difficult as possible for Marian to claim the money due to her. She was reduced to working on him through an intermediary. From Berlin in November 1854 she wrote to Bray: 'I shall be obliged to you if you will talk to my brother about the investment you mention, since you are so good as to be willing to take this trouble for my sake. Isaac is always at the King's Head [Coventry] on Friday to transact business, and I enclose a letter to him introducing the subject . . .' This was to humiliate herself.

She was even more upset and humiliated by the very cool reception which Cara and Sophia gave to the news of her going joyously off alone with Lewes. She wrote an urgent, deeply felt letter to Sophia about all this from Weimar on October 31 1854. 'Cara, you and my own sister [Chrissey] are the three women who are tied to my heart by a cord which can never be broken and which really *pulls* me continually. My love for you rests on a past which no future can reverse . . . I must repeat, that I can feel no bitterness towards you, however you may act towards me . . .'

The dire, and not perhaps wholly foreseen, consequences of her escape from London journalism bore down rather on the ardours and delights of Weimar and Berlin. It couldn't have been the time for her to launch out into modes of writing never previously seriously practised, but the fact of her earlier vague plans for some sort of novel was

104

something that Lewes bore in mind. Meanwhile he went ahead with his life of Goethe. He was talking to people who had known the master, who had stories to tell of him. His book was going to be livelier, more immediate than the one some way towards completion which he'd brought out with him from England, and which now, in the light of new knowledge and insights, would need to be re-cast.

But in the summer of 1856, in Tenby, six months after their return from Germany, Marian described in a later article – 'How I came to write Fiction' – being urged by Lewes: 'He began to say very positively, "You must try and write a story."' And that was the beginning of *The Sad Fortunes of the Reverend Amos Barton*, the first of the *Scenes from Clerical Life*. Lewes coached her and encouraged her. How much of it belongs to him and not to her we shan't ever know, but more of it, I would say, than is generally thought. It was Lewes throughout who conducted the negotiations with John Blackwood which led to the publication of the *Scenes*. He discusses the collection freely and frankly with the publisher; Lewes knows those stories astonishingly well. He criticises defects with the enjoyment of someone looking at his own handiwork under cover of an alias. (Lewes had his defects, but self-importance was never one of them.) 'Perhaps the author falls into the error of trying too much to explain the characters of his actors by descriptions instead of allowing them to evolve in the action of the story. . .' he tells Blackwood; but in another letter a few days later he praises *Amos Barton* '. . . as exhibiting in a high degree that faculty which I find to be the rarest of all, viz, the dramatic ventriloquism . . .' Lewes himself always had this knack of dramatic ventriloquism. Did he write some of the dialogue himself? Or did he simply teach her the tricks?

When, much later on, Lewes as editor of the *Fortnightly Review* came to write the series of essays which he collected and published under the title, *The Principles of Success in Literature*, he wrote in the second chapter:

No sunset is precisely similar to another, no two souls are affected by it in a precisely similar way. Thus may the commonest phenomenon have a novelty. To the eye that can read aright there is an infinite variety even in the most ordinary human being. But to the careless, undiscriminating eye all individuality is merged in a misty generality. . .

To set against Lewes's *Fortnightly* essay you have this from *Amos Barton*:

These commonplace people – many of them – bear a conscience, and have felt the sublime prompting to do the painful right; they have their unspoken sorrows, and their sacred joys; their hearts have perhaps gone out towards their first born, and they have mourned over the irreclaimable dead. Nay, is there not a pathos in their very insignificance – in our comparison of their dim and narrow existence with the glorious possibilities of that human nature which they share? Depend upon it, you would gain unspeakably if you would learn with me to see some of the poetry and pathos, the tragedy and comedy, lying in the experience of a human soul that looks out through dull grey eyes, and that speaks in a voice of quite ordinary tones . . .

Who wrote that? Lewes or Marian? In both passages it sounds like the same voice speaking. Of course it might be argued that what is being said in both passages is trite enough to have come from many a hack, but it stands out none the less as one example amongst many of a very close literary alliance.

There can be no doubt that he coached her to begin with. And the pseudonym they chose between them is further evidence of partnership. 'George' asserts equality. Lewes was eager to demonstrate that – perhaps even more than she was. 'Eliot' was a code name and the one she wanted. According to Cross in his biography Marian thought of it simply as 'a good, mouth-filling, easily pronounced word'; but it was more than that – a not too deeply concealed acknowledgment of debt. 'It is to L [Lewes] that I owe it' – I. O. T. Lewes would have jokily invented the *nom de plume* in an effort to alleviate the intense seriousness that was part of her. As her writing life developed, the collaboration probably became less close, but right to the very end there were always discussions, debates, suggestions, amendments. Marian noted in her journal: 'read the opening of my novel to G.' In the printer's manuscript the Introduction is paged 1 to 10, and the page numbering begins again at 1 with the novel proper. Furthermore, the printer's introduction is on unlined paper of a quality different from the rest of the book. This seems to argue that the introduction as read to Lewes didn't satisfy him and that a second attempt at it was made in compliance with his wishes. After *Adam Bede* came out there was gossip galore on the subject of the identity of George Eliot. Chapman pressed Herbert Spencer, who knew, to tell him was it true that the author of the book was Marian. Recalling all this a long time afterwards in his autobiography, Spencer wrote: 'I made no answer; and of course my silence amounted to an admission.' When he told Marian and Lewes of this encounter and of how he had allowed silence to mean assent, they were neither of them at all pleased. ' . . . if the thing is to be denied at all,' Lewes confided to his journal, 'I am for distinct, effective denial rather than equivocation.' And, anyway, by what right had Chapman been so inquisitive? The same day as the diary entry, Lewes wrote to Chapman a letter which lacked nothing in bluntness. 'After the previous correspondence, your continuing to impute those works to Mrs Lewes may be *meant* as a compliment, but *is* an offence against delicacy and friendship. As you seem so very slow in appreciating her feelings on this point, she authorises me to state, as distinctly as language can do so, that she is not the author of *Adam Bede*.'

It is tempting to theorise about this very strong reaction on the part of the not properly married couple. 'She' is not the author of *Adam Bede*' – and the insistent implication is that George To-Whom-I-Owe-It Lewes is. Why otherwise should there have been the tremendous to do, which in fact there was, over the question shall we, shan't we, say that

107

George Eliot equals Marian Evans? The debating and the questioning can't reasonably be explained except on the assumption that, for both of them, what they were doing (if they did it) was blowing a code or destroying a secret pact. Barbara Smith, natural daughter of the wealthy MP for Norwich, Leigh Smith, and a strong figure in the story of nineteenth century female emancipation, had been introduced to Marian by Bessie Parkes when Marian was living with the Chapmans at 142 Strand in 1852. (Barbara by the way was yet another of the women drawn by Chapman's sexual magnetism.) Marian and Barbara became close friends; they were both unsubjugated, unorthodox, intelligent and independent (Marian strugglingly, Barbara very comfortably indeed). Barbara's talent – a considerable one – was for landscape painting. On April 26 1859 Barbara wrote to Marian from Algiers (by then she was Mme Eugène Bodichon):

My darling Marian! Forgive me for being so very affectionate but I am so intensely delighted at your success. I have just got *The Times* of April 12th with the glorious review of *Adam Bede*. . . Now you see I have not yet got the book but I *know* that it is you . . . I . . . read one long extract which instantly made me internally exclaim that it is written by Marian Evans, there is her great big head [Combe and his phrenology] and heart and her wise wide views. Now the more I get of the book the more certain I am, not because it is like what you have written before but because it is like what I see in you. It is an opinion which fire cannot melt out of me. I would 'die in it at the stake' . . . I can't tell you, my dear George Eliot, how enchanted I am . . .

There is much more of this. Barbara becomes almost incoherent in the excited certainty of her discovery.

Marian and George seem both to have been delighted by Barbara Bodichon's bull's eye intuitions. It helped forward, in the most natural way, the transition from Marian Evans (because she could never legally be Marian Lewes) to

George Eliot. And it was important that some sort of certainty should be established because of the Reverend Joseph Liggins. Liggins, a Warwickshire parson, not in any way a notable person, seems to have had imposture thrust upon him and to have lacked the decisiveness to quash it at the beginning. People in Nuneaton and districts round about, reading *Adam Bede* and the *Scenes*, must have realised, reading slowly and carefully and often aloud as people did in the mid-nineteenth century, that the author was talking of places and people familiar to them. They decided that Joseph Liggins, from his country parsonage, must be the child amongst them taking notes. The rumour spread quickly and far enough to become an embarrassment, and Blackwood published a letter in *The Times* denying the rumour.

The letter of thanks was written, by both of them, to Barbara on May 5.

God bless you, dearest Barbara, for your love and sympathy. You are the first friend who has given any symptom of knowing me – the first heart that has recognised me in a book which has come from my heart of hearts. But keep the secret solemnly till I give you leave to tell it and give way to no impulses of triumphant affection. You have sense enough to know how important the *incognito* has been, and we are anxious [the 'we' should be noted] to keep it up a few months longer . . . I read aloud my manuscripts – to my dear dear husband, and he laughed and cried alternately and then rushed to kiss me. He is the prime blessing that has made all the rest possible to me – giving me a response to everything I have written, a response that I could confide in as a proof that I had not mistaken my work . . .

And Lewes himself added at the bottom:

You're darling, and I have always said so! . . . you are *the* person on whose sympathy we both counted . . . The success of the book is *inoui* – over 3,000 copies have been sold already and as 500 is a good success for a novel, you may estimate by that detail what my Polly has achieved . . . you must not call her Marian Evans again: that individual is extinct, rolled up, mashed, absorbed in the Lewesian magnificence! . . .

Doesn't this sound like the gentleman generously giving pride of place to the lady?

The moral awfulness of what she'd done weighed on her, even though intellectually she could brush guilt feelings aside as invalid. She wanted her novels to stand in their different ways as signposts pointing to moral excellence and social betterment; she wanted to be convinced that living with Lewes was the means whereby these aspirations of hers could and did become realities, so that for her – and for him? – there was a figurative as well as a real sense in which Lewes as much as she was the author of those eight novels. She was tormented by the way her beloved family – above all, Isaac, but Chrissey too – was taking her flaunting of the proprieties. Coping with her distress was hard work for Lewes who felt no scruples at all in his own person. With entire justification, he considered his loyalty to Agnes to be at an end, although his material support both of her and of his family by her never wavered to the very end of his life.

The letter Marian wrote to Cara from Jersey on June 6 1857 is full of that torment. Envy and perturbation are in the first part of it, even though concealed. ' . . . I like to think of you as a happy wife and mother,' she says, and the un-spoken words underneath are: 'Happy? Well, yes, I suppose I can say that I am, but I can never be a wife and never, therefore, a mother.' (This isn't to say that Lewes and Marian didn't have normal sexual relations. They certainly did. But there must be no conception. That would never do. Contraception was no unusual practice amongst the educated of the mid-nineteenth century. Mrs Grote, the Egeria of her generation, went further than this and taught the overburdened, under educated women of her village how to go about it. But all the same there were strong elements of uncertainty about the methods. Marian and Lewes were careful, had to be careful, about how often and about exactly when they slept together.)

After the congratulations, Marian gossips on. She is glad that her liberated friend Bessie Parkes is travelling in Italy, because 'the Savile Row establishment is not richly provided with [hearts and souls].' 'Savile Row establishment' refers to Bessie's Radical politician father, Joseph, who kept a mistress there and whose unprotesting wife had no sympathy at all for the feminist assertiveness of her daughter. Then at the end of the letter Marian talks of the way she is dealing with the ostracism she is enduring.

I have written to my brother and my two sisters telling them that I have changed my name and have a husband. Fanny has already answered me in a very kind letter. I have not yet heard from my Brother. [the upper case B should be noted] I feel satisfied to have done this, for they are now acquainted with what is *essential* in my position, and if any utterly false report reaches them in the first instance, their minds will be prepared not to accept it without reserve. I do not think Chrissey will give up correspondence with me in any case, and that is the point I care most about . . . The 'rumours' you mention have I dare say come through the Smiths – friendly headshakings and regrets which are meant in the best spirit. I have kept the subject so long before my mind, and have learned to see how much of the pain I have felt concerning my own family is really love of approbation in disguise, that I look calmly on the most disagreeable issues. If I live five years longer, the positive result of my existence on the side of truth and goodness will outweigh the small negative good that would have consisted in my not doing anything to shock others, and I can conceive no consequences that will make me repent the past.

The defiant conclusion here (followed by 'thine in headachiness') is moving. Marian is asserting that her talents for 'good', as she conceives the word, have been released by her alliance with Lewes. He is the one her

111

womanliness must rely on – for moral support, for guidance, and more particularly for that direct help in the work she has begun and sees ahead of her, the help that comes, where the writing is concerned, from his wide experience and his literary dexterity.

But now, in the 1980s, there is immediate trouble staring anyone in the face who wants to hold this particular literary line. And the trouble stems from this glorification of Marian, this Ascension into a Heaven which Leavis has all ready waiting for her. Is it reasonable, the Marian-idolaters will ask, to assign near-Eliotian eminence to this little journalist, this busy populariser, this novelist who wrote *Rose, Blanche and Violet*, about which Carlyle complained in a letter to his wife, 'Oh my dear, be sorry for me! I am nearly out of my wits. From 3 o'clock until now (11 pm) I have been in a tempest of twaddle.' It's important to note, though, as we read this, that Carlyle by his own admission had been tempest tossed for eight solid hours. If he felt such nausea couldn't he have thrown the thing to the waves after, say, an hour? Does a vastly experienced writing man like Carlyle stay with twaddle for the whole of one working day? Or isn't it perhaps more likely that little Lewes, taking deft evasive action as the Carlylean thunderbolts drop around him, nevertheless has the invaluable trick of knowing how to beckon the reader on?

There is no intention of suggesting that Lewes was a novelist of genius hiding behind the skirts of a neurotic lady who put a fake masculine name down as the author of eight novels. The more modest, and perhaps not wholly foolish, intention is to suggest that Lewes had a somewhat larger share of talent than is usually allowed him and Marian a somewhat smaller. This makes her still a vastly better novelist than Lewes could ever have been on his own, but still not quite the lioness dreamt up by Leavis – Leavis who is inspired to write about *Adam Bede*, for example, and to see in it

an illuminating case of one of the major original artists learning from predecessors. For George Eliot is widely and deeply rooted in the literature of the past as well as

112

decisively influential on major novelists succeeding her – eg James, Hardy, and Lawrence. She is at the centre of the creative achievements of the English language in the phase of its history to which we still belong, and incites to pregnant reflections on vital continuity in art: we see that there is indeed in English literature – something more than an assemblage of individual masterpieces or separate authors. . .

Here surely is an Eliot-intoxicated man. 'Deeply rooted in the literature of the past'?

Marian was no great novel reader, and had a way of telling worshippers at the shrine that she'd no stomach for any novels later than *Rasselas*. She wrote in 1877 to Elizabeth Stuart Phelps, a strong and independent minded American novelist, and spoke of her reading habits.

. . . I am usually studying some particular subject and reading I take outside that line is done aloud to Mr Lewes. I daresay you will understand that for my own spiritual food I need all other sorts of reading more than I need fiction. I know nothing of our contemporary English novelists with the exception of Miss Thackeray's* and a few of Anthony Trollope's works. My constant groan is, that I must leave so much of the greatest writing which the centuries have sifted for us, unread for want of time . . .

That was written when she was getting towards the end of her time, but it reflects closely the attitudes of the young woman of twenty when she was writing to Maria Lewis, most influential of all her teachers, whom she first came to know when at the age of nine she went to Mrs Wallington's school in Nuneaton.

As to the discipline our minds receive from the perusal of fictions I can conceive none that is beneficial but may be attained by that of history. It is the merit of fictions to

* Lady Richmond Ritchie, Thackeray's elder daughter.

113

come within the orbit of probability; if unnatural they would no longer please. If it be said that the mind must have relaxation, 'Truth is strange – stranger than fiction.' When a person has exhausted the wonders of truth, there is no other resort than fiction; till then I cannot imagine how the adventures of some phantom conjured up by fancy can be more entertaining than the transactions of real specimens of human nature . . . The weapons of Christian warfare were never sharpened at the forge of romance. Domestic fictions, as they come more within the range of imitation, seem more dangerous. For my part I am ready to sit down and weep at the impossibility of my understanding or barely knowing even a fraction of the sum of objects that present themselves for our contemplation in books and in life. Have I then any time to spend on things that never existed?

Like Prospero? Or the Wife of Bath? Or Xanadu? Or Mrs Veal? No, Marian was interested in facts and in abstract cerebration. She preferred Spinoza to Spenser. Leavis's picture of her as deeply rooted in the literature of the past (and by 'literature' here one takes him to mean 'creative literature') doesn't seem to keep its nose to the known facts. She did read novels of course. She read Benjamin Constant's *Adolphe* with the greatest interest and marked her text closely. But then *Adolphe* is the sort of arid, cerebral novel you'd expect her to respond to. Her own novels are the product of a formidable intelligence, but they are overburdened with planning and plot. The old discredited view that the early ones are the best will come to be seen again as the right one. Dragged along by an enthusiastic Leavis and his talk of specificity – an ugly sounding, elusive little abstract – you may struggle on to the end of *Daniel Deronda*, but you'll have established yourself as a very accommodating reader indeed if you haven't experienced quite longish periods of tedium along the way.

Lewes, always the quick, adaptable little Lewes, doesn't after all look so impossible in the role of collaborator. For one thing, his faults and her faults resemble each other so closely. They are both, for example, addicted to the long

114

pause for the homily. For example, in *The Mill on the Floss*, Tulliver, the obstinate, stiffnecked miller, suddenly realises that his money difficulties are closing in on him with a speed he hadn't reckoned on. Perhaps Bessy, his wife, might approach her not poverty stricken sister Pullet to see if help might be on offer from that quarter? At this point the novelist squares her shoulders, starts a fresh paragraph, and mounts the pulpit steps.

It is precisely the proudest and most obstinate men who are the most liable to shift their position and contradict themselves in this sudden manner: everything is easier to them than to face the simple fact that they have been thoroughly defeated, and must begin life anew. And Mr Tulliver, you perceive, though nothing more than a superior miller and maltster, was as proud and obstinate as if he had been a very lofty personage, in whom such dispositions might be a source of that conspicuous, far-echoing tragedy, which sweeps the stage in regal robes and makes the dullest chronicler sublime . . .

And so on, and so on, blank verse and all, for another two hundred words of trite generalised maundering. Perhaps Leavis skipped sketches like this: at any rate he makes no mention of them so far as I am aware. And yet surely he should, because they come very frequently indeed.

Lewes was a martyr to the same complaint. Ranthorpe, in the novel named after him, is a young man with no favourable accidents of birth to foster his ambitions. He writes a book of poetry called *Dreams of Youth*, and this, lucky for him, has a surprising success. Overblown with confidence, Ranthorpe dashes off a second volume which he simply calls *Lyrics*, and this the critics take their knives to. The collection is rough, ill considered, unpondered. Ranthorpe's gorgeous palace of promise comes tumbling down. He is upset enough to consider suicide. Lewes begins Book Three of his novel at this point, and calls it *The Unsuccessful Author*. Chapter one, 'The Aristocracy of the Intellect', begins:

Ranthorpe stumbled at the threshold of his career. His mistake was fatal, though common. He misconceived his own position in the world: he belonged by nature to one aristocracy, and he aspired to the other; born a member of the great aristocracy of the intellect, he misconceived his rank, and yearned for recognition and fellowship in the great aristocracy of birth. Let me explain.

And, my word, Lewes does explain. The rest of the chapter, not a very long one but still a whole chapter, becomes an essay setting out Lewes's view that the old Chesterfieldian world of the Aristocracy and the Rest is quite outdated now in this reformist, humanist, Comtist mid-nineteenth century, and the Aristocracy of the Intellect has won its rights. 'Rousseau was the son of a watch-maker – D'Alembert was picked up in the streets – Burns followed the plough. Had these men no nobility?' These are some of the questions you come to if you read so far. But where has Ranthorpe got to? Ranthorpe has to wait till Lewes has pronounced the benediction (and the congregation has dispersed). Neither Lewes nor Marian are perhaps solely to be blamed for grievous faults such as this in their novel writing. There was a current fashion and some novelists followed it – but not many as slavishly as Mr and Mrs Lewes.

Both of them were capable of false pathos of the Little Nell kind. In the first story of the *Scenes, Amos Barton*, for example, Milly the young mother is on her deathbed; husband Amos and the young brood are gathered round.

. . . They all stood by the bedside – Amos nearest to her, holding Chubby and Dickey. But she motioned Patty to come first, and clasping the poor, pale child by the hand, said – 'Patty, I am going away from you. Love your Papa. Comfort him; and take care of your little brothers and sisters. God will help you.' Patty stood perfectly quiet, and said 'Yes, mamma.' The mother motioned with her pallid lips for the dear child to lean towards her and kiss her; and then Patty's great anguish overcame her, and she burst into sobs. Amos drew her towards him, and

116

pressed her head gently towards him, while Milly beckoned Fred and Sophy, and said to them more faintly – 'Patty will try to be your mamma when I am gone, my darlings. You will be good and not vex her.'

And the rest of the numerous little tribe are pushed forward for the final audience and the little hearts swell and '. . . Dickey . . . cried aloud.'

And here is Lewes's handling of the scene in which Isola, wakening from a premonitory dream, finds, Oh rapture, her long parted lover Percy Ranthorpe marvellously at hand.

Oh joy! O rapture. It was indeed Percy; – it was indeed her lover! It was her dream realised! . . . She took his head between her hands, and gazed intensely at him . . . She twined her fingers in his silky hair with a sort of impatience and gazed upon his lovely face upturned. [Notice the blank verse creeping in and up like convolvulus] . . . He began to stammer his excuses: 'Dearest Percy,' she said, 'do not recal [sic] the past – not even to weep over it as an error.' . . . 'Blessed one!' he exclaimed, 'You forgive me then? You give me again that heart which this time I shall know how to prize? You are again my love – my wife?' 'WIFE!' she shrieked . . . She fell senseless at his feet. Alarmed and surprised [Well, who wouldn't be?] he took her in his arms, and raised her to the sofa . . . 'I have killed her,' he frantically exclaimed. A deep sigh heaved her breast, and she slowly opened her eyes. He was so overjoyed at this sign of life that he nearly stifled her with kisses. She pushed him from her, with a convulsive effort, exclaiming: 'Percy! Percy! – do not touch me – I am another's!' 'Another's,' said he, puzzled yet alarmed. '. . . I am engaged.' 'Impossible – you?' 'Too true! – too true!' A long silence ensued . . .

Here are two writers reaching mindlessly for their clichés, and writing stuff so bad as to be almost hilariously enjoyable. Allowance must be made for the conventions of the time they were writing in. Allowance has to be made in

117

a similar way even for Shakespeare. And doubtless the routine writhings on non nuptial beds which breathe hotly on the 1980s novelist's page almost without the writer's being aware of it will arouse jeers and laughter a hundred years on when come upon in a dusty corner of a secondhand bookshop. But that all said, it still remains reasonable to suggest that the writer of the first passage might have been the writer of the second, and vice versa.

So far as Lewes is thought of at all in these days he's thought of as the subordinate, the dedicated acolyte. This is as foolish a notion as the one still prevailing, thanks to Lytton Strachey, of Clough as the insignificant fetcher-and-carrier for Florence Nightingale. In different ways both Marian and Florence were greedy and arrogant ladies. Both Lewes and Clough were generous men and neither of them was in the least given to jealousy. Florence Nightingale, so far as her homosexual tendencies allowed her, was in love with Clough. When he died untimely she wrote: 'Oh Jonathan, my brother Jonathan, my love for thee was very great, passing the love of women.' You don't talk like that about a runner of messages and a doer-up of parcels. Marian, in the privacy of a letter to Harriet Beecher Stowe written in 1872, is prepared to admit, talking about *Middlemarch*,

> But do not for a moment imagine that Dorothea's marriage experience is drawn from my own. Impossible to conceive any creature less like Mr Casaubon than my warm, enthusiastic husband, who cares much more for my doing than for his own, and is a miracle of freedom from all author's jealousy and all suspicion. I fear that the Casaubon-tints are not quite foreign to my own mental complexion . . .

Here she is looking first hard at Lewes and then at herself and in both examinations showing considerable insight. She was right, certainly, to see a little of herself in Casaubon, but the real model behind the fiction is the more than a little fraudulent Dr Brabant of Devizes with whom she dallied in 1843, when she was twenty-four.

There are two entries in Marian's journal for March 25 and 26 1865, when the couple were by now established and successful. Here is how the entries go:

25. During this week the commencement of the *Fortnightly Review*, of which George has been prevailed upon to be the editor, has been finally decided on. I am full of vain regrets that we did not persist in original refusal, for I dread the worry and anxiety G. may have. About myself, I am in deep depression, feeling powerless. I have written nothing but beginnings since I finished a little article for the *Pall Mall* . . . Dear George is full of activity yet is in very frail health. How I worship his good humour, his good sense, his affectionate care for every one who has claims on him. That worship is my best life . . . 29 . . . *I have begun a Novel*.

This can be seen as describing not a collaboration exactly but nevertheless an important writing relationship. This pair, by now in their late forties, are extremely closely bound to each other. She is sorry that 'we' did not persist in Lewes's refusal to take on the editorship of the *Fortnightly*. And then, after her announcement that she has begun *Felix Holt*, comes a journal entry of Lewes for June 13 1865: 'Sat with Polly for two hours in the garden discussing her novel and psychological problems . . .' Who can doubt that her trust in him, her admiration of him, meant that Lewes played an important part in the shaping of the *oeuvre* to which Leavis has accorded so high a place?

When they were dealing with John Blackwood over the Amos Barton novella from the *Scenes*, Blackwood wrote to say that some of his friends, someone called Colonel Hamley in particular, weren't happy about the treatment of him as a character. '. . . He thought,' Blackwood wrote, 'the Author very possibly a *man of science* but not a practical writer . . .' Marian reacted strongly to this. '. . . against this sort of condemnation, one must steel oneself as best one can.' She's willing to accept that her 'scientific illustrations must be at fault since they seem to have obtruded themselves disagreeably.' But then she comes out with something that can only be described as coy. ' . . . if it be a sin to be at once a man of science and a writer of fiction, I can declare my perfect innocence on that head, my scientific knowledge being as superficial as that of the most "practised writers".' Marian may have been a scientific innocent, but Lewes most certainly was not; indeed, over the whole period of their life together his interests could be described as predominantly scientific.

It was Lewes who tided her over her bouts of uncertainty about herself as a writer which persisted all through her career and weren't in any way mitigated by huge success and large cash advances.

> After the publication of *Adam Bede*, [he told Cara] Marian felt deeply the evil of talking and allowing others to talk to her about her writing. We resolved therefore to exclude everything as far as we could. No one speaks about her books to her, but me . . . excessive diffidence which prevented her writing at all, for so many years, and would prevent her now, if I were not beside her to encourage her . . .

Marian was never the vigorous, independent, campaigning woman. She was eager to have help, willing to accept advice. Her books, and more especially the earlier ones, slowly grow and are the products of continuous close and private conversations and consultations, with Lewes always the single helpmeet, the guiding and always encouraging critic. Page by page, chapter by chapter, the work she produced was read to him; he commented, discussed – and altered. His pronouns are 'we' and 'our'. Marian could be assertive, and was always greedy for gain, but Lewes was her mentor and in his company she enjoyed submissiveness. 'Walked in Kew Park,' she noted in her journal on August 18 1856 – the year of the *Scenes* – 'and talked with G. of my novel . . .' The conversations prolonged themselves through the years, and they were productive conversations.

Does insistence of this kind on the importance of Lewes's role in the creating of an *oeuvre* as weighty and important as Marian's diminish her achievement? If *Middlemarch* and the rest were the wholly incomparable masterpieces which so much recent criticism says they are, it would. But good though her novels are they aren't quite as good as that. Lewes, the quick, clever, limited, generous man, produces his star turn. She responds fully well enough to satisfy him. This is to say much, but it is not to say that here are fictional peaks which once scaled leave you, on all sides, with nothing but a descent.

6

For both of them it must have felt like a defiant adventure. True, they had both long before got used to the idea of being rebels. Marian had lived in Chapman's seraglio and, almost for certain, been his mistress. Shaggy little Lewes and his Agnes had both stuck their tongues out at convention, but Agnes's turn-and-turn-about between himself and Thornton Hunt had shaken his faith in sexual freedom of action. By 1854 he was ready for someone prepared to play the game somewhat less recklessly. Marian's mental powers far exceed Agnes's. As editor of the *Leader* he was fully in the swim of London journalism and would know that although Chapman was nominally in charge of the *Westminster* it was Marian's behind-the-scenes spadework which had lifted the paper into its position as required reading amongst the intelligentsia of the left. He was ready to settle down with her. He had had enough of roaming about with no settled roots anywhere with no opportunity to see his own children except when taking on the odd, unacceptable role of occasional visitor. In Marian's company he looked forward to harmony and a relationship which would satisfy him not only sexually but intellectually as well.

They spent three months in Weimar, Lewes scratching away at his re-writing of the Goethe biography, she supporting him because he was far from well, though not seriously enough to force him to abandon the busy, socialising role which he enjoyed and did so successfully. It's important to realise that right from the beginning of the relationship the two were remarkably adept at propping each other up. Marian worked at a long Macaulayish review of Victor Cousin's *Madame de Sablé*. She called this 'Woman in France', and took a long time before sending it off to Chapman. Lewes, under whose scrutiny the article must first pass, thought that the points made in it were '. . . crowded and would impress the reader if they were diluted a little', and so she set to work to make her introductory section fuller. They pleased each other. They delighted each other. They were happy.

What neither of them at first realised was the extent and depth of the shocked dismay which was felt at home by their quick, scarcely announced, departure together for Germany as man and wife, or at any rate as man and mistress. It was wonderful for them to meet such a celebrity as Liszt – 'the first really inspired man I ever saw,' Marian thought – who was living, Marian told Bray, 'with a Russian Princess, who is in fact his wife, and he is a Grand Seigneur in this place . . .' Whether Liszt paid any closer attention to formal ceremonies of marriage than she had herself doesn't seem to have occurred to her; there is no mention of the Comtesse d'Agoult. It was enough that Liszt, saintly looking and sweetly singing, should be floating around amongst ordinary folk in pot hats or hooped skirts.

It was not so wonderful to get news of what Marian in her journal called 'a painful letter from London [which] caused us both a bad night'. This was a letter from Thomas Woolner, sculptor and minor poet, to Bell Scott, the friend of Lewes's youth.

> . . . By the way – have you heard of two blackguard literary fellows Lewes and Thornton Hunt? They seem to have used wives on the ancient Briton practice of having them in common: now blackguard Lewes has bolted with a —— and is living in Germany with her. I believe it is dangerous to write facts of anyone nowadays so I will not further lift the mantle and display the filthy contaminations of these hideous satyrs and smirking moralists – these workers in the Agapemone – these Mormonites in another name – stinkpots of humanity.

We don't know how Scott took that. Probably for old times' sake if for nothing else he was mildly expostulatory, because a dozen years later Woolner had come round and used to call when the Leweses had become famous enough

123

to hold what can only be called a salon. But beyond doubt Lewes and Marian were greatly perturbed. How could such opinions be entertained about them, let alone be put down on paper? And, more particularly, how could such opinions come, not from the mob, not from the incapable generality of persons, but from their own highly literate and, as they'd thought, sensibly emancipated circle? Even Harriet Martineau, archdeaconess of emancipation, seems to have sniffed. And Marian appears to have written her a sharp letter about her remarks – although the letter no longer exists and has to be guessed at. At all events, Lewes sat down on Thursday night October 19 in Weimar and wrote to Carlyle a long and loud exculpation of himself and Marian.

The insistent question which asks itself is: why should Carlyle have so readily taken up the role of go-between in all this? The answer might be that Carlyle, a tortuous man and given to envy, might not have been above a bit of mischief making. He would have been perfectly well aware that Lewes was pushing ahead with a biography of Goethe, that Lewes's normal habit as a writer was to move fast, whilst he, Carlyle, at that very time, was thrashing laboriously about in the Valley of the Shadow of Frederick the Great. He might well have felt that, as the leading mediator between Germanism and Anglo-Saxondom, he had, on his side of the Channel, won personal rights in Goethe, and what was Lewes doing, poking his nose in? Lewes, with that sprightly mixture of knowledgeableness and innocence which was characteristic of him, wouldn't have recognised the eruptive potential of the craggy eminence of Cheyne Row. So Lewes began his letter by saying, effusively, how glad he was that Carlyle, whilst being careful to pass on the Woolner stuff, hadn't explicitly allied himself with it. '. . . and *now* to find that you judge me rightly, and are not estranged by what has estranged so many from me, gives me strength to bear what yet must be borne!' At this point Lewes quite stops being effusive and gets down to business. 'So much in gratitude. Now for justice: On my *word of honor* there is no foundation for the scandal as it runs. My separation was in no wise caused by the lady

124

named, nor by any other lady. It has always been immi-
nent, always *threatened*, but never before carried out, because of those assailing pangs of anticipation which would
not let me carry resolution into fact . . .' And he went on to
assure Carlyle that Marian had written no letter to Harriet
Martineau. '. . . this letter is a pure, or impure, fabrica-
tion – the letter, the language, the purport, all fiction . . .
Where gossip affects a point of honour or principle I feel
bound to meet it with denial; on all private matters my only
answer is *silence . . .'*

Four days later Marian wrote to Charles Bray, at slightly
longer length.

I yesterday wrote to my brother to request that he would
pay my income to you on the 1st December. I also
requested that, in future, he would pay my half yearly
income into the Coventry and Warwickshire Bank, that I
might order it to be sent to me wherever I wanted it, as he
has sometimes sent me a cheque which I could not get
cashed in London. Is there anything to be done – any
notice given to the Bank in order to make this plan
feasible?

It is possible that you have already heard a report
prevalent in London that Mr Lewes has 'run away' from
his wife and family. I wish you to be in possession of the
facts which will enable you to contradict this report . . .
Since we left England he has been in constant correspondence with his wife; she has had all the money due
to him in London; and his children are his principal
thought and anxiety. Circumstances, with which I am
not concerned, and which have arisen since he left England, have led him to determine on a separation from Mrs
Lewes, but he has never contemplated that separation as
a total release from responsibility towards her. On the
contrary he has been anxiously waiting restoration to
health that he may once more work hard, not only to
provide for his children, but to supply his wife's wants so
far as that is not done by another. I have seen all the
correspondence between them, and it has assured me
that his conduct as a husband has been not only ir-

125

reproachable, but generous and self-sacrificing to a degree far beyond any standard fixed by the world. This is the simple truth, and no flattering picture drawn by my partiality.

I have been long enough with Mr Lewes to judge of his character on adequate grounds . . . He has written to Carlyle and Robert Chambers [a journalist and publisher who wrote *Papers for the People* in 1851] stating as much of the truth as he can without very severely inculpating the other persons concerned; Arthur Helps [Helps was a lettered, comfortably off man who was in the process of becoming, and thereafter remaining, a close friend of Lewes's; he was appointed Clerk to the Privy Council in 1860] who has been here since we came, already knew the whole truth, and I trust that these three rational friends will be able in time to free his character from the false imputations which malice and gossip have cast upon it.

Of course many silly myths are already afloat about me, in addition to the truth, which of itself would be thought matter for scandal. I am quite unconcerned about them except as they may cause pain to my real friends. If you hear of anything that I have said, done, or written in relation to Mr Lewes beyond the simple fact that I am attached to him and that I am living with him, do me the justice to believe that it is false. Mr and Mrs Chapman are the only persons to whom I have ever spoken of his private position and of my relation to him, and the only influence I should ever dream of exerting over him as to his conduct towards his wife and children is that of stimulating his conscientious care for them, if it need any stimulus . . . I am ignorant how far Cara and Sara may be acquainted with the state of things, and how they may feel towards me . . .

In this most interesting letter it's possible to see signs of rising alarm in her – a reflection perhaps in part of rising alarm in Lewes himself. They knew of course that in a small way the hornets of orthodoxy would swarm and buzz, but their rational, humanistic, forward looking friends? Would

126

they too look the other way? Why, for example, should ferocious, enlightened Harriet Martineau show such disgust? 'Do you know that Lewes is likely to die?' she wrote in a letter. 'What will she do? Take a successor, I shd expect.' Contempt or envy? A little of both one suspects.

But the first paragraph of the letter deserves first comment because it tells us much about the realities of a woman's situation in the mid-century. It didn't matter whether the woman was strong in intellect and respected by virtue of personal achievement – a Marian, a Mrs Grote, a Jane Carlyle – or simply a timid governess trained to curtsey and keep her place: a woman was still a woman, and man was her lord. Isaac Evans, the so strictly evangelical brother whom Marian looked up to and leaned upon, had in no way accepted Marian's breakaway from orthodoxy, still less her consorting, independently and away from home, with such atheistical riff-raff as Chapman. Isaac was the trustee of his father's will. What was due to Marian by it came through him and was doled out by him. She had to ask for it – and ask nicely. When she went abroad to live in sin Isaac dragged his feet and deliberately made it as difficult as he could for her to get her hands on her own – and this at a time when money was important and hard to come by. They were away from London where their sort of salaried action lay; Lewes, ailing, had been obliged to rest for a while from his usual swift laboriousness; her day-to-day earnings didn't amount to much. Yet she is obliged to be reasonable and appealing in tone when addressing her brother through the medium of another. '. . . Is there anything to be done . . . to make this plan feasible?' And there's no hint anywhere in the paragraph of justified impatience on her part.

On the question of living adulterously with a married man she is frantically disingenuous: 'if you hear of any thing that I have said.' This is a sentence put together in confusion and alarm. 'The simple fact' isn't all that simple, and she knows it isn't. She is saying in one breath that she has done everything and that she has done nothing. She reassures herself as much as her correspondent that she feels secure in well doing. She is unconcerned about

127

silly myths, but the unconcern doesn't ring true.

Lewes had worries too, especially worries about money. But as for the rest, he wasn't going to be hurt as Marian might be hurt – simply because he was a man. Her strong defence of him, of what he had done and of what he was doing, has its pathos. Certainly it was right that then, as always, Lewes never left either Agnes or the children in the lurch. Thornton became more and more improvident and useless so that his, quite real, responsibilities in the business had to be shouldered by Lewes and Marian. There is no hint anywhere that Agnes felt herself to have been wronged and robbed. The correspondence between her and the husband she'd rejected in favour of Thornton is never harsh in tone, hints at no quarrels.

Did Lewes ever regret his break with Agnes? There's no evidence that he did, unless, perhaps, in the *Life of Goethe* which he was working on in Weimar, where he produced one of those little moral asides he was always too fond of. He was talking of Frau von Stein's feelings of resentment against Goethe after he had married, and pronounced: 'A nature with any nobleness never forgets that once it loved and once was happy in that love; the generous heart is grateful for its memories . . .' If he was thinking of his own situation, then his is the generous heart and Agnes's the spirit of resentment. Certainly he kept in touch with Agnes throughout his life (she outlived him by almost twenty-five years) and he regularly paid her an allowance. Money is the usual great bugbear in marital estrangements, and this caused him to show impatience in his journal. In March 1858, for example, he wrote: 'Another very painful proof that my kindness to Agnes has not been appreciated. In spite of last year's affair, she is £184 beyond her increased income this year. Resolved to change my line of conduct altogether until I see a different character in her. I feel she is quite hardened . . .' The difficulty was that the liaison with Thornton Hunt didn't last, and he, just as unreliable as his father over money matters and much less talented a writer, didn't accept his responsibilities as father of some of Agnes's children as punctually as fixed arrangements provided for. In December 1856 Lewes noted: 'Have been agitated and distressed lately by finding Agnes £150 in debt, mainly owing to T's defalcations. Angry correspondence and much discussion. Jervis [Agnes's father, that is] has, however, given some temporary aid and more is hoped.

Thornton didn't take at all kindly to Lewes's angry accusations. Ten days later Lewes has this:

This evening Thornton sent me a challenge . . . as I would not withdraw the 'offensive expression' of my disbelief in his statements and promises. There is something ludicrous in the extravagance of this. [The Hunt-Lewes friendship is clearly wearing thin by this time; insouciant and good natured to begin with, Hunt could become trying when lived close to over a long while] A challenge from him to me, and on such grounds! Wrote . . . declining to withdraw the expression and declining to name a friend, but offering as an alternative that Thornton should name some gentleman to act as a Court of Honour before which my charge and his explanation could be heard.

Hunt would have nothing to do with this suggestion and the squabble fizzled out, but it never became easy to get money out of him. There was never, however, any lasting estrangement between Lewes and his legal wife.

Lewes and Marian spent three months in Weimar, and Marian wrote an article about it which appeared in *Fraser's* in 1855. Money wasn't plentiful and they had to be thinking constantly about ways of earning it. Obviously there was no question of Marian's raising personal questions in this article; it is simply a dogged, very flat run-through of what they did and whom they saw. The only surprise comes from the fact that *Fraser's* should have thought it worth buying. The theatre opened in September and gave *Lohengrin*, with Liszt conducting; but Wagner, even early Wagner, was too much for them and they both became restive after the first two acts. They read Goethe to each other and lived a frugal life. 'Our expenses,' Marian tells *Fraser's* readers, 'including wine and washing, were £2.6s per week . . .'

At the beginning of November they left Weimar for Berlin, spending three months there over the city's unwelcoming winter. Lewes went on harvesting his Goetheana. Here he met the elderly Varnhagen von Ense, wounded warrior of Wagram. The old gentleman hadn't quite lost his late wife – the actress Rahel's – passion for cultured sociability and Lewes was made welcome at serious minded gatherings held in Varnhagen's house. Here again Goethe was a talking point as well as the subject for personal reminiscence. Varnhagen was courtly and carried a gold headed cane and sported an order ribbon round his neck. He was no reactionary, however, knew Carlyle before Carlyle began all his backtracking, and professed sympathy with his views. Carlyle for his part, though, preferring as usual to grumble and mock, reported on him without much enthusiasm. 'A very vigorous old fellow,' Carlyle thought, 'with cunning grey eyes, turn-up nose, plenty of white hair, and a dash of dandy, soldier-citizen and Sage . . . and he goes to Miss Something's soirée every night – whither I would never follow him, and "don't intend to".' 'Miss Something' would have been Fräulein von Solmar, who kept open house every night of the week except Thursday and carried on where Rahel had long left off. Lewes had none of Carlyle's objections to parties. He went along, noted what might be useful to him for his biography, and, as usual, was quite ready to speak up for himself and to assert that German cultured society had much to learn from its English counterpart. The salon habitués read *The Merchant of Venice*, doubtless in Schlegel's translation, and Lewes, always loving to act, did the best he could for them in the role of Shylock. But the Germans were stolid and solid and hard to move – all except for old General Pfuel who was ready with 'appreciatory groans always in the right place'. Marian was kindly received, and, from their rooms in the Dorotheengasse, thought she might set to work on an essay, 'Women in Germany'; she wrote to Chapman about this early in January, but it came to nothing. They both worked hard, saw the sights, met the

130

academics, withstood the cold. As for society in general, Marian seems surprisingly to have found the Germans harder to bear than Lewes, but this may well have been because she lacked his linguistic fluency. For the seven months of their German stay, 'we never heard,' she says, 'one witticism, or even one felicitous idea or expression from a German.' On March 11 1855 they set off to face the music back in England.

Dover, Marian thought, looked 'very lovely under a blue sky'. She had plenty of time to admire it because Lewes left her there on her own for a month or more whilst he went up to London to reconnoitre. Where were they to live? Cambridge Street? Bayswater? Kensington? The Strand? Perhaps it would be wiser to put a little distance between themselves and old acquaintances until they could form an accurate opinion of what the temperature of their reception was likely to be. Lewes stayed with Arthur Helps at Vernon Hill whilst he took stock. Marian from Dover lodgings wrote to Bessie Parkes who wasn't the shockable sort, but even with her she took a defensive line.

> . . . if you knew everything, we should probably be much nearer agreement even as to the details of conduct than you suppose. In the mean time believe no one's representations about me, for there is not a *single* person who is in a position to make a true representation. My mind is deliciously calm and untroubled so far as my own lot is concerned, my own anxieties are sympathetic ones . . .

'Deliciously calm' sounds very much like whistling to keep her courage up. Isaac was still being awkward about her half yearly payment. '. . . it is difficult to know what he will do' she told Charles Bray on April 4. And difficult to know what she would do if he continued to play stubborn in order to mark his huge disapproval of the way she had behaved. (By June 17, however, Isaac had relented, her money came in, and his accompanying letter lacked reproof.) At least it is permissible to guess that this

131

was how it was, although Isaac's letter hasn't survived. Marian may well have been too eager to read signs of unbending into any letter received from her brother, because he remained icy and aloof until John Walter Cross made an honest woman of her a quarter of a century later.

Meanwhile Lewes looked for somewhere to live. They had decided it would be unwise to risk London proper. '. . . on his return,' she told Bray, writing from Dover, 'I shall join him in London where – that is, in the environs – we shall establish ourselves till the big books are fairly through the press . . .' The big books were Lewes's *Life of Goethe* and her translation of Spinoza's *Ethics* which didn't, after all, get fairly through the press.

He found what he thought would do at number 7 Clarence Row, East Sheen, and Marian was determined to be pleased about it.

A charming village so close to Richmond Park . . . far less trouble to get there than to Bayswater. You have only to jump into the train at the Waterloo Bridge station and in ten minutes you will be at Mortlake where you must get down. Mortlake, as I daresay you know, is a lovely village on the banks of the Thames and East Sheen is its twin sister lying close to it. Ask the way to East Sheen and in three minutes you will be at our door. Then you shall have a nice dinner and a nice snooze after it, and then a stroll, along the river or in the Park, such as you can't get at Coventry even by the help of a carriage . . .

Lewes had had a tiring search and still wasn't well. One evening quite soon after they'd got there he fainted away. This alarmed her greatly. She'd never seen anyone faint before. She was to see much of Lewesian ailments as the years went by. As with so many of the Victorians, it's difficult to discover quite what was the matter with him – until his last few months, that is, when cancer claimed him and all difficulties about diagnosis dropped away; but he was often ill, and as soon as they'd come back to England there happened, in part at least, an exchange of roles. So far Lewes had been the male and the protector. He had

132

escorted her to theatres, introduced her to his friends who were so numerous, and helped her to acclimatise to life abroad which he knew and understood so much better than she did. But now, in East Sheen, a long way from his old ground, having Agnes still on his hands so far as finances went, having to rebuild a new kind of relationship with his own children whom all his life he never ceased to love devotedly, he began to discover that Marian was sturdy as well as uncommonly gifted, that she was a woman who, whilst herself always needing and demanding support, was also ready to give it.

It would be a mistake to suppose that the alliance, once they'd both embarked on the *Ravensbourne*, was necessarily to be a life long affair. Certainly Lewes wanted a change from the 'wasted' life he had been leading; certainly Marian wanted a man, and 'Vivian' was sprightly and amusing and intelligent and could take her around. These desires on the part of both of them don't in themselves, however, form a cement strong enough to bind two people together for better for worse through all the days remaining to them. But writing to Cara in September 1855 from East Sheen after four months, on and off, in this rural place, Marian shows herself unfaltering, and even defiant, about the rightness of what she has done. She feels surer than ever about Lewes. She wants to go on with it. Cara, one of her closest friends, is disapproving, she knows. She isn't shaken by this – regretful, yes, but not shaken. 'I feel no levity,' she says, about 'marriage and the relation of the sexes . . .' Her relation with Lewes 'is and always has been profoundly serious'. Cara has been thinking of Lewes in his Vivian role, but Marian has a strong, even brusque, reply to this.

. . . not only are you unacquainted with Mr Lewes's real character and the course of his actions, but also, it is several years now since you and I were much together, and it is possible that the modifications my mind has undergone may be in quite the opposite direction to what you imagine . . . [She accepts that her views on marriage, and Cara's, don't tally even if once they did] . . . *How far we differ I think we neither of us know; for I am ignorant*

133

of your precise views and apparently you attribute to me both feelings and opinions which are not mine [here the claws start to come out] . . . but one thing I can tell you in few words. Light and easily broken ties are what I neither desire theoretically nor could live for practically. Women who are satisfied with such ties do *not* as I have done – they obtain what they desire and are still invited to dinner . . .

The bitterness of banishment to East Sheen works strongly on her at this point. But she rallies. First there comes a stab at Cara:

That any unworldly, unsuperstitious person who is sufficiently acquainted with the realities of life can pronounce my relation to Mr Lewes immoral I can only understand by remembering how subtle and complex are the influences that mould opinion. But I *do* remember this, and I indulge in no arrogant or uncharitable thoughts about those who condemn us, even though we might have expected a somewhat different verdict. From the majority of persons, of course, we looked for anything but condemnation. We are leading no life of self-indulgence, except, indeed, that being happy in each other, we find everything easy . . .

Marian is a woman embattled. She insists that everything is well between her and Lewes. Is she whistling to keep her courage up? She, a woman of thirty-six, unmarried, with an elder brother Isaac, executor and head of the family, who had more or less disowned her, had put herself, at that moment of the mid-century, in a very perilous position. Lewes faced no such risks. He was cuckolded but he could, probably, go back to Agnes. He had children. He had contacts enough to earn a sufficient living. If Agnes still preferred to cling to her fallible Thornton, Lewes could keep a mistress, and still be invited to dinner, something not possible for Marian as she sees clearly, and somehow – this is surprising – not ruefully. It is no surprise therefore to find Marian insisting to Cara – and to herself? – that she and Lewes 'find everything easy'. If Lewes were to abandon her, then her situation, in the middle 1850s, would be grievous indeed. All doors – almost all doors – would be closed to her. Her family? Isaac was unrelenting. The Brays? Sophia and Cara would find it an embarrassment to welcome her in quite the old way. She would have to run for cover to Chapman – but Chapman, she knew by now, bent very easily in the wind, a very whoreson bulrush, as Matthew Arnold said of himself.

But it worked out well. During those months in Germany they managed to create a relationship firm enough to withstand any shock, any disapproval, any anxiety. Sexually Lewes discovered, perhaps to his surprise, that this heavy jowled, serious minded woman was a far more eager, far more deeply satisfying partner than ever Agnes had been. And she loved him because he was quick, sprightly, intelligent. He discovered that although she could talk learnedly about Spinoza, she needed to have her hand held. She needed in fact to be dependent. Physically, it's true to say that the two of them were great deceivers. Lewes had something of the look of an effeminate dancing master, whilst Marian, born a hundred and thirty-five years on, would, to judge from outward appearances, have been going along to the National Health Service to enquire about the possibilities of a sex change. Yet it wasn't like this at all. Lewes was a strongly masculine man, and Marian a strongly feminine woman. They must both have had reassuring intimations of this in the London days before the dash to the continent and whilst she was lodging at Cambridge Street, Hyde Park, after October 1853: the German months provided the confirmation.

They worked hard at East Sheen. 'I hope you think the supplement of the *Leader* a respectable turn-out,' Marian told Charles Bray in mid-June. 'Mr Lewes wrote the articles on Sydney Smith, Owen Meredith, Newton's Boyhood, and How to Live a Hundred Years and I wrote the one on Menander and Greek Comedy . . .' This meant that the June 16 supplement was filled to half its capacity by their combined efforts. They were hard-up, and money had to be earned, but she insists in the same letter that:

we like East Sheen better and better, and are happier every day – writing hard, walking hard, reading Homer and science and rearing tadpoles. I read aloud for about three hours every evening, beginning with Boswell's Johnson, or some such enjoyable book, not unfriendly to digestion, then subsiding into the dreary dryness of Whewell's *History of the Inductive Sciences* and winding up with Heine's wit and imagination. We breakfast at ½ past eight, read to ourselves till ten, write till ½ past 1, walk till nearly 4 and dine at 5, regretting each day as it goes . . .

It needs to be remembered that 'hard-up' is a relative term. The chores – the cooking, the shopping, the cleaning – in 1855 there were always women a lot lower down the pyramid than you. When she had been on her own in Dover, and apprehensive, Marian apparently did take up sewing, but soon went back to translating Spinoza. Of Marian the novelist there is still very little sign. In Berlin she had shown Lewes a short fictional fragment, but Lewes then had given no encouragement. He thought she lacked dramatic power. This must have set her back seriously because only very rarely, if ever, did she run counter to Lewes's judgments.

Not many people were brave enough to risk obloquy by calling on them in their quasi-banishment. Bessie Parkes, mother of Hilaire Belloc, called. An early campaigner for women's rights and always on the watch for a chance to flout convention and authority, even she couldn't bring herself to call Marian Mrs Lewes. She was still Miss Evans, and that was that. Marian took a firm line over this.

Your address to me as *Miss Evans* was unfortunate, as I am not known under that name here. We find it indispensable to our comfort that I should bear Mr Lewes's name while we occupy lodgings, and we are now with so excellent a woman that any cause of removal would be a misfortune. If you have occasion to write to me again, please to bear this in mind.

136

In September Herbert Spencer invited them to meet him in Paris. Spencer was administering to himself a six months' cure at Le Tréport. That June 'my nervous system finally gave way' he tells us in his *Autobiography*, a condition that persisted until well into the autumn when he was back in England where he took to self-help. He invented a method of 'keeping up the cerebral circulation through the night', and did this by dousing his head in salt water and then clamping on a waterproof cap which put a stop to any risk of evaporation. What a constitution Spencer must have had, living into his eighty-fourth year and all the while taking such hideous care of himself. Lewes and Marian felt, however, that there were too many claims on their slim resources for them to consider a trip to the Paris exhibition of 1855. '. . . neither our inclination nor our pocket says yes, so we content ourselves with not seeing either him or the Exhibition, and shall go to seek polyps and health at Worthing.'

After Worthing – one of their so-frequent breakaways from outer London – they crept a little closer in. Acceptance, they must have felt, might by now be not quite so distant. At the beginning of October (they had been in East Sheen since May 2) they found lodgings at 8 Park Shot, Richmond. They stayed there for three years. Everything was tidy and clean, but they were cramped and had to work in one room together. On October 30, Lewes published *The Life and Works of Goethe* and Marian wrote three pages about it in the *Leader* of November 3. 'For reasons which will easily be divined,' she wrote, 'we have received an injunction to deliver no judgment on this work, but simply to make the reader acquainted with its general character and purpose.' In his thirty-ninth year Lewes had produced the work by which he is best remembered.

7

Countless pages about Goethe have been written since 1855. Researchers have scrambled over the dust heaps, discovering facts which throw doubt on the authenticity of earlier, accepted, facts. Huge biographies have been written – one thinks for example of Gundolf's vast and indescribably boring tome published in 1920. But a good case can be made for saying that Lewes's book, very far from a small one, remains the best comprehensive biography of Goethe in English, and one for which German scholars, as well as German general readers, still have a regard.

The Victorians liked pomp and amplitude in their biographies of eminent persons and Lewes supplied these trimmings. They aren't obtrusive, however, because his subject is a person of soaring genius. A certain admixture of reverence and awe isn't out of place in treating of him. It's only when the same kind of treatment is accorded – as it often was – to inconsiderable bewhiskered creatures of small account that the wounding Stracheyan ridicule at the beginning of *Eminent Victorians* strikes home. Lewes begins with a sandstorm parable. According to Quintus Curtius, Bactria in certain seasons used to be darkened by whirlwinds of dust. The roads merged with the sand and travellers had to wait for the stars before getting their bearings. How aptly, Lewes goes on, this applies to literature. A star suddenly arises above the confusion of Grub Street. The way is pointed. Goethe was the way. Or a way, at any rate. Two to three thousand words of this exordium-cum-ancestry have to be got through before little Johann Wolfgang appears on the scene precisely on the strike of noon August 28 1749, and biography proper can begin.

He is always quick – too quick? – to defend his hero. At the end of the 1875 edition (the last to appear in his lifetime), after 566 large, closely printed pages, he prints an

George Lewes and his Agnes with Thornton Hunt behind
making up the triangle. Thackeray, who drew it, shines down
on the scene like a sun.

Above: Mary Ann and George in middle life.

Below left: John Blackwood, the faithful publisher.

Below right: George Lewes and the pug who was Marion's substitute for the child she never had.

The Priory (top) and Whitley Heights (bottom), the properties that came with their prosperity.

To my dear husband, George Henry Lewes,
I give this MS of a work which would
never have been written but for the
happiness which his love has conferred
on my life.

Marian Lewes

March 23. 1859

The first volume was written at Richmond, the second at
Munich & Dresden, the third at Richmond again. The
work was begun on the 22ⁿᵈ October 1857, & finished on
the 16th November 1858. A large portion of it was
written twice, though often scarcely at all altered in
the copying, but other parts only once, & among these
the description of Dinah & a good deal of her sermon,
the love scene between her & Seth "the Hall farm world", most
of the scene in the Two Bedchambers, the talk between Adam
& Bede, various parts in the second volume which I can not
now specify, & in the third, Hetty's journeys, her confession & the cottage
scenes.

Marion wrote this on the manuscript of *Adam Bede*.

appendix. Herman Grimm (Lewes spells him Hermann but his father, Wilhelm, one of the brothers of the fairy tales, gave him only one 'n') had published an article in 1869 in the *Preussische Jahrbücher* about Goethe's friendship with Marianne Willemer and about how she had a hand in the Suleika poems of the *West-Östlicher Diwan* volume produced in his sixty-fifth year. Herman Grimm knew Marianne when she was old and had the story directly from her. Counting this a slur on the memory of one of the greatest of men – that he should take over a line or two allegedly breathed into his ear by a young woman and use them as his own – Lewes rushed furiously into print in an article he called 'Goethe Exploded', which appeared in the *Pall Mall Gazette* of October 4 1869. When it came to the 1875 reprint of his fine book he slammed the little piece, all huffing and puffing, on to the end; the reader closes it regretfully, wishing he hadn't done so.

Grimm lectured in Berlin University and was to go on, in 1877, to publish his twenty-five lectures on Goethe, given before the university. Added together, these remain to this day one of the finest books on Goethe ever written. What Grimm reported was mildly put, with no hint whatsoever of malice or cantankerous-denigration. For Grimm as for Lewes, Goethe was a hero, a supreme creature. Goethe was the polymath they both admired.

Lewes hammers away at the point that Marianne was old when her allegations were made. '. . . When Grimm made her acquaintance not many years ago she was widowed, old, garrulous, living in the far golden past when she had been pretty . . .' Grimm's narrative conceded that 'Marianne was over seventy when she made these communications to me.' Lewes pounces on this. 'No, we will not forget it. Neither shall we forget that it is a scion of the Grimms, himself a distinguished writer, who has thus dared to bring such a charge before the world – a charge suggested (let us not forget this either) by himself to that dear and queer old lady of Frankfurt.' To hear him, one might suppose that Marianne had been ninety and Grimm a charlatan out for a scoop. The whole appendix is tremendously irate and exaggerated. Where, after all, would poets be, if they didn't take a little bit from here, a little bit from there? Where would be Shakespeare's description of Cleopatra enthroned on her barge if he hadn't chanced to take a look, many a look, into Plutarch? It should be added, though, in fairness to Lewes, that he was an ailing man when he came to write this testy little addendum.

Espinasse says that for Lewes the publication of the Goethe biography, 'very much strengthened his literary position'. And this was no understatement. He became less dependent, from that moment, on the incessant scramble to place articles. Indeed he felt able, whilst still contributing to it, to give up his editorship of the *Leader*. He dedicated his book to the arch-apostle of Germanism in England, Carlyle, and Carlyle was much mollified. Carlyle had helped him with the proofs, and wrote immediately to him on the book's appearance.

> . . . I am dashing athwart it in every direction; *truanting*; for I won't wait a time to read the work with such deliberation as I well see it deserves. My conviction is, we have here got an excellent biography, – altogether transcendently, as Biographies are done in this country. Candid, well-informed, clear, free-flowing, it will certainly throw a large flood of light over Goethe's life, with many German things which multitudes in England have been curious about, to little purpose, for a long while. It ought to have a large circulation, if one can predict or anticipate in such matters. On the whole I say *Euge*, and that heartily – though dissenting here and there . . .

The book sold nine hundred copies in the first six weeks and never after that did Carlyle judge it appropriate to refer to 'that body Lewes'.

Carlyle's adjectives – well-informed, clear, free-flowing – are certainly just. Something else we can see in the book is a deep personal concern. His book isn't at all an objective task for him. He winds himself into it. He binds himself to it. When for example he talks of the twenty-two-year-old Goethe's love affair with Friederike Brion, sixteen-year-old daughter of the Pfarrer of Sesenheim, he talks of it with the insight and vigour of a man personally involved. Goethe's story for the time being is somehow also his. Goethe jilted the girl, as he was to jilt many another, but Lewes comes strongly to his defence. '. . . It is a mistake to speak of faithlessness at all,' says Lewes, husband of Agnes Swynfen Jervis,

> . . . It is a mistake to speak of faithlessness at all . . . he [Goethe] was perfectly right to draw back from an engagement which he felt his love was not strong enough properly to fulfil . . . the pain which a separation may bring had better be endured, than evaded by an unholy marriage, which cannot come to good. Friederike must have felt so too, for never did a word of blame escape her . . . He had experienced, and he could paint (no one better), the exquisite devotion of woman to man; but he had scarcely ever felt the peculiar tenderness of man for woman, when that tenderness takes the form of vigilant protecting fondness. He knew little, and that not until late in life, of the subtle interweavings of habit with affection, which makes life saturated with love, and love itself become dignified through the serious aims of life. He knew little of the exquisite *companionship* of two souls striving in emulous spirit of loving rivalry to become better, to become wiser, teaching each other to soar . . .

All this is perfectly reasonable comment on the very youthful affair between Goethe and Friederike Brion, but it also reveals as clearly as anything could his feelings about his own situation, both as the young lover and young husband of Agnes and also the settler down, in young middle age, with Marian Evans, ready to face, and outface, the embarrassed stares of the Londoners he'd long known, although obliged, probably for Marian's sake rather than his own, to do the facing from a prudent distance. (Neither Richmond nor East Sheen sound at all like banishment now, but in 1855 they could count as the modern equivalent of (say) Aylesbury or Royston.) In particular, his stressed talk of the exquisite companionship of two souls points to how he and Marian gradually – he probably more gradually than she – came to see their relationship.

For roughly the first third of his book Lewes relies very much on Goethe's own *Dichtung und Wahrheit*. For us, a century and a quarter on, heirs to much vast and vigorous research into Goethe's early days, this is the least valuable third of his book – although Lewes is skilful enough in distinguishing the Dichtung from the Wahrheit.

On November 7 1775, however, Goethe, at the age of twenty-six, had put in his first appearance at Weimar. Weimar was then no more a seething metropolis than now. In a poem to the Duke of Saxe-Weimar, Karl August – the remarkable man he was to serve and be served by for upwards of fifty years – Goethe candidly admits:

Klein ist unter den Fürsten Germaniens freilich der meine,
Kurz und schmal ist sein Land, massig nur was er vermag.
(Small I confess is my Prince, compared with some of the
    Germans,
Brief and narrow his plot, hampered in what it can do.)

But Weimar, Goethe aiding, was to develop into an Athens, an incomparable model demonstration of how small can become beautiful. And Lewes knew Weimar well. He and Marian had paced it up and down, and he had known it well before Marian came into his life. He had the entrée into society. Lewes always had the knack of getting the entrée into society. There were innumerable people of substance and acumen still alive and vigorous who had been able to form their personal impressions of the master, and, confronted by Lewes's devoted curiosity, were willing, even delighted, to pass these on. At Varnhagen's house – Varnhagen had himself written a life of Goethe – he was able to collect personal first hand opinions about Goethe which gave strength and vivacity to the second two thirds of his biography. Tributes also came from the very old. He had, for example, a useful meeting with the sculptor Christian Daniel Rauch, born in 1777. Four years before Goethe's death, in 1828, Rauch had partnered Ernst Rietschel in a curious sculpturing job. Frock coated, Goethe had stood between them as Rauch saw to the front half and Rietschel, less rewardingly, laboured on the back. Was the great man in a hurry for the finished artefact? Or did he – he was seventy-nine by then – have a dislike of standing too long on his feet? Himself a very old man by this time, Rauch doesn't seem to have been questioned by Lewes on this, but he was fulsome in his assurances and details as to Goethe's lovable nature.

In Lewes's own country, opinion united pretty solidly in approval. One came upon occasional little murmurs of dissent. But the infrequent objections were scarcely audible, drowned as they were by vocal and printed approval which went on and on right down the century, so that Jowett, writing a letter of condolence to Marian after Lewes's death, is able to say:

> I am so glad that I knew him and was able to appreciate him. He was so very kind and disinterested and he was one of the first literary men of the day: His life of Goethe to say nothing of his other works was the second best biography in the English language, and as you have told me that it was by his encouragement you were induced to write we are indebted to him for a great deal more than this . . .

This is high praise indeed, but, casting round even now, you would have to think hard to cast effective doubt on Jowett's order of merit.

Boswell comes first, but Boswell had the luck to be in the company of his subject. Because he had the art of immediacy, and because Johnson was so wonderfully quotable, he gives the reader the impression that he and Johnson walked down the years side by side talking to each other. (This was very far from the truth but there was enough of truth in the impression for Boswell's genius to give it credibility.)

Lewes had no such opportunities. Goethe had been six years dead when Lewes first visited Germany. All he had to go on was elderly reminiscence, but the book is a wonderfully lively performance all the same. How surely he places the character of Karl August alongside Goethe's, and gives life to that unique alliance lasting between these two men for over half a century.

In a letter [unprinted], he [Karl August] writes to Goethe, then at Jena, saying he longs to be with him to watch sunrise and sunset in Gotha, hidden as it is by the crowd of courtiers, who are so *comme il faut*, and know their 'fish duty' with such terrible accuracy, that every evening he feels inclined to give himself to the devil. His delight, when not with soldiers, was to be with dogs, or with his poet alone in their simple houses, discussing philosophy, and 'talking of lovely things that conquer death'. He mingled freely with the people. At Ilmenau he and Goethe put on the miners' dress, descended into the mines, and danced all night with peasant girls. Riding across country, over rock and stream, in manifest peril of his neck; teazing the maids of honour, sometimes carrying this so far as to offend his more princely wife; wandering alone with his dogs, or with some joyous companion; seeking excitement in wine, and in making love to pretty women, without much respect of station; offending by his roughness and wilfulness, though never *estranging* his friends – Karl August, often grieving his admirers, was, with all his errors, a genuine and admirable character . . . Once, when there was a discussion about appointing Fichte as professor at Jena, one of the opponents placed a work of Fichte's in the Duke's hands, as sufficient proof that *such* a teacher could not hold a chair. Karl August read the book – and appointed Fichte. He had great aims; he also had the despotic will which bends circumstances to its determined issues. 'He was always in progress,' said Goethe to Eckermann; 'when anything failed, he dismissed it at once from his mind. I often bothered myself how to excuse this or that failure; but he ignored every shortcoming in the cheerfullest way, and always went forward to something new.'

A passage such as this gives the tone and quality of Lewes's book: he makes his two principal characters rise convincingly from the page.

As has already been seen, Lewes, without ever relapsing into any sort of *folie de grandeur*, did see in himself parallels with the Master. He is discussing Goethe's liaison with and ultimate marriage to Christiane Vulpius, who bore him a son, August, at the end of 1789, when Karl August, of course in full possession of the facts, was glad to stand as godfather. (Goethe had after all given his son his patron's name.) They lived long together and eventually married, with son August, by then in his seventeenth year, acting as one of the witnesses of the marriage. Lewes comments:

. . . Public Opinion has not forgiven this defiance of social laws . . . But let us be just. While no one can refrain from deploring that Goethe, so eminently needing a pure domestic life, should not have found a wife whom he could avow, one who would in all senses have been a wife to him, the mistress of his house, the companion of his life: on the other hand, no one who knows the whole circumstances can refrain from confessing that there was also a bright side to this dark episode. Having indicated the dark side, and especially its social effect, we have to consider the happiness it brought him at a time when he was most lonely, most unhappy. It gave him the joys of paternity, for which his heart yearned. It gave him a faithful and devoted affection . . .

What Lewes meant to suggest in saying that Goethe 'so eminently needed a pure domestic life' isn't exactly clear. One is tempted to give it the meaning one might attach to the remark: 'What that boy needs is a damned good hiding.' But all the rest of it reflects, even though confusedly, Lewes's own problems and vicissitudes. His Agnes-Marian relationship is clearly running through his mind, though one has to stress that no exactness can be claimed for the parallel. Agnes and Marian are here made to share the Christiane Vulpius role, but all the same he's stirring Goethe's sexual life – a territory of vast dimensions – into a modest mix-up that includes his own. And the 'joys of paternity' is a very relevant phrase here too. Despite the strong difficulties which Agnes and he created for them-

145

selves, all the emotions that can be associated with paternity were always very strong indeed in Lewes.

The range and strength of Goethe's appetites are well brought out. Goethe was a great gorger of himself – of his five senses and of his intellect equally. Lewes puts this all before us with exactly the right kind of wholeheartedness. We can feel a touch of the envy of a smaller spirit rising in him – and this adds to the point of it all.

[Goethe] rose at seven, sometimes earlier, after a sound and prolonged sleep; for, like Thorwaldsen, he had a 'talent for sleeping', only surpassed by a talent for continuous work. Till eleven he worked without interruption. A cup of chocolate was then brought, and he resumed work till one. At two he dined. This meal was the important meal of the day. His appetite was immense. Even on the days when he complained of not being hungry, he ate much more than most men. Puddings, sweets and cakes were always welcome. He sat a long while over his wine, chatting gaily to some friend or other (for he never dined alone), or to one of the actors, whom he often had with him, after dinner, to read over their parts, and to take his instructions. He was fond of wine and drank daily his two or three bottles . . . [Here Lewes springs to his defence] . . . I hasten to recall to the reader's recollection the habits of our fathers in respect of drinking. It was no unusual thing to be a 'three-bottle-man' in those days in England . . . [And Lewes insists that Goethe's Rheinwein was in any case weakish stuff by English standards] . . . The amount he drank never did more than exhilarate him . . . Over his wine he sat some hours: no such thing as dessert was seen upon his table in those days . . . His mode of living was extremely simple; and even when persons of very modest circumstances burned wax, two poor tallow candles were all that could be seen in his rooms. In the evening he went often to the theatre, and there his customary glass of punch was brought at six o'clock. When he was not at the theatre, he received friends at home. Between eight and nine a frugal supper was laid, but he never ate anything except a little salad or preserves. By ten o'clock he was usually in bed . . .

Lewes makes you feel that this is the way of a very great man, who has fulfilled himself and caught that elusive jewel we all chase after, and might best be called – if you're willing to condone three bottles of Rheinwein a day – balance.

The Pecksniffian cover-up, the dodging which taints so strongly the normal Victorian attitudes towards conduct and behaviour, was always something which Lewes was prepared not only to deplore but to defy in his own personal life. In 1855, and in the years before, he and Marian were feeling the hot Pecksniffian breath strong on the napes of their own necks. Goethe's view, lofty yet earthy too, of the good, the true, the right and even the acceptable, seemed to Lewes wholly right, wholly healthy. His response to it is genuine and quickens his book. He himself, in his comparatively small way, had been following the Goethean path ever since the time in his teens when he shook off the despotic glare of Captain Willim and worked his way, through trials and errors, into a career which had made him known and respected. For him Goethe is a hero, and he is able to make us feel that he is a hero for the right reasons.

His [Goethe's] worship was Nature worship, his moral system an idealisation of Humanity. The human being was the highest manifestation of the Divine on earth, and the highest manifestation of Humanity was therefore the ideal to which morality tended. We must first learn Renunciation; we must learn to limit ourselves to the Possible; in this first restraint lies the germ of self-sacrifice; in giving up claims too high for attainment, we learn to give up claims for the sake of others. True piety springs from human love.

The Goethean position is too large and too many sided to be boxed into a few sentences. But what Lewes says here is close to what is central to Goethe's conception of things, and central too to Lewes's own way of looking at the

147

dauntingly difficult business of living one's life and avoiding – to some extent anyway – finishing up with grief and
self-disgust.

Lewes is always – in this his finest work and indeed in
everything he wrote – brisk, decided, and never prepared
to be unqualified and adoring without what appears to him
as due cause. This makes his biography of Goethe a re-
freshing book to read. He mentions, for example, the fact
that Goethe and Beethoven, by far the greatest German
geniuses of their time, 'were together for a few days at
Töplitz, with the most profound admiration for each other's
genius'. That was in about 1812. Lewes goes on to say how
Beethoven later wrote to Goethe, asking him to persuade
Karl August to subscribe to his *Missa Solemnis* – and got no
reply. Lewes splendidly refuses to make heavy weather of
this.

> . . . It was doubtless very mortifying not to receive a
> reply; such things always are mortifying, and offended
> self-love is apt to suggest bad motives for the offence. But
> a bystander, knowing how many motives may actuate
> the conduct, and unwilling to suppose a bad motive for
> which there is no evidence, will at once see the inferences
> of Goethe's 'not deigning to reply', and of having 'forgot-
> ten-the-great-composer,' are by no means warranted by
> the facts. We know that Goethe was naturally of an active
> benevolence; we know that he was constantly recom-
> mending to the Grand Duke some object of charitable
> assistance: we know that he profoundly admired Beet-
> hoven, and had no cause to be offended with him; and,
> knowing this, we must accept any interpretation of the
> fact of silence in preference to that which the angry
> Beethoven, and his biographer, have inferred.

This is straightforward talk. Lewes was an experienced
practising journalist. Perhaps the letter had got lost in the
post. Perhaps Goethe had stuffed it into the hinder pocket
of his tailcoat and it had been emptied out by some officious
wench. Because one of the smaller mischances of life has
befallen a towering genius – who was bedevilled by mis-

chances infinitely more grievous – it still remains one of the smaller mischances and no valid spur to righteous wrath. The matter disposed of, Lewes marches on, and the reader feels pleased with him. As counsel for the defence he does a good job.

He is also quite prepared to prosecute if he sees occasion. When it comes to the master's *Wilhelm Meisters Wanderjahre*, Lewes has reservations and makes no secret of them. He accepts that there is inimitable Goethean stuff in the book,

but I cannot bring myself to regard the whole book as anything better than a collection of sketches and studies, often incomplete, and sometimes not worth completing . . . much of what is symbolical seems to me only fantastic; and as a composition the work is feeble, and careless even to impertinence. Not only are the various little stories 'dragged in' with the transparent artifice of juvenile productions; not only are these stories for the most part tiresome and sometimes trivial, but there is one story [*Nicht zu weit*] which, beginning with considerable animation, is actually left unfinished in the work, just as it lay unfinished in his portfolio. Observe it is not given as a fragment – the conclusion is promised but never comes. This is an impertinence to the public; all the more remarkable as coming from a writer who thought so much of Art . . .

Not many people, in the England of 1855, would have dared to give the venerated Colossus such a dressing down. About the second part of *Faust* Lewes is equally candid. It takes a brave man to state that outstanding genius has been wasting its time. How many critics today would be found willing to talk in such terms about Joyce's *Finnegans Wake*? But Lewes, having gone over the ground honestly and carefully, has no hesitation. He thinks, to put it bluntly, that *Faust* Part Two is the work of an ageing man who has lost his grip. *Faust* One and *Faust* Two shouldn't be thought of as parts of a whole, he thinks. They are separated for one thing by too great a gap in time.

149

. . . we have seen . . . the gradual development of a tendency towards mysticism and over-reflectiveness which . . . shadowed and perplexed his more vigorous concrete tendencies, and made this clearest and most spontaneous of poets as fond of symbols as if he had been a priest of Isis . . . It is quite true that Modern Art, as representative of the complexity of Modern Life, demands a large admixture of Reflection; but the predominance of the reflective tendency is a sign of decay . . . The poet who has only profound meanings, and not the witchery which is to carry his expression of those meanings home to our hearts, has failed . . . The Second Part of *Faust* . . . is a failure, because it fails in the primary requisite of a poem. Whatever else it may be, no one will say it is moving . . .

Here perhaps Lewes's fighting mood carries him away a bit. His quick, practical, honest, impatient mind shied away from the hesitant, fragmented quality of *Faust* Two. He failed to see – though not from want of trying – that the whole of the *Faust* opus is an unending act of confession; that it is a deliberate and conscious translation of Goethe's own life into poetic form, and that that form, under the huge weight of long years and vast experience, can become strained and distorted – as undoubtedly it sometimes does in *Faust* Two. Lewes is prepared to accept 'the occasional charm of the writing', and agrees that 'there are many passages of exquisite beauty,' but these seem tributes grudgingly given, and far too swiftly passed over. It's strange, for example, that he can't find time to pause over the exquisite metrical manipulations over which Goethe lovingly works in *Faust* Two – as when Helen appears, with immortal words on her lips:

Bewundert viel und viel gescholten, Helena,
Vom Strande komm' ich, wo wir erst gelandet sind . . .

And yet, by contrast, with what exact impartiality Lewes seizes on the weakness of the *Italienische Reise*:

[It] wants the charm of a collection of letters, and the solid excellence of a deliberate work. It is mainly interesting as indicating the effect of Italy on his mind; an effect apparently too deep for utterance. [Lewes might usefully have added here, but doesn't, 'at the time'.] He was too completely possessed by the new life which streamed through him, to bestow much time in analysing and recording his impressions . . .

It was at about the age of thirty, in 1779, that Goethe seriously started on what Lewes calls 'the passionate study of science'. On Goethe's preoccupation with science, the advanced and wide ranging researches he carried out, and the motives underlying these activities of his which went on hand in hand with all his other multifarious engross-ments for upwards of half a century – on all this Lewes is excellent. When it came to writing, he knew perfectly well that he was a hillock and Goethe a mighty, and even in places unscalable, peak. But when it came to science, to investigation of the natural world Lewes could face his subject on something more like level terms because he, too, was an investigator; after 1855 scientific exploration came to matter more and more to him, and literature – as Leigh Hunt, Slingsby Lawrence, or Dickens, or even Carlyle, saw it – began, Lewes says, to take second place.

He [Goethe] was trying to find a secure basis for his aims; it was natural he should seek a secure basis for his mind; and with such a mind that basis could only be found in the study of Nature . . . Saussure, whom he had seen in Geneva, led him to study mineralogy; and as his official duties gave him many occasions to mingle with the miners, this study acquired a practical interest, which soon grew into a passion – much to the disgust of Her-der, who, with the impatience of one who thought books the chief objects of interest, was constantly mocking him for 'bothering about stones and cabbages'. To these studies must be added anatomy, and in particular oste-ology. . . To improve himself he lectures . . . on the skeleton. And thus, amid serious duties and many dis-

151

tractions in the shape of court festivities, balls, masquerades, and theatricals, he found time for the prosecution of many and various studies. He was like Napoleon, a giant-worker, and never so happy as when at work. . .

Lewes manages with vivid accuracy all this highly important side of Goethe's all embracing love of life; and it isn't surprising that this should be so. If the blood and guts of the medical schools of the 1830s hadn't been too much for his squeamishness, he might well have been the one to have edged Lister – ten years younger than Lewes – out of his place as the founder of modern surgery in this country. Anatomy, biology – all the sciences of life in the rudimentary stages of when it began – were always a passion with him, and tended to take precedence over all his other activities as he grew older. Whenever and wherever in the *Life* he talks of Goethe's similar interests in the field of science, Lewes's own passionate interests are reflected in the writing. Lewes's *Life of Goethe* can claim to count as a very far from negligible substitute for what he might have achieved as a pioneering surgeon, had not chance and a weak stomach swung him into another direction.

8

The polyps ensconced among the Worthing pebbles with which Marian had to content herself were one of the signs of Lewes's new preoccupations. It was as though, having had the perceptiveness to see, before her, that Marian's potentialities as a writer might serve to take care of their joint career on the literary side, he felt freer now to flex his scientific muscles.

He was much concerned at this time about the education of his two elder sons, Charles Lee and Thornton Arnott. Agnes couldn't be persuaded to think very seriously about them, and Thornton couldn't be persuaded to think seriously about anything. Marian wrote to Charles Bray on March 31 1856 about his decision to give up his Coventry business and invited him to visit them at Park Shot. 'We can give you a bed – not a sumptuous one' – and boating upstream was delightful. She adds that they're uncertain about summer plans – money was still tight – but thought they might have to take the two boys out to Germany at midsummer to place them at school. This journey was in the end postponed until September and the two boys stayed on at a private school in Pembridge Gardens, Westbourne Park, until then.

Hofwyl School, up in the Alps about two hours' walk north of Bern, was an interesting place, and there was quite a little fashion for English parents who had split up to send their offspring there. It had been set up by von Fellenberg and Pestalozzi in 1806. To begin with Pestalozzi followed the educational principles laid down by Rousseau in *Emile*, and later came more and more to stress the importance of psychology as a guide in the bringing up of the young. His influence upon teaching was, and indeed remains, strong, but the schools he started suffered in time from his tendency to go bankrupt. Fellenberg, however, though influenced, did not go bankrupt, and when he was succeeded in 1855 – the very time when Lewes was pondering what to do with his boys – by Dr Eduard Müller, the school was flourishing and had a reputation. Earlier it had been supported by Brougham* and Lady Byron. Müller, a capable and strenuous innovator, kept the school's name before the British public, and in 1867 Meredith†, by then re-married, sent his motherless Arthur there and was glad of the relief.

Lewes and Marian, still shy of reintroducing themselves to the London society they'd known, spent the summer of 1856 away: the first half of the summer at Ilfracombe, the second at Tenby. They got back to Park Shot on August 9 and on the 25th Lewes set off alone with his two sons for Hofwyl.

The summer of 1856 was therefore a summer of exile for both of them, but it was also perhaps the most important summer of both their lives. Lewes had just published his most successful book and was getting acclaim for it; he also began in earnest his bid to be taken seriously as a natural scientist. And Marian was at last being encouraged. Having told her what she lacked as a writer of fiction Lewes now began apparently to have second thoughts, and when, long afterwards, she wrote her *How I Came to Write Fiction*, she said:

He began to say very positively, 'You must try and write a story,' and when we were at Tenby he urged me to begin at once. I deferred it, however, after my usual fashion with work that does not present itself as an absolute duty. But one morning as I was thinking what should be the subject of my first story, my thoughts merged them-

* Henry, Lord Brougham (1778–1868). Highly successful Whig lawyer and polymath. Lord Chancellor 1830–34. But he was arrogant and quarrelsome. The Whig aristocracy never really took to him. A great orator, his verbal tussles with Canning in the House of Commons are still remembered.

† Meredith, George (1828–1909). The reigning English novelist between 1880 and 1910. His reputation has plunged since then – undeservedly. He will make a return. His first marriage, to Mary Ellen Peacock (daughter of Thomas Love), was unhappy and they parted.

selves into a dreamy doze, and I imagined myself writing a story, of which the title was 'The Sad Fortunes of the Rev. Amos Barton'. I was soon wide awake again and told G. He said, 'Oh, what a capital title!' and from that time I settled in my mind that this should be my first story.

She didn't begin it till the autumn. But Lewes had given the nod. She was provisionally launched. In the meantime there was Lewes's splashing about in marine biology – Lewes's interests must come first.

It wouldn't perhaps be wise to make too much of Lewes's dedication to natural science. He was, and always remained, a working writer. And although there's no reason to suppose that his scientific interests weren't entirely genuine and lively, it has also to be said that, to begin with at any rate, he was cashing in on a market. In 1855 Kingsley had published *Glaucus: or the Wonders of the Shore*. This is a refurbishment of an article he wrote for the *North British Review* for 1854. The theme is the same as Lewes's *Seaside Studies*, which didn't reach publication in book form till 1858 although the articles composing it began to appear in the autumn of 1856. The handling of the subject matter in both books is closely parallel. Both authors leave London for a holiday. There's no need, they say, to be a hunter with rod or gun in order to find enjoyment; reading poorish novels or staring through a telescope are both also quite inadequate substitutes for wandering attentively along the seashore. Kingsley went to Paignton, Lewes to Ilfracombe. Both examined and dredged. Polyps and medusae and anything else that took their fancy were brought back to their lodgings, put into jars, and then looked at closely with the help of Arthur Helps's microscope. On August 23 he wrote in his journal: 'Before dressing this morning ran to look at my medusae – found all alive so dressed with "equal mind".' When he wrote up his findings in successive articles for *Blackwood's*, it's difficult to avoid the conclusion that he had Kingsley's *Glaucus* very much in mind. Both writers are recommending a new hobby, proposing to their fellow countrymen a new and worthwhile pastime for

155

their holiday leisure. Both describe careful, inspecting walks along the shore. Both lever up rocks with crowbars – and they do this rather blithely, rather carelessly, in a way that would cause a modern marine biologist to shake a disapproving head. Both – it should be stressed again – were going at the thing in a writer's way rather than a scientist's. Both had become aware of a market and as journalists were shaping up to supply it.

Both also make reference to Philip Gosse's *The Aquarium*, published in 1854 – and indeed Kingsley quotes extensively from Gosse, who was a scientific originator in a way that neither Kingsley nor Lewes could ever claim to be. Gosse indeed, quite apart from his fathering of that clever, capable, mischievous literary mandarin Edmund Gosse, has a genuinely earned place in scientific history. He made original contributions to marine zoology, was elected a fellow of the Royal Society, was entirely self-taught as Lewes must have been apart from his brief early brush with medicine. But Gosse was a scientist first, and a writer only in so far as he found it necessary to communicate his findings. It would be quite unjust to accuse Lewes of plagiary – either of Kingsley or of Gosse – but it wouldn't be unfair to suggest that he did take himself too seriously as a scientific enquirer, both at the beginning in the comparatively light hearted *Seaside Sketches* right on to the concluding, somewhat ponderous, *Problems of Life and Mind* to which Marian, the faithful and admiring relict, put the finishing touches after Lewes had died. And their choice of Ilfracombe and Tenby as places of refuge from the rather lonely, unsocial, ostracised hours at Park Shot isn't without significance. Ilfracombe and Tenby were both places that Philip Gosse had explored and written about.

Parts Three and Four of the *Seaside Sketches* deal with the long visits made by Lewes and Marian, first to the Scilly Isles and afterwards to Jersey, between March 15 and July 25 1857. Here he becomes more technical – surprisingly so indeed, because the material now, like the earlier, first made its appearance in the form of articles for *Blackwood's Magazine*, a paper catering for the educated general reader and not at all for the specialist. The explanation for this probably lies in the fact that by then Blackwood was willing to take Lewes provided he could have Marian as well. Lewes's ability – astonishing and exceptional – to read quickly and widely becomes apparent in these later sections, as it had in the *Biographical History of Philosophy* of the previous decade. He quotes for example from something he calls *Mémoires sur un genre de Polypes d'eau douce* which appeared in Leyden in 1744. The correct title of this work is much more charming: *Mémoires pour servir à l'Histoire d'un genre de Polypes d'eau douce à bras en forme de cornes**; but one forgets his misquoted title in amazement at his having unearthed at all a book so ancient and obscure. Where he contrived to lay hands on some of the books he mentions is a mystery. He acknowledges his debt to the London Library as have so many thousands of others since his time, but some of the obscure foreign titles he mentions weren't, so far as is ascertainable, in the Library's catalogue at the time of Lewes's writing: founded in 1841, the Library had after all had only fourteen years in which to work at its accumulation of treasures. He thanks Mr Trübner for lending him an Italian book which he couldn't afford to buy – what a busy, resourceful man he was. And however suspect we may find his zoology now, Charles Darwin found time to make a courteous bow in his direction. Francis Darwin, in his biography of his father, quotes a letter from him to Hooker about *The Variation of Animals and Plants* which had just been published. '. . . There has appeared a review in the *Pall Mall* which has pleased me excessively . . . if by any chance you should hear who wrote the article in the *Pall Mall* do please tell me; it is someone who writes capitally and who knows the subject . . .' Francis Darwin adds, 'I am indebted to Messrs Smith and Elder for the information that these articles were written by Mr G. H. Lewes . . .' And so they were, appearing in the issues of February 10, 15 and 17, 1868. The two never came to know each other well, but they did meet after that – at a party to investigate claims made by spiritualists.

* Study notes making a contribution to the History of a species of Polyp frequenting fresh water and having hornlike arms

As you read through Lewes's scientific output – and there's a vast deal of it – you get the impression that he modified his intentions, or perhaps enlarged them, as he went on. In the earlier material he doesn't escape the pervasive Victorian tendency to moralise. It isn't of course moralising along the lines his generation was accustomed to; he doesn't exactly preachify, but he is none the less at pains to point out that collecting sea anemones is good for you. It's a rather vague sort of good. Kingsley made no bones about insisting that while you were poking about looking for sea anemones you were assisting in the praise of God. Lewes wouldn't accept this for an instant, yet although he formulates nothing very precise to set against Kingsley's view, the inextinguishable journalistic spark in him kindles in response to the popular mood. There are also frequent patches of what a modern, thin lipped scientist would dismiss as comfortable, easy-to-read padding. On the other hand, Lewes does insist on the necessity for experiment as well as for observation before any valid advance in scientific knowledge can become possible. In the second and third chapters of Part Four of the *Sketches*, for example, he ceases to be simply a collector for his aquarium, and provides technical discussion of the structure of the retina in molluscs. Indeed he claims here to have made a tiny advance across the frontiers of human ignorance and dares to criticise the conclusions of the great, such as Richard Owen, and substitute conclusions of his own. On such matters of detail both Owen and Lewes alike are equally discredited: neither of them knew enough, neither possessed techniques sufficiently sophisticated. (The modern expert would, however, probably find that Owen was nearer the mark than Lewes.) It's worthwhile here noting surprise that scientific detail of this kind should appear in a magazine such as *Blackwood's*. But scientists of Lewes's generation, even outstanding ones, couldn't expect the deference, and eager receptivity, accorded to them now. James Prescott Joule, one year younger than Lewes, wrote a famous paper on the equivalence of heat and work which was refused by all the physical journals and came out in a church periodical. Lewes claims further, in these later

Sketches, to have discovered a new species to which he gives a convincing Latin name. But this would now be dismissed as unacceptable because he provides no proper description of his discovery.

It's obvious that Lewes knew a lot, and his wide reading bore him up; he was familiar with the dissection techniques current in his time. But as with the *Biographical History of Philosophy* you are left with the impression of an intelligent and enthusiastic amateur. Darwin, as we've seen, respected him and made some small use of him. But it wouldn't be wrong to place Darwin himself in the category of amateur – even though amateur of genius.

In the manner of the vast majority of journalists he was very good at sounding more knowledgeable than he was. This isn't at all to say that he was fraudulent. He took the high handed line because that was, almost always, the preferred line in nineteenth century journalism. *The Times* wasn't called 'The Thunderer' for nothing. The grievous bodily harm inflicted upon Keats's 'Endymion' at the beginning of the century by the critical hit men of *Blackwood's* and the *Quarterly* set a fashion in journalism which was to last pretty well through the century. When Lewes dismisses the phrenological notions of Charles Bray and George Combe, both of them friends of his and even closer friends of Marian, he does it roughly, in a manner that suggests contempt; even this might possibly be justified if he'd been as thoroughly qualified and clued up on the stage reached by his time in all branches of scientific research as he claimed to be. But he wasn't, and, as can happen to all journalists, his boomings sound louder than he probably meant because of the hollowness underneath.

This same characteristic, which sounds now in our ears much more unpleasantly than he ever intended, is apparent in the scientific books he produced after the *Sketches*: *The Physiology of Common Life*, 1859–60, *Studies in Animal Life*, 1862, and *Problems of Life and Mind*, five volumes of them, which appeared between 1874 and 1879. He is capable of shouting his wares like the barker at the entrance to a circus tent. 'Come with me,' he says in *Studies in Animal Life*, 'and lovingly study Nature, as she breathes, palpitates, and

159

works under myriad forms of life – forms unseen, unsuspected, or unheeded by . . . ordinary men . . .' He goes in for the harangue – because generally speaking Victorians enjoyed being harangued. 'Avert your eyes a while from our human world, with its ceaseless anxieties, its noble sorrow, poignant yet sublime, of conscious imperfection aspiring to higher states and contemplate the calmer activities of that other world with which we are so mysteriously related.' One can have too much of this sort of thing, and Lewes – and Marian too, come to that – is always eager to provide it.

He was quite willing to take on Darwin in 'Mr Darwin's Hypotheses' – four articles in the *Fortnightly* between April and November 1868. Here it has to be remembered that Darwin in 1868 was very far from being the renowned and revered figure he was to become a century later. Lewes's attitude is never that of the pupil looking up at and deferring to the master. The implications of Darwin's theories, so disturbing to many, weren't ever likely to shake or bewilder anyone possessing Lewes's cast of mind.

The reason why Darwin upset the Victorians so thoroughly was that he became the first man who was prepared – not theoretically (there had been plenty before him willing to do that), but demonstrably – to elbow the Creator out of the way. Darwin left First Causes to look after themselves, and concentrated as it were on what happened, or at any rate on what quite conceivably might have happened, after God had rested on the Seventh Day. This gave Lewes, filled as he was with Comtist explanations of the mysteries of life, nothing to jib at. When he reviewed the *Origin*, it was clear that to him, as to Darwin, the theory of the variation and multiplicity of types was a perfectly reasonable one. He felt no wish to postulate a Great Original whose creatures chanted in seemly harmony: As it was in the beginning, is now, and ever shall be. A horse was a horse and a Shetland pony was – well, something else again. Indeed Lewes rejoiced in the notion of flux. In *Studies in Animal Life* he falls in with the Darwinian view completely. Living creatures, he thinks, develop, adapt and alter in much the same way as Latin has fathered strongly differing

160

descendants in the modern Romance languages. He even claims in *Animal Life* that he had himself put forward the theory of the development of species ten years before Darwin. But now, he's willing to admit, the Darwinian version is sounder and more solidly buttressed than his own had been. What Lewes had said derived in fact from Herbert Spencer – in matters of science and philosophy it could never be claimed that Lewes is a true original. Spencer's views, just like Lewes's restatement of them, were always 'in the mind'. That's to say they were based on nothing which, in the modern sense, could be called scientific. Spencer never experimented, except in medicaments to soothe his hypochondriac body; he didn't observe, didn't nose his way down faint tracks to see where, if anywhere, these might lead him. What Spencer, and Lewes with him, really believed in was the abstract notion of 'progress' – something which could support their social and political creeds and their scientific pronouncements alike. Lewes's aim, sincerely and genuinely held, was to bring scientific study into a system of general ideas. The patient accumulation of details was to him a hindrance. As he said in the *Seaside Studies*, 'The observations of Chaldean shepherds . . . produced no astronomy in centuries of watching . . .'

And if Darwinian theory, or the implications of it, put Victorians into a great tizz, well, *tant pis* – as he might have said, because he was a great lover of intrusive and unnecessary French. He was delighted to see portly middle aged Victorians being pressed into doing mental somersaults after a reading of the *Origin*. His was the type of mind – and there are many more of the type around now than there were in his time – that finds apes much easier to swallow than Adam and Eve. He considered that to talk of a soul which inhabits man was to play with a word and make it do enforced duty as an explanation. Obviously there was a difference between men and animals. He accepted this. But he inclined to the view that the difference lay simply and exclusively in the matter of language. He suggested that language amongst human beings in general resembled the nervous system in the individual.

161

By the time he came to be talking in this way he would have thought of himself as having far outdistanced Philip Gosse. Ilfracombe, Tenby, the Scilly Isles and Jersey, the crude crowbars, the big jars, Arthur Helps's microscope – all these lay behind him. He was working on his last long book, *Problems of Life and Mind*, five volumes of it which appeared between 1874 and 1879. He died before it was quite finished. Marian greatly admired it. Had she been asked, she would almost certainly have said that here was a work which far outstripped *Middlemarch* or *Daniel Deronda* or *Romola*, and it would have been an opinion held with genuine sincerity.

You need fortitude, even heroism, to get through this book now – a remark it would be entirely false to make about his other large size work, the *Biographical History of Philosophy*, which despite its too snip-snap pungency remains thoroughly entertaining and informative. The first of his Problems is one which ought perhaps to be reserved for the ultra brave, the ultra talented – or, some might think, exclusively for the foolhardy. Lewes took the view that living and non-living mind and matter were two aspects of the same thing. This puts him outside the mechanist camp and outside the vitalist camp as well. He would call himself a reasoned realist. What he says is pretty much in line with what Haeckel says in his *Morphology* of 1866. But the parallels between the Jena professor, seventeen years younger than Lewes, and the Englishman's problems could be accidental. Haeckel nowhere mentions Lewes, but the views expressed by both of them still stand up pretty well. Modern scientists, although they (rightly) keep clear of philosophic abstractions, would, if they had to, choose a position very close to Lewes's. As he wrestles with his Problem he says things which sound simple enough but which were worth saying then just as they are worth saying now: an hypothesis is a guess which must be tested and perhaps verified; science is concerned always with How and never with Why. If it is objected that here he is offering no more than a statement of the obvious, then the reply must be that this is a statement too often conveniently forgotten in scientific circles even today. Lewes concludes this part with a discussion of Darwinism. There's much confusion in what he says here: it's as though he still can't make up his mind about *Origin*, but what Lewes says about 'Perception in the lower animals' still has value.

Problem two concerns itself with the nervous system. A modern expert would deposit all of this instantly on the scrap heap. The populariser of knowledge was here faced with a body of knowledge too scanty and ill founded to be worth popularising. Lewes's main contention is that all nervous action involves sensibility. The modern response to this would be to say either that it was wrong or that it was meaningless. This isn't at all the same as branding Lewes as a nincompoop. Knowledge of the action of the nervous system was in his day virtually non existent, so that whatever he said amounted to no more than a guess, and if he guesses incorrectly he stands in excellent and numerous company.

The third of his Problems concerns animal automatism. In this section he discusses the question of consciousness, and in what he says about the subconscious and the unconscious he comes very near to Freud. It has to be presumed that these remarks of his gained no very great currency at the time of his writing – in the 1870s – or if they were widely read then their significance wasn't widely realised. This is how it must have been, because otherwise there's no adequate way of explaining why Freud's theories, once they became generally known, should have caused so much shock and dismay. When he comes to Problem four, the reflex theory, there is too great a lack of essential knowledge for his remarks to have any significance worth mentioning for the modern expert.

Lewes's *Problems of Life and Mind* can be dismissed as a disposable book. It is inexact, unscientific in the modern sense, shaky in its definitions, but full of an enthusiasm which he often conveys and not without its bits of prophecy. He was always at pains in it to reassure his nervous Victorian readers. Science, galloping forward, needn't ever rob human life of its nobility and its idealism. What he thought would happen was that science would in the end invade morality's ground and, in a manner perfectly de-

163

cent, proper and unifying, take that ground over. In the last article he was ever to write, a piece in the *Fortnightly* of June 1878 called 'On the Dread and Dislike of Science', he poured these reassurances into receptive ears. In all his scientific writing, in fact, Lewes sticks to being a journalist, going this way and that, sometimes leading but sometimes following the ebb and flow of current opinion. Reassurance is indeed the primary aim of *Problems*. Lewes the positivist, Lewes the man prepared to give accepted views on sexual morality a brisk shake, treads carefully and is ready with comfort: the divine mysteries of creation aren't to be belittled in any way by the scientists' bit-by-bit taking to pieces of all the vast and intricate machinery. Although in the 'Dread and Dislike' article he did in the end come round to thinking that natural laws, as gradually they'd come to be unravelled, were all that human beings could reasonably and safely cling to, what he really sought was the 'ultimate package'. (The great temptation in most of us is to light our lanterns and go stumbling after this.) He longed to fight through to that blessed summit where hard, discoverable fact and revelation could live harmoniously together side by side. Comte and Herbert Spencer were the fallible leaders in whom he continued to put his faith as they pushed their way towards a synthesis which he couldn't, or wouldn't, accept as shaky or in any way faked.

In *Problems* he shows himself to be, right to the end, a metaphysician, even if an unoriginal one, rather than a scientist. What he longed for all along was not discovery but proof. Proof was what really mattered. But he shuttled between the two, hedging and qualifying, and was never himself an originator of abstract notions capable of changing men's habits of thought. He maintained, in Volume One of *Problems*, that for any philosopher, 'the power of *abstaining* from forming an opinion where the necessary data are absent' is the one that must be exercised in the interests of safety and credibility.

All through he is an uncertain man, groping about, but keeping up his spirits. He is certainly intelligent, certainly also amazingly knowledgeable, certainly capable of grappling more satisfactorily than most with the problems, seeing how difficult, how self-contradictory these problems are. A true Victorian, he wants, like Tennyson's Ulysses, to seek and to find. But even his considerable self-confidence falters when faced with the task of formulating a system that will hold together and resist onslaught from any quarter. He thinks, or at any rate he wishes, that the scientific explorers and the religious no-compromise men like Newman or Pusey can be brought together to 'sit round a table,' as we put it, that Huxley and Darwin can amicably confer with the Tractarians and the Evangelicals and come out of the room with a formula acceptable to both sides. But Lewes backs away from framing this formula with any precision or authority. His later work, in fact, lacks the solidity and permanence of Marian's – because she built, if never trustingly enough, on her imagination.

Lewes was never at all concerned with that favourite Victorian occupation – doing good. There was nothing of John Ruskin about him. The just society, that mirage that Ruskin pursues with bewildered pertinacity through the multitudinous jottings of *Fors Clavigera*, doesn't find any place in what Lewes wrote. Yet to make up for this, the variety of his interests, and his considerable mastery of a very wide range of subjects are quite exceptional. He isn't a polymath as Milton was – by his time the world had moved on too far and too fast for that to be possible – but few if any men of his generation could rival his capacity to know more and more about more and more.

But in the end he was always guided by his sure journalistic sense of what the public at any given moment was looking for. His science, as well as his literary and dramatic criticism, his philosophy, his novels, stocked the shelves of the Victorian mind with what that Victorian mind felt it ought to have in readiness for bleak, surprising times that might lie ahead. His Wellsian faith in what science was surely going to be able to accomplish quite soon, as social manipulation would achieve human betterment – no part of this faith had to struggle through the calamities which brought the eager, pulpiteering Wells down at last to the derelict self-abandonment of *Mind at the End of its Tether*.

Marian thought he was a wonder. He was also all she

165

had. Lewes made no capital out of the strength of his position, but his role – unconsciously taken up – was none the less that of leader, hers that of follower, of grateful recipient of advice.

This aspect of the early part of their relationship is clearly seen in the matter of her translation of Spinoza's *Ethics*. She wrote an enthusiastic review of Meredith's first book, *The Shaving of Shagpat*, in January 1856, and then in February finished her translation. At the end of March she wrote to Bray: '. . . By the way, when Spinoza comes out, be so good as not to mention my name in connection with it. I particularly wish not to be known as the translator of the *Ethics*, reasons which it would be "too tedious to mention".' She refers mysteriously to 'reasons'. Why should there be even one reason, let alone two or more? The likeliest guesses would be that, first, she didn't want her name to appear much in public, situated as she then was – this admittedly is a bit thin but it will have to do. The second reason is stronger and has to do directly with Lewes. He had in 1853 published with Bohn an exposition of Comte's positivism. After that there had been talk of a translation of Spinoza: he would edit and annotate a translation done by another hand. Then in 1854, before the dash to the continent, Lewes had come to an altered arrangement with Bohn's son. For an altered, and increased, fee, Lewes would supply the translation as well as be responsible for the auditing. But then Bohn senior had objected, considering the fee now arranged between Lewes and his son as being excessive. Bohn thought the business should be re-negotiated. Lewes thought Bohn guilty of wriggling and backsliding, and told Bohn so in the tart manner he could employ, and indeed frequently did employ, when he felt there was occasion for it. He broke off all dealing with Bohn.

But apparently he had already farmed the work out on Marian, and neglected to tell her of the brush with Bohn, leaving her quite ignorant of the fact that she was going to be working on a very difficult and demanding task uncommissioned and totally at a venture. She went obediently ahead. If Lewes told her to do something she did it. He, a sanguine man always, probably felt confident that he knew his way about literary London sufficiently well by then to place anything by himself or subcontracted. But, as it turned out, Spinoza's *Ethics* in Marian's translation proved to be an unsalable product. As late as 1859 Lewes was trying it on publishers A. and C. Black but getting only No for an answer. Nowhere in Marian's correspondence is there any hint of irritation on her part over this, no word to suggest that Lewes had treated her shabbily. It seems incredible that he should have kept from her his hoity-toity rejection of all dealings with Bohn, but the assured certainty of publication which is suggested by her words in that March letter to Bray must mean that that was how it was. He, the man, disposed. She, the woman, accepted. She never took the role of feminist, of liberated woman. Never, neither then nor much later when she had become famous and admired, when, in the summer of 1863, they'd bought The Priory and she was paid court to as the High Priestess of Regent's Park. And her acceptance of the fact that she had struggled through a vast deal of very hard work for nothing is the more surprising because, in 1856, they were both of them pressed for money. In that same letter to Bray she tells him: 'You don't know what a severely practical person I am become, and what a sharp eye I have to the main chance. I keep the purse and dole out sovereigns with all the pangs of a miser.' They were both busy with articles, mainly for the *Leader*, but they must both have been very conscious of having been shunted into a backwater – and this when Lewes had responsibilities towards a wife and children.

Only a few days before Marian's letter to Bray, Mrs Anna Jameson of Ealing had sat down to write to her friend Ottilie von Goethe, the great man's daughter-in-law. Mrs Jameson was a clever, advanced lady who in 1838 had written a book which Marian had reviewed. It was called, not very enticingly, *Winter Studies and Summer Rambles in Canada*, and the young Marian, writing to Patty Jackson at Griff – the girls had been friends at school in Coventry – had spoken of this volume by a '. . . clever authoress, but I fear of no fixed religious principles, if I may judge from an apparent affectation of a liberalising, philosophising manner of

167

speaking about religion and morals . . .' Now it was Mrs Jameson's turn to take a lofty line.

The story of Lewes and his Wife is true, I fear. The lady who is with him I have seen before her [known] liaison with him. She is first-rate in point of intellect and science and attainments of every kind, but considered also as very *free* in all her opinions as to morals and religion. In the first, I think there are certain duties not to be thrown overboard; in the second, certain principles to be recognised; so that I do not well understand how a good and conscientious woman can run away with another woman's husband . . .

Three weeks after this, thumbing his nose at money worries and ostracism, Lewes haled her off to Ilfracombe and the molluscs.

9

They were away till August. Lewes dragged her round –
Ilfracombe, then Tenby, and she splashed after him. By
June, in addition, she'd finished two articles and was 'determined to pay some attention to seaweeds'. This was pure
wifely dutifulness. Levering up sharp, green slime-coated
rocks with a crowbar wasn't Marian's line, but Lewes,
playing the directing role which came naturally, and not
unpleasantly, to him, willed her to be enthusiastic, and
enthusiastic she forced herself to be. He smoked cigars, had
nervous headaches, mastered Helps's microscope, and
cultivated nice Mr Tugwell, curate of Ilfracombe, who was
himself very good on sea anemones.

Up till now he'd thought of her as an outstandingly
capable, serious journalist, prepared to work hard in order
to tackle serious books embracing a wide range of subjects
and able to write thoroughly adequate notices of them of a
length – very considerable – to suit the tastes of the intelligentsia of the 1850s. But did she have the dramatic power
necessary for the writing of novels which might command
the attention of people like Jane Welsh Carlyle or Mrs
Grote? No, he had felt that this would be to give her a run
over a course not suited to her considerable powers.

But now for some reason – perhaps because every day he
was getting to know her better – Lewes changed his mind.
The ex-novelist and continuing playwright decided that,
perhaps after all, here was a novelist in the making. And
novels properly done could make you rich: look at Dickens,
look at Thackeray, look at hosts of others. And as head of a
double ménage there could be no doubt that Lewes needed
to be, if not rich, at any rate much richer than he was. If
these were his thoughts – and to suggest that they were is
guesswork and no more – there's no need at all to accuse
him of cynicism or self-seeking in thinking them. A literary

editor is nothing if he isn't a talent spotter and Lewes was closely familiar with such duties. Pigott, one of Lewes's closest assistants on the *Leader*, came to visit them in June, and it was agreeable to find in this way that they weren't going to be wholly barred from the society of old companions. Barbara Leigh Smith, liberated, freethinking, shortly to become Madame Bodichon, and with an income of £300 a year, which was all her own, ever since 1848, came too. She was a robust flouter of all conventions and the Leweses loved her always. Ilfracombe was a success. In fact it was almost an idyll. They felt reassured. Tenby, where they had moved at the beginning of July, wasn't at first quite such a success. Lewes missed Mr Tugwell. Marian set to work on an article on 'Silly Women's Novels', and then Lewes began prodding her towards novel writing. He even said she was to sit down then and there and make a start.

Marian, though, didn't accept this switch in direction immediately, but she did turn obediently from facts and abstracts and gave her imagination a preliminary airing. It is almost incredible to think that it had lain unexercised within her for thirty-six years and eight months.

Odd too that Lewes should have been so excited by a title so humdrum as *Scenes from Clerical Life*. But probably what he was saying to himself was: 'Anything to get her started.' It's clear from his journal that there had been talk of this kind of project before and that Marian had been showing uncertainty. They got back to Richmond on September 4. Lewes busied himself with a revision of his *Biographical History* which would bring a projected fresh edition up to date. He also, in a *Blackwood's* article on sea anemones, translated some of his summer researches into print. In October he bought a microscope for himself so that he could return Helps's. Marine biology and the problems it raised still greatly exercised him, and an October entry in his journal expressed fears: 'Tormented with doubts as to whether the bodies I took for embryos *were* embryos or whether they had any spontaneous motion.' Thornton Hunt also contributed to his torments: he was holding back on the payments he was due to make to help towards the maintenance of Agnes and the family which she was bringing up in Kensington. With constant advice, Lewes fostered the gestation of *Amos Barton*, and early in November, when it was finished, he wrote to John Blackwood about it. Lewes took these first fruits over because he felt, with entire justification, that they were as much his as hers. He had been the tutor and she the student. She had written, he had criticised, and she had gone back to her desk to re-write. When it came to a pathetic scene – the death of Milly Barton for example – could she manage it? He made suggestions, gave hints, and then he went off to London for the evening leaving her to get on with it. By the time he got back the work had been done and was read to him. It passed this test. This was an important moment in both their lives. Marian remembered it and much later on recorded the reaction of the man she loved. 'We both cried over it, and then he came up to me and kissed me, saying "I think your pathos is better than your fun."'

His letter to Blackwood expressed the confidence he now felt. 'I confess that before reading the Ms I had considerable doubts of my friend's power as a writer of fiction: but after reading it those doubts were changed into very high admiration . . .' He went on to say that *Amos Barton* was planned as the first of a series, that all the pieces would be set in country places, centre round the life of country parsons and would refer back to life as it was being lived in the early 1830s – when Marian herself was beginning the transition from childhood to young womanhood. The tone, Lewes said, was to be human, not theological, but, 'He begged me particularly to add that – as the specimen sent will sufficiently prove – the tone throughout will be sympathetic and not at all antagonistic.' Finally, 'He calculates the present story will make two parts for *Maga**. . .' So the new author, thus promoted, was to be a He. Why had Lewes and Marian decided, and were long to insist, upon anonymity? The reason was simply that the name Marian Evans had become – not generally but in close, cultivated circles both in London and the main provincial centres – a name associated with scandal. They both wanted success

* The alternative title of *Blackwood's Magazine*.

for the newly launched novelist and the safe, solid, masculine anonymity of George would keep the chance of that success open.

Lewes chose to negotiate with Blackwood because he was having dealings with him over his zoological articles. Otherwise Blackwood wasn't a natural choice because he and his paper took the Tory line, quite counter to the views of Lewes and Marian as set out often enough in the *Westminster*, in the *Leader* and elsewhere. But John Blackwood was a generous, straight dealing as well as thoroughly able man. He served the Leweses well, published all of Marian's novels except *Romola*, and blame for the one brief spell in their relations when they were at odds rested wholly on their side and not on Blackwood's. He was just a year younger than Lewes. His Edinburgh business had been founded by his father, William Blackwood, in 1817, and John, sixth of seven sons, had by 1852 become the principal figure in a prospering concern. His handling of its affairs enabled it to prosper and flourish ever more widely. Joseph Langford was the firm's London manager between 1845 and 1881 and he too was a man of many sided ability. He found time to write dramatic criticism for the *Observer* as well as to look after Blackwood's interests devotedly, and he was always a staunch upholder of Lewes and Marian.

In the early stages all the negotiations between the two parties were conducted by Lewes. The shy mysterious 'He', Lewes said, wanted to remain anonymous, and Lewes, to avoid the shadowy repetitiveness of 'him' and 'he', mischievously and misleadingly referred to 'our clerical friend'. 'I am glad to hear that your friend is as I supposed a Clergyman,' John wrote, perhaps with his tongue in his cheek. 'Such a subject is best in clerical hands.' That was on November 18 1856. He was willing to take *Amos Barton*, but he had reservations and said so. The clerical person explained his characters too much and was a bit sparing when it came to the essential novelistic business of showing characters in action; the ending was lame because too much attention was paid to the settling of the fortunes of a host – too many? – of minor characters. But it would do, none the less. 'If the author is a new writer I beg to congratulate him on being worthy of the honours of print and pay.'

What more could a new writer – new at any rate to Blackwood – expect? Nothing but gratitude, one might think. But Lewes, characteristically, was stand-offish as well as a bit brisk in his reply. His protégé had been rather put off by Blackwood's words but in spite of this he would, obedient to Lewes's advice, submit a follow-up story to Blackwood, although 'At present he has only written what he sent you'. In his opening letter Lewes had contrived to suggest, without exactly putting it into words, that Marian had plenty of material all ready and waiting in a drawer, but when Blackwood replied he made no reference to this apparent contradiction although shrewd Blackwood must certainly have noticed it. His reply was generous in the Blackwood way. He hadn't meant to discourage his new author and what was more – this was handsome – he was sorry he had nothing more already written, 'but if he cares much about a speedy appearance I have so high an opinion of this first tale that I will waive my objections and publish it without seeing more . . .' He couldn't, naturally, commit himself to accepting something that didn't yet exist, but 'I am very sanguine that I will approve.' After this reply Lewes warmed up, became even expansive. His friend was more anxious about *excellence* than about appearing in print '. . . afraid of failure though not afraid of obscurity; and by failure he would understand that which I suspect most writers would be apt to consider as success – so high is his ambition.'

Lewes kept on with his persistent headaches. Over Christmas and the New Year 1857 he paid one of his increasingly regular visits to Arthur Helps at his house, Vernon Hill, in Hampshire. Marian began the second *Scene** on Christmas Day and on January 1 *Amos Barton* was published. Blackwood sent her his cheque for fifty guineas

---

* The three *Scenes* are made up of three novels, shorter than George Eliot's others except for *Silas Marner*. The separate titles are: *The Sad Fortunes of the Rev. Amos Barton, Mr Gilfil's Love Story* and *Janet's Repentance*. They were published by Blackwood in two volumes in January 1858.

on December 29, with a generously appreciative letter to go with it. He made it clear that he was hoping for more. He made the cheque payable to Lewes. What else could he do? That January also Lewes looked back over the year and put down a summary of his journal.

> The past year has been a happy and successful one and will be memorable to me, not only as the year in which my greatest literary success – *The Life of Goethe* – was assured, but also as the year in which I learned to employ the *Microscope*, and inaugurated by *Seaside Stories* the entrance into the vast field of marine zoology. I resumed also my contribution to *Blackwood* this year, which formed the proximate cause of Marian's introduction to fiction. We had long discussed the desirability of her trying her powers in that direction, and the temptation of appearing anonymously and successfully in *Blackwood* induced her to begin a series of tales, the first of which appeared this month. Revision of *Biog. Hist.* – schemed 'Ariadne, Principles of Success and Failure in Literature'.

When Lewes got back they both set hard to work. Marian's *Mr Gilfil's Love Story* was finished on January 17 – which means she was very quick indeed with it. The review articles from both of them continued coming. Both of them got bilious, and Lewes's glands swelled. *Amos Barton* got off to a quiet start, but Blackwood's faith in his new author grew stronger none the less. He wrote to her on January 30. 'My Dear Amos' he began – he had after all to call her something – and went on to tell her that Thackeray had been staying with him and that he (Blackwood) had told him: 'Do you know I think I have lighted upon a new Author who is uncommonly like a first class passenger.' By mid-February praise in the press for this new first class passenger began to increase markedly and Lewes wrote to Blackwood to assure him that reports he was getting in London were encouraging. The reaction, he admitted, wasn't large in size, 'but it is unanimous, and from *typical* readers, namely *foolometers* and men of intellectual eminence.' Helps had said it was 'pestilently clever' and

Richard Owen 'does not remember when he has read a better story'. Owen's high repute as a scientist would have made this verdict particularly valuable to Lewes because his own scientific preoccupations were by now more and more taking hold of him. Indeed in the same letter Lewes immediately goes on to talk about his January paper in *Blackwood's* called 'New Facts and Old Fancies about Sea-Anemones' and informs his publisher that 'Owen, in spite of being controverted in it, thinks it masterly and convincing . . .' Lewes concludes his letter by saying:

I am panting for the Scilly Isles, and every gleam of sunshine makes my uneasiness greater; but printers, rightly named diabolic, keep me proofbound inland, and I shall not be free till the end of the month; but early in March I take wing. After Scilly I think of Guernsey and Brittany – in the two latter places I have hopes of having the company of Eliot . . .

It sounds here – as it pretty well always does sound – as if Lewes was the one who took the decisions. The Scilly Isles didn't particularly beckon her but in the end she went, though in the February letter there are hints of resistance. They were very much on their own, and Lewes seems happy to have been so. The fact that he was less than well – swollen glands still troubled him – probably made it easier for him to accept the lack of the busy social life and the gossip going with it which he loved. They walked in Richmond Park; in the evenings they read to each other, and constantly, over a long spell of time, they discussed, plotted and planned the long Warwickshire novel which they hoped would follow on after the *Scenes – Adam Bede*. On August 15 – not a Day of Obligation for either of them – they set out on what Lewes firmly called 'our zoological expedition'. They spent the night at the Great Western Hotel, Paddington, to be poised and ready for the 10 o'clock Plymouth express next morning. In Plymouth they stayed at the Globe Hotel where, having arrived at 5.30 pm, they gave orders for a chop tea to be prepared. Then they went out on to the Hoe, admired the sea (although

Lewes always got painfully sick on it) and after tea Marian read Mrs Gaskell's *Cranford** aloud to him. In 1857 the GWR hadn't yet crossed the Tamar so from then on it meant a coach. They had outside seats, which in mid-March couldn't have been good for Lewes's glands, and took superior pleasure in the company of a pretentious surgeon. Lewes, feigning ignorance, drew him out on anatomy in order to mock in private. They reached the Union Hotel in Penzance at 8.30 pm where they ordered another chop tea after which they retired much fatigued to bed. The next day was a wild wet one so they decided to wait before crossing and found themselves lodgings (cheaper) at 1 Marine Parade. This proved to be a ramshackle dump. The bedpole fell when Lewes drew the curtains. All day it had rained, so they sat it out indoors and Lewes read Draper's *Physiology*.

Still it blew and they had to sit it out at Marine Parade till the 26th. In the dry intervals they learnt by heart 'all the hedgerow beauties of March in this country'. Eventually the packet *Ariadne* sailed on a bright morning at 6 am. There was nothing either to eat or drink for breakfast on board, so they munched biscuits on deck, and soon the rain came on, and the wind and swell with it. They ducked below – they were the only passengers – and lay in their berths. But the 'swell and roll of the Atlantic soon produced a terrible commotion, and we lay sick, at times semi-delirious, icy cold, and with pain in the intestines of a very unpleasant kind.' 'Nevertheless,' Lewes noted, 'between intervals – when lucid – I mentally wrote passages in my contemplated article for *Blackwood's*, and reproached myself for the cowardly twinges of remorse extorted by suffering . . .' The last remark here comes as something of a surprise. By this time he and Marian had been together for two years and eight months but he still apparently hadn't reconciled himself to his abandonment of Agnes. And the abandonment of his children? No. There, surely, he could feel no guilt. Hofwyl was a good school and the cost of supporting

Cranford, scenes of village life in Cheshire (Knutsford), came out in 1855. The book had a success. The tone is that of gentle-sharp, quiet comedy.

two sons there lay entirely on his shoulders. But Agnes? That wasn't the same thing at all. Agnes remains always an elusive figure, difficult to get to know. As Lewes lay clutching his intestines on the wallowing packet, she was within two months of being brought to bed of her fourth child by Thornton Hunt. This was to be a girl – Mildred Jane. And the surname was still of course to be Lewes, which was probably one reason why he should call his twinges of remorse cowardly. Her liaison with Hunt broke off after the birth of Mildred Jane. Lewes stayed on, to be – what he'd always been – her prop and stay.

On Scilly they stayed at St Mary's with Mrs Scadden, the postmistress. Life was pretty rough and tough. Mrs Scadden charged them fourteen shillings a week with one and six for fire. She was no cook, but Marian gave her 'a culinary lecture every morning, and we do in the end get fed'. Lewes scrutinised his molluscs, zoophytes and annelids. He worked on a fresh series of *Seaside* papers for Blackwood and buried himself in '. . . big physiological books,' Marian recorded, 'German, French and English, with broad pages spreading like a prairie, unbroken by paragraph or quotation.' On March 31 Lewes noted: 'Walk. No fowl, meat or fish to be had. Called on Mrs Tregarthen who cut off steak from beef she was keeping. One dines by stratagem!' At the end of April Blackwood sent him proofs of the opening article of his new series and had an interesting objection. 'Your enthusiasm,' he said, 'prevents you from seeing the peculiar effect of the analysis of the faeces of the Actiniae and I wish you would delete or alter a portion of this. The quotation from your clinical authority is painfully minute and could not be otherwise than distasteful, especially to ladies who form a large section of the readers of such papers.' Blackwood was in the entertainment business – and so was Lewes. Faeces were nasty and unladylike and best not discussed, however scientific the tone, and Lewes agreed immediately that they should be cut out, '. . . but you must confess it is an awful wet blanket on a writer's shoulders, that terror of lady readers, and what they will exclaim against. I am tempted to exclaim with Charles Lamb "Hang up the ladies! I will write for antiquity."' He ended this letter of May 3 with: 'I strike my tents on the 11th for Jersey.'

The sea was smooth for once, and St Helier was interesting to him because of his boyhood schooldays there twenty-nine years before. 'The Square seemed so *much* smaller! Broad Street, the theatre, the market and a few other places were revived; but for the rest the place seemed as much changed as I.' They found rooms at Gorey, looking across at the Carentan twelve miles away, in Rosa Cottage, 13/- a week for three rooms and attendance, which was better than Mrs Scadden, and after the rigours of Scilly they enjoyed lush plentifulness. Having booked in, they returned to St Helier, and 'bought wine, brandy, groceries, paper, map etc hired an easy chair, and a bath'. Then they dined at the Union Hotel and returned to Rosa Cottage in a fly, equipped to indulge themselves. At the end of May Marian braced herself to write to her brother Isaac to tell him that now she had 'someone to take care of me in the world'. She told him further that they'd be in Jersey, or else Brittany, for some months because her health was frail. When winter came they'd go to Germany. 'We are not at all rich people, but we are both workers, and shall have enough for our wants.' It's a moving letter, proud yet also supplicating, eager to be reunited, and accepted, by all the Evanses, yet seeing the perhaps-impossibility of this and prepared to face a long period of non-acceptance.

Blackwood wrote to Lewes two days later, saying he'd addressed an earlier letter simply to Lewes in St Helier, telling the postmaster 'to find out a maniac answering to your name hammering rocks and dissecting Sea weeds on the shore.' He was pleased with them both, with the *Scenes* and with Lewes's new series of *Seaside Sketches*. Lewes wrote to him breezily, not in the tones of an exile at all. They'd be back in London early in July, and he would 'organise a quiet dinner and persuade our excessively *umbrageous* friend to peer from beneath his *umbra*, join our party and show himself to you in the flesh.' He was beginning to see that the masquerade couldn't be continued indefinitely. Isaac replied to his sister's letter, but coldly and unforgivingly – through his solicitor. She remained quite unshaken about the rightness of what she had done: Lewes's zoology must sometimes have been a trial, but she was willing to adjust herself bravely to that. 'Moreover, having myself a slight zoological weakness, I am less alarmed than most people at the society of a zoological maniac.'

By July 24 they were back in Richmond. Lewes went to see Agnes in Kensington many times; there was much to see to, in particular he had to arrange for his youngest son, Herbert to join his brothers at Hofwyl. On August 24 he took him off to Switzerland, and stayed a few days while the boy settled down. Then he returned, 'gloating over the cathedral' at Strasbourg, he said, and settled to work to pay the fees. *Adam Bede*, long brooded over and discussed by both of them, was begun on October 27. By New Year's Day Lewes could write:

The last year has been one of the happiest and most successful of my whole life, the effect of domestic happiness obviously telling on my intellectual efforts. I have done scarcely any journalism, only an occasional review for the *Leader* and about a dozen and a half for the *Saturday Review*. Have dissected an immense quantity of animals and used the microscope with daily diligence. Several not unimportant discoveries have rewarded this labour and the effect of *Seaside Studies* in increasing my reputation has been very appreciable . . .

He could perhaps justifiably feel pleased with himself because on January 19 1858 he was able to note: 'Last night received a very complimentary letter from Huxley on the *Seaside Studies*, this morning one still more complimentary, but not of course so gratifying, from Sir Henry Holland.' Holland was physican to the Prince Consort and a busy writer himself, but the approval of Huxley would clearly count for more with Lewes.

But when April came round they were off again. They were finding living in Richmond expensive, so they did go to Germany, only later than Marian had predicted. They found lodgings at 15 Luitpoldstrasse, Munich, with an old maid, the rooms overcrowded with *biedermeierestil* furnishings but short on washbasins. They preferred the 'glorious mass' being celebrated in the Frauenkirche to the Lutheran St Sebald's where 'a Protestant clergyman was reading in a cold formal way under the grand gothic arches'; they enjoyed the Rubens masterpieces in the alte Pinakothek. They had colds, though, and didn't on the whole respond very joyously to Munich – the general aspect was 'distasteful' – but it was good to hear from Blackwood on April 30 that he was quite 'ready to meet [Lewes's] wishes by the publication of *Adam Bede* as a separate work at once'.

But Lewes had the knack of quickly getting into the swim wherever he was, and by mid-May he was dining with the great chemist Liebig, 'the skin begrimed and the nails black to the roots. He looks best in his laboratory with his velvet cap on, holding little phials in his hand and talking of Kreatine and Kreatinine in the same easy way that well-bred ladies talk scandal.' Karl von Siebold, the professor of anatomy at Munich university, was also affable. Lewes was permitted to watch wonders through his microscope, to watch the great man dissect, and to listen to him playing difficult Schubert accompaniments whilst his wife, much younger than he and still pretty, did the singing. They stuck it in Munich till July 7 – at 10/- a week the Luitpoldstrasse rooms were the cheapest yet – and *Adam Bede*, so long and carefully planned between them, went very rapidly ahead there, but vague ill health plagued them both so they decided to move on. Von Siebold saw them off, proof enough of how much Lewes had impressed him; indeed von Siebold had been 'much interested by the discoveries therein described' and 'will quote [from the articles] in the new edition of his *Comparative Anatomy*'.

Before he went, Lewes found time to get across to Zurich to see his youngsters, and also spent a day, whilst there, with Jacob Moleschott, recently appointed professor of physiology in Zurich. Moleschott invited some celebrities of the scientific world to meet him there and he had 'quite a little ovation'. Lewes, in fact, was making a name for himself at an astonishing speed, both at home and abroad, in the world of science. (It has to be remembered that a scientific reputation was infinitely easier to achieve then than now. No long years of arduous preparation were necessary; there was no vast body of knowledge to master before you could acquire your licence to launch out on your own and announce personal achievement.) 'I have been doing some capital work in the laboratories of my friends here,' he cheerfully tells Blackwood at the end of June, 'where an extensive apparatus and no end of frogs are at my disposal!'

Then they were off on a leisurely, roundabout journey to Dresden, going by way of Linz, Vienna (where Lewes says 'saw my old lodgings in the Kârtner Tor'), and Prague where they visited the Jewish quarter, the alte Friedhof. There, 'The Jew who showed us over the Synagogue explaining everything and reading a bit out of the old parchment copy of the Book of Moses was a very decent quiet man for whom I felt quite a liking.' It was a beautiful journey and for Lewes Dresden was 'the most habitable of German towns'. By now his scientific obsessions went with him everywhere. And 'it was so very amusing to find myself thinking of nerve cells amid the grand mountains, and of physiological processes on the shores of a lake. But after all the two went perfectly together.' Dresden was a *ville d'art* and had no labs for Lewes to be given the run of. 'We live like hermits here,' he told Blackwood. 'Not a soul will I see and our society is strictly limited to Raphael, Titian, Correggio, Veronese, and the other "gents" of painting. In Munich we had too much society; it was pleasant but prevented work . . .' Later he goes on to talk to Blackwood about the latter's golf.

So you are golfing again? I must learn that golf, some day to ascertain what its fascinations are. Do you *really* find it as thrilling as molluscs? How many days could you spend doing *nothing else*? That is the test. In Munich I made the acquaintance of a Russian anatomist who for *six years daily* has done nothing but make preparations and observations on the Spinal Cord – and with 50,000 preparations he couldn't convince me of the truth of his 'discovery'. What say you to that?

181

It wasn't all science. Quite apart from the articles which were to form the basis of *The Physiology of Common Life*, published in 1859–60, and *Adam Bede* which was in sight of completion, they returned to Richmond, on September 2, having 'brought back a goodly heap of M.S.', including his essay on modern German novelists in which he talked interestingly about Gustav Freytag and Paul Heyse amongst others. Lewes immediately set about preparing for the twenty-eighth meeting of the British Association a paper called 'The Spinal Cord a Sensational and Volitional Centre', which was read on September 27 by the great Richard Owen in person. Lewes had come far fast, which was his way. Blackwood sturdily refused to be mocked out of his golf, and early in October Lewes told him: 'Your dithyramb on golfing stirs my desires. "Thou almost persuadest me to be a golfer." Who knows but some day I may develop in *that* department too – and write you a book the "Golfing of Common Life"?'

In November Blackwood offered Marian £800 for a four years' copyright of *Adam Bede*, which he said he found 'capital'. A fortnight later he offered Lewes £250 for the first 5,000 copies of the *Physiology of Common Life*, and £3 per thousand of each sixpenny part sold over and above this. Lewes accepted. 'Physiology is not so remunerative as *romans*,' he told him. But there was no envy in his remark. Lewes was always beautifully free of envy. And, anyway, the partnership was beginning to do splendidly – and it was he, after all, who had planted the seed of 'the Bedesman' as he called it. Marian's Aunt Samuel had once long ago told her of how she had visited a condemned criminal, a very ignorant girl who had murdered her child and refused to confess. She told this remembered tale to George in December 1856 and George had pointed out how promisingly a story might be built up around that. From then on Lewes had watched over the slow expansion. She was making Adam's role too passive, he insisted, and out of that came the scene in the wood between Arthur and Adam . . . Yes, the partnership was doing well.

On February 1 1858 the full novel was published. On the final Ms for Blackwood was a heading: 'To my dear husband,

182

George Henry Lewes, I give the M.S. of a work which would never have been written but for the happiness which his love has conferred on my life.' Here, then, the truth about her union with Lewes was joyously proclaimed. The words didn't appear on the printed sheets. This satisfied her needs and uncertainties. Let Isaac Evans and anyone else who cared shake their heads over the liaison until they were dizzy.

Ten days after *Adam Bede* was published the couple crept closer in to London – to Holly Lodge, in Wandsworth. Lewes was surprised that the subscription for the new book should have been 'small', but remained confident that the book would be a hit. He became busy with the practicalities of moving house and with the preparations for bringing out his *Common Life* book. He was also planning an article on 'The Novels of Jane Austen' which appeared in the July 1859 issue of *Blackwood's*. 'My frogs mutely reproach me for neglect. My microscope gathers the dust of disuse. My hand forgets its cunning, and does nothing but write checques [sic] and open purses.' It was lucky that thanks to their united labours the cheques had backing and the purse the means of replenishment. *Adam* made ground. By March Mudie's had ordered 700 copies. Lewes was poorly again around this time, though neither he nor Marian make mention of what precisely was the matter. He began to take a closer look at the breezy, self-confident manner of writing which he had made his own.

> Latterly I have taken to re-write almost everything . . . This I formerly never did – or only quite by exception. But I find it necessary: the defect of my style is want of largo: it is too brief, allusive, hurried. In re-writing the defect is in some degree remedied. I notice also that since my illness the power of rapid composition has very materially diminished; en revanche the result is better.

Slowly the banishment was being relaxed. On February 24 1859 Marian noted that she'd had a letter from her sister Chrissey, who was ill in bed with tuberculosis, and regretted 'that she ever ceased to write to me. It has ploughed up my heart.' They were also surprised to find themselves not totally isolated at Holly Lodge. Their purpose in renting it had been still to find some harbourage where they could be isolated and at the same time comfortably domestic. The landlord had offered reassurance. Look at the Congreves, he had said, now to be near neighbours, how admirably their taste for seclusion was being indulged. Richard Congreve was an earnest Warwickshire man, just a year younger than Lewes, who had given financial support at the launching of the *Leader* but had withdrawn in June 1851 when the launching partnership – consisting of Lewes, Ballantyne, Thornton Hunt, Linton (Eliza Lynn's husband) and others, had been dissolved. He had been elected to a fellowship at Wadham in 1844, but he resigned this ten years later on becoming a convert, wholly and without reserve, to the Comtist doctrines, accepting therefore Comte's *Religion of Humanity* as expounded in the *Cours de Philosophie Positive*, which couldn't, of course, at all be countenanced in the Oxford senior common rooms of the mid-century. Being sufficiently well off to afford to make a gesture, he marched off to London to found the Positivist community. He had married Maria Bury, daughter of a Coventry surgeon, who when young had met Marian and been deeply impressed by her, as women so often were. The two always remained close friends.*

The Congreves called, and 'We called on the Congreves,' Lewes noted in his journal on the last day of February, 'and found them both charming and likely to be agreeable neighbours.' John Bridges, then a young doctor at St George's Hospital, also joined this little coterie, and Bridges and Lewes talked about the spinal cord which was pushing Lewes's never quite unreserved Comtism more and more into the background.

He was still suffering from prostrating headaches and that March noted: 'My head too full and hot to permit work, so I went upstairs and performed experiments on my

* Maria Bury's father had attended Marian's father and by virtue of this she had known Marian if only slightly since early youth. Maria could be called Marian's closest woman friend after 1859, second only to Barbara Leigh Smith (Barbara Bodichon). She lived to be old, dying as late as 1915.

tritons.' *Adam Bede* was getting admiration and beginning to go well; it was even quoted in the House of Commons, and Lewes was able to be highhanded when considering publishers' offers. 'If Tauchnitz won't give fifty pounds now – he will in a few months, and so he had better do it at once.' Herbert Spencer visited them, but he was cool. The moods of that strange man were always unpredictable, but Marian, though not Lewes, felt rebuffed. Lewes was preoccupied with the shaping of *The Mill on the Floss*. The day after his visit the couple rambled on Wimbledon Common: she wanted to puzzle out why Spencer should have chosen to come and then, once arrived, be at pains to be aloof. Lewes was for leaving Spencer alone and for keeping the talk to the next novel. It's clear that a sense of isolation was strong in Marian during those first months at Holly Lodge, whilst Lewes, going frequently into London, meeting people to talk of tasks and prospects, chatting with his innumerable friends, was affected hardly at all.

That month he met Meredith, sifter of manuscripts for Fred Chapman.* It was a year of loneliness for Meredith as well as for the Leweses – a bond that may have helped bring them together. Two years earlier Meredith had separated from his wife, Mary Ellen Peacock, and was living in Hobury Street off the King's Road in Chelsea and making great play of how he was devoting himself to the bringing up of his five year old son by Mary Ellen, Arthur Gryffydh. Meredith and Lewes, rambling together on Wimbledon Common, must have discussed together the perils and pains of broken marriages, but they coped far differently. Lewes was buoyant, chock-full of physiology and of the glorious promise afforded by the prospect of future novels he'd be able to prise out of Marian. He was prepared to face the world and make it love him; he was prepared also to stand by Agnes and his children and see them all safely provided for through his own exertions. Meredith, even

* 1823–95. He was head of Chapman and Hall, publishers, from 1864. He was a shrewd business man and prospered much, especially through the firm's close association with Dickens. When choosing his list Fred relied much on the advice of George Meredith, q.v., who was his principal reader over three decades.

186

though he had *The Ordeal of Richard Feverel* due to appear in three months' time, was bitter and resentful.

By the end of June it was becoming clear that the pseudonym George Eliot couldn't be maintained much longer. The notion of Warwickshire Liggins as author had gained ground absurdly and would have to be scotched. Many people had guessed. Perhaps even – there's no certainty of this – Blackwood at some moment might have been indiscreet. Barbara Bodichon back from Algiers had guessed. On the 30th Lewes wrote to her.

> . . . we have come to the resolution of no longer concealing the authorship. It makes me angry to think that people should say that the secret has been kept because there was any *fear* of the effect of the author's name. You may tell it openly to all who care to hear it that the object of anonymity was to get the book judged on its own merits, and not prejudged as the work of a woman, or of a particular woman . . . PPS. *Entre nous*. Please don't write or tell Marian anything unpleasant that you hear unless it's important for her to hear it. She is so very sensitive, and has such a tendency to dwell on and believe in unpleasant ideas that I always keep them from her. What others would disregard or despise [Lewes is thinking of himself] sinks into her mind.

Nursemaid? Trainer-manager? Collaborator? – what was his role exactly? The answer must be that he combined all three functions and sustained an active and prospering literary-cum-philosophic-cum-scientific life for himself into the bargain. The duty of the male to protect – this was a concept strongly rooted in him: humanism, libertarianism, sex equality – these were notions, however sincerely embraced, which never succeeded in quenching that primitive certainty of his. And Marian took her feminine pleasure in seeing him in this role. She was never resentful of protectiveness; it was what was due to her; she even asked for it.

That summer they were off abroad again, this time not obliged to hunt determinedly for cut-price lodgings. They boated on Lake Lucerne with the well-heeled Congreves, and Lewes made his usual one-man deviation to Bern and Hofwyl to see his boys. 'Dined at the school. Coffee and fruit in the drawing-room, followed by cigar in the shade. The boys then accompanied me to the wood and there, lying on the moss, I unburthened myself about Agnes to them.' Charles, Thornton and Herbert were by now seventeen, fifteen and fourteen respectively. It was time – today one might think high time – that they should be given, clearly and without hedging, the details of the broken marriage of George Lewes and Agnes Jervis. 'They were less distressed than I had anticipated and were delighted to hear about Marian. This of course furnished the main topic for the whole day.' Lewes particularised not only about what had happened but about what was going to happen. When the Hofwyl days were over for them home would no longer be with Agnes in Kensington but with himself and Marian until they could be launched. When he got back to Lucerne, where Marian had stayed on with the Congreves, they had a long talk, 'mainly about the domestic changes and future arrangements'. She was willing to act as *mère de famille*, but one senses a certain hesitancy. After all it was a considerable undertaking for a woman in her early forties with a rich and highly promising career beckoning. There's no doubt though that, career or no career, what she'd have genuinely liked, had she not been a bit old for it and in uncertain health, would have been a child of her own. But they both agreed that prudence should be allowed to triumph over longing. To compensate her, Blackwood would be looking out for a pug dog, and on July 8 he wrote from Edinburgh to say that his cousin, Colonel Steuart, 'an excellent fellow knowing in horses and dogs', had been entrusted with the getting of such a pet.

Soon after they got back to Holly Lodge at the end of July the pug arrived and Lewes assured Blackwood that 'Mrs Lewes feels greatly benefited by the trip, and will rock the cradle of the new "little stranger" with fresh maternal vigour.' Marian acknowledged the gift with more Eliotian ponderousness. 'Words fail me about the not impossible pug, for some compunction at having mentioned my unreasonable wish will mingle itself paradoxically with the hope that it may be fulfilled.' In September Lewes 'took Pug to Agnes who was delighted with him as were the children'. Here, plain to see, is Lewes the least rancorous of men. Agnes and he were still to be friends. The children, too, were delighted with the pug; these being Thornton's children, not his. There was a second visit to Kensington not long after this and talk of Agnes's taking over occupancy of Holly Lodge towards the end of August when Lewes and Marian – or at any rate Lewes; there are signs that Marian might have preferred to stay home in Wandsworth and contemplate *The Mill on the Floss* – were planning a visit to North Wales.

He wrote a couple of popular scientific pieces, returned to an earlier love with an article on 'Actors Off the Stage' for *Once a Week*, and then on August 25 they set off. Although *Adam Bede* was beginning to do amazingly well – a fourth edition of 5,000 copies was exhausted in a fortnight – they couldn't shake off the conviction that cheap lodgings were a necessity. But North Wales was full of holidaymakers. Prices in Llandudno were very high, so down they went to Llandudno Junction and on to Penmaenmawr. But the 'no vacancies' signs were out everywhere, so back then to Conway where they eventually found lodgings over a grocer's in Castle Street – 'not the place for us,' Lewes noted, 'but it will do to rest in and look about. Dined and went to bed at eight thoroughly knocked up.' The winds blew cold and no comfortable quarters were anywhere on offer, so they fled south to Weymouth, breaking their journey in Lichfield to visit Marian's nieces who were at school there, and put up at 39 East Street, Marian working away at the *Mill* in a room at the top of the house.

Apart from Liggins there were others who made nuisances of themselves over *Adam Bede*. A big literary success almost always attracts people of this kind, and Bracebridge of Wandsworth, amongst others, had to be written to. '. . . it is unequivocally false to say there is *a single portrait among the characters of Adam Bede* . . . Mrs Evans is not Dinah . . . It is notorious that "everybody" said his mother was Mrs Nickleby, and every Yorkshire schoolmaster Squeers . . .'

Unused to a big success in fiction, both Marian and Lewes seem to have over-excited themselves over the kind of imbecile correspondence which a more experienced hand would have thrown into the fire and forgotten about. Lewes wrote long elaborate letters in the tone of one addressing the jury in a court of law. Blackwood, who was used to funny letters, took it all imperturbably. 'I regret very much that you should allow yourself to be so disturbed by an old fool like Bracebridge . . . Quirk's mode of appealing to your feelings was most unjustifiable [Quirk was another one] . . . No whisper of your persecutions has reached me. I fancy I have choked the crew off.'

On October 24 Lewes wrote again to Blackwood 'in hot indignation'. Mr Newby of Welbeck Street was advertising 'Adam Bede Junior', and this was to be a 'sequel in 1 vol. 10s.6d'. 'What can be done?' asked Lewes in anguish. '. . . legal proceedings? At all events it ought to be tried. Do see to this matter at once.' Again Blackwood was surprised by such feverishness and wrote to his brother William: 'I was surprised that our friends in Holly Lodge should lose so fine an opportunity of putting themselves in a fever as this Adam Bede Junior . . . Lewes of course exaggerates the importance of the matter and I have endeavoured to tone him down by recalling Pickwick Abroad and the many similar felonies on popular authors.'

But by way of consolation Lewes's own affairs were going ahead without hiccups. George Smith of Smith Elder wanted him to cooperate in the forthcoming *Cornhill Magazine*, wanted to discuss terms, and wanted papers from him on natural history. Smith drove down himself to Holly Lodge to put proposals to him, which was very handsome. Lewes accompanied him back to town, called on Smith and Beck, the scientific instruments people, and 'changed my old Microscope for one of their first class instruments'. The cheques from Blackwood were already beginning to have their uses. Beck told him he'd been in Aberdeen the previous month to hear the British Association papers being read, Lewes's of course among them. They hadn't sent anybody to sleep – Lewes's writing skills would always see to that – but instead had caused quite a row, but Allen

Thomson the anatomist and indeed Huxley* himself had come down on Lewes's side. 'I expected the papers would create a disturbance,' Lewes wrote on getting home, 'but hardly expected these eminent men to stand up for me.' And in the same journal entry he says: 'The proposal of George Smith becomes very seductive.'

On November 10 he was able to write to his sons at Hofwyl.

You have heard I dare say that Mr Thackeray is about to edit a new magazine. Well, as soon as he had begun to make arrangements, he wrote to me to ask me to help him. I replied that I should be very willing indeed, if I saw clearly that I could do so, and if the payment was tempting. Whereupon Mr Smith, the publisher, drove here in his carriage, and made me a tempting offer, which I accepted. I am going to write a book for him, *Studies in Animal Life*, which will appear as a series of articles in the Magazine . . . Yesterday I dined with Mother, Agnes was there. From her I learned that Vivian had the meazles; Edmund was still away with the coastguardsman at Goring; and the baby was very poorly. Captain Willim has been suffering severely from the gout, several *chalk stones* having come from his foot! Imagine that! Mother was in good spirits but very feeble . . . To-day we are to have Charles Dickens to dinner. He is an intense admirer of your mother, whom he has never seen . . .

Lewes writes quite easily and without embarrassment or circumlocution, clearly confident that the Hofwyl boys will be able to sort out the various uses of the word mother in what their father is saying. The first 'Mother' is Lewes's mother, and their grandmother. Agnes – well, Agnes is Agnes, dismissed, in Lewes's eyes anyway, from her biological position as mother to them, but still a perfectly nice little person whom he meets and greets and gets on with.

* Thomas Henry Huxley (1825–95). Amongst the greatest of England's nineteenth century scientific investigators. A notable upholder and developer of Darwin's evolutionary theories.

Edmund is a half brother, packed off to the coastguardsman because Agnes's family number two was getting too much for her, with Thornton no longer on the scene prepared to do fatherly duty. And Captain Willim? The elusive Captain Willim? To the Hofwyl boys he would probably have been an overbearing, ill tempered step-grandfather rarely seen by them and not much talked about by their father. Chalkstones! Imagine that! Lewes puts it down as a little item, but there isn't much warmth of loving kindness behind the exclamation marks. The feeble but cheerful final 'Mother' is the first one all over again, obviously an accepted and acceptable figure and one the Hofwyl boys would want to know about. As for Charles Dickens – well, it wasn't a certain indication that by dining with them the Inimitable was signalling that the Leweses were back in the swim. Dickens by now was beyond convention and could do as he liked. But none the less it was evidence of a sort that George and Marian had begun their long climb back to top social (as opposed to Chapmanite) acceptability. When he tells his sons that Charles Dickens is 'an intense admirer of your mother' he is obviously making use of 'mother' as an expression prearranged; the young Leweses had by this time grown to accept it as normal and natural. Marian, after all, to put the thing at its lowest, had become a safe provider.

The end of 1859 shows both of them in pettish, assertive mood. Success had gone a bit to the head. Their outrage over Newby and his Adam Bede Junior burned red and long. It was no use Blackwood's telling them that this was the sort of thing that writers of successful books had to learn to put up with. They were receiving attractive offers from other publishers. Dickens after dining with them wanted her to write a novel for serialisation in *All The Year Round*, and Lewes was in demand too.

Dickens, [he wrote] having written to ask Polly if she could on her own terms write a story . . . we have turned the matter over and almost think it feasible. Today I went by appointment to see Lucas and Evans who wanted me to write a novel for *Once A Week* on my own terms; but having agreed with Polly that it was desirable I should not swerve from Science any more, at least just now, I declined. They then asked me to contribute articles on my own terms. After this they approached the subject of a story from Polly and wanted to know whether her new novel was in the market. I told them it was unlikely that she would publish in *Once A Week* and that she felt bound to give Blackwood the refusal; but they assured me that *whatever* Blackwood offered they would give more. We parted on the understanding that they were to make an offer.

Once A Week understood, as did everyone else, that the way to Marian was through Lewes; if he gave the nod, then any deal might go ahead.

It's interesting to see him rejecting, for the time being, the commission to write a novel for himself. He seems to have decided that scientific research, scientific journalism, collaborative editing and fiction-coach would be enough, in his forty-third year, for his far from vigorous health. His willingness to play one publisher off against another, however, brought a strong reaction from Blackwood. Blackwood felt he'd acted generously by Marian, as indeed he had. He felt that now, if there was to be a reward, he had earned the right to have a share in it. It's impossible not to sympathise with him; it's also difficult to see Lewes in the role of one testing the market for bids. He could be sharp, testy and combative in his dealings with people, but it was never in his nature to be ungenerous. But over-excitement can lead people to act out of character.

Blackwood wasn't long in telling them quite clearly how he felt about what was going on. He got an irritating letter from Lewes dated November 18. 'Maggie [*The Mill on the Floss*] goes on gloriously and Mrs Lewes does *not* suffer herself to be much bothered by external things . . . My precious time is occupied with declining offers on all sides – everyone imagining that he can seduce George Eliot . . .' Blackwood rightly felt that they were both of them allowing themselves to be bothered a very great deal by external things, and on November 28 he wrote to 'My dear Madam' – and he was cold, and dignified, and justified.

193

. . . I was very much annoyed or rather, I should say, hurt at the tone in which my offer for the new novel was replied to and also at the very dry way in which our conduct in doubling the purchase money of *Adam Bede* was acknowledged. In regard to the new novel . . . I would be the very last man who would wish for a moment to stand in the way of your doing what you thought best for yourself, but I think I should have been told so frankly instead of having my offer treated as if it were not worth consideration at all . . .

In reply to this Marian wrote the long confused sort of letter of someone without a leg to stand on. They made it up, but a couple of years later – by then they'd moved on up from Holly Lodge to Blandford Square – recriminations began again when, over *Romola*, Blackwood was definitely dropped in favour of George Smith for a handsome sum.

All this sheds interesting light on the Marian-Lewes-Blackwood triangle. Beyond doubt Blackwood comes best out of the dust-up. He talks of the 'voracity' of Lewes, but here I think his judgment is astray. Lewes was brisk, businesslike, sharp and a bit inclined to dash off an uppity letter. But he was never a grabbing man, never an ungenerous one. His mother adored him, and his concern for Agnes, his regular visits to her, his refusal ever to be mean or revengeful towards her in his role of cuckolded man – a wronged husband could, in the mid-century, cause the most grievous suffering and humiliation to be heaped on his once-partner if he so chose – must have caused her to wish many times that she had stuck by Lewes and never allowed herself to be beguiled by the undependable Thornton Hunt. The picture of Marian – the shy, dedicated one, hiding behind her man and leaving mundane business matters to him – is true in part but only in part. Certainly she lacked confidence in herself; certainly Lewes was the one who gave her confidence and gave her the seminal ideas which she was able to work on; but Marian was the daughter of Robert Evans, a man who did well in his chosen sphere of life and a man who drove hard bargains. Marian liked money and was most anxious to heap together as much of it as she could. Money was the power which helped her to shore up the shaky social position which her unsanctified marriage condemned her to and of which she remained always conscious, though never guilty about, right on into the days of triumph, right on to the day Lewes died, leaving her bereft but at the same time blessedly free to put a despised little crown on her swift and splendid career, achieve the full and final re-establishment of herself in the eyes of the world, and receive the ultimate blessing – a letter from Isaac.

They wondered about the title. Lewes argued for the disastrous *The House of Tulliver, or, Life on the Floss*. Both of them hesitated long over *Sister Maggie*, but it was John Blackwood's choice which won in the end and *The Mill on the Floss* was published in three volumes on April 4 1860. The month before that Lewes had taken time off from his microscope in order to turn literary critic again, and had published in *Blackwood's* 'A Word about Tom Jones', 'a subject,' he noted in his journal, 'I have had *in petto* ever since the last reading of that over-praised work.' It's an article that shows him at his worst – over confident, over quick, over reaching himself. He hated that famous plot which has been so much admired: it was, he thought, simply a web of foolish coincidences. So it is, if you look at it like that. What Lewes couldn't or wouldn't see was that form is simply what the author makes of it: the artificial formality of a pattern dance can be just as acceptable as the sexual meanderings of the half awake Mollie Bloom, and certainly more acceptable than those vitally important, accidentally unopened letters which cause such dire extremes of suffering in Casterbridge, The Hintocks and stations beyond. Blackwood didn't altogether like the piece. 'Coarse drollery is too low a term for humour such as his which has made so many generations of us shout with laughter,' and '. . . shallow circumscribed nature seems to me a phrase which should not be applied to a man who has done so much as Fielding.' Lewes replied to this in a don't-carish mood. '. . . I am busy finishing the Physiology . . . you will see I have modified the article according to your suggestions.' He sounded busy, and he was. 'Will you

195

please "put on the steam" with the printing now [of *The Mill*]' he told Blackwood on February 28. '. . . I don't know whether I ever explained to you our object in having the printing done in advance – we want to reach Rome by Holy Week and in fact want to be there as soon as possible . . .'

To Madame Bodichon, living in Algiers, he wrote on the 6th to say, 'we are girding up our trunks for Italy . . .' *Adam Bede* was still selling well, *The Mill* would do better. *The Physiology of Common Life* came out in two volumes after its serialisation . . . The firm of Lewes and Evans was doing well: it deserved a holiday and it could afford one. If it hadn't been for their common dread of seasickness, they'd have crossed the Mediterranean to Algiers, but as it was, Rome would have to do. They set off on Saturday March 24, and in Paris on Sunday morning Lewes noted: 'Strolled out and bought a pretty bonnet for Polly. Notre Dame – very bad taste of inside . . .' And the next day, 'Paris is a place to spend your grandmother's ransom, 'tis so seductive!' They crossed the Alps by sledge and diligence and were in Rome by April 1. What tireless travellers the Victorians were in spite of their headaches, their biliousness, their fevers; these two especially, so beset by physical frailty, and yet, so early in the season, prepared to be packed in a sledge over the Mont Cenis pass, and then down by diligence into Italy. Out of Genoa Lewes got 'a sense of voluptuous enjoyment quite indescribable,' but Rome he thought 'mean and ugly, so poor, dirty and without colour or picturesqueness'. Perhaps where Rome was concerned English expectations were always too high. Clough had been there eleven years earlier, and

Rome disappoints me much; I hardly as yet
   understand, but
Rubbishy seems the word that most exactly would suit it.

They went to St Peter's on Good Friday but everything that happened there was 'a hollow show of sham'. But once they got a chance to look closely at the art enthusiasm crept in. They saw the Vatican statues by torchlight and there raged a 'fierce appetite for more' in them both, but their rational, Benthamite, Comtist souls found the manifold forms of ritualism and ecclesiasticism simply deplorable. Raphael was perfectly all right, but a 'procession of miracle-working crucifix, sham, sham, sham!' Lewes thought it would be 'a very dangerous place for any *young*, enthusiastic mind'. It's characteristic of him that he should see it like this. For him progress was the thing, 'advance', and it was natural and proper that it should be for the young to take the lead because progress could only happen when you looked forward, with a lifetime ahead to gambol about in. In Rome there was a danger that the young adventurous ones, with creative possibilities in them, could be 'oppressed with the immensity of the achievement . . .' Rome might be a noble stimulus, of course, but only when principles had matured, 'or when the nature is naturally rebelliously independent'. These last were the strong young souls whom Lewes all his life approved of – the ones to whom even now, in his often ailing forties, he liked to think of himself as belonging.

Early in May they went on to Naples, Lewes still with 'a terrible oppression in his head'. There he got what he called 'chequered news' about *The Mill*: '. . . the sale is about 5,600 – immense . . .' By now it must have been becoming clear to this shrewd yet somehow never calculating man that his Marian was going to turn out to be a money spinner on a quite colossal scale. What were his thoughts about his life and what he had made of it at this point? Whatever they were, they were entirely private thoughts, never spoken of, never committed to paper, even although he was a man who committed so much to paper. Did he feel so much as a hint of self-contempt? Was he by way of becoming a kept man? Superficially his actions and attitudes might have suggested that this indeed was how it was. He ran errands, he looked after his queen bee, he shielded her from the rough-and-tumble of bargaining – which had to be gone through, even with such a decent, open, prompt and straightforward fellow as Blackwood. His own work – there was no point in trying to conceal the fact – was beginning to take a back seat. The letter Blackwood sent

197

him on April 24 is full of *The Mill* and Mudie, and the swiftly diminishing 6,000 stock, and 'Mrs Lewes' genius'. A one paragraph sentence further down informs him that 'Rather better than a thousand have been subscribed of the 2nd volume of the *Physiology.*'

Well, that wasn't so bad, but could he now, without the risk of seeming fatuous, continue in his role of senior partner? When they got back to Holly Lodge on July 1 he was busy and confident. The tones of second fiddle aren't anywhere apparent. He was busy with his own bits and pieces. He wrote an article based on the currently very popular spiritualist experiments of Daniel Home which he called 'Seeing is Believing'; he abridged his *Physiology*, thinking it might serve as a school textbook but Blackwood flatly rejected this when he saw it as being wholly unsuitable; they had become too wealthy and important for Holly Lodge and he rambled about in search of somewhere closer in and more prestigious as an address, finding at last 10 Harewood Square, close to Regent's Park and moving there on September 24; he put the idea of an Italian historical novel into Marian's head, but this time, for the moment at any rate, could only produce a spark too feeble to light a fire; instead, barely a week after moving to Harewood Square, she set to work on *Silas Marner*. This was her own idea. Lewes had implanted no seed. Was he losing his influence? Was he going to have to give her her head?

The answer must be that Lewes, though no more than a journalist if you looked at him squarely, was still wholly in control. Without him she was nothing. She clung like ivy to a sturdy little tree. If the tree was cut down, or became enfeebled, she would wither. Admittedly he took charge of the chores; but he took charge of the big decisions as well. In February 1861, when she had got nearly to the end of *Silas*, she told Blackwood:

> I have felt all through as if the story would have lent itself best to metrical rather than prose fiction, especially in all that relates to the psychology of Silas; except that, under that treatment, there could not be an equal play of humour. It came to me first of all, quite suddenly, as a

198

sort of legendary tale, suggested by my recollection of having once, in early childhood, seen a linen-weaver with a bag on his back; but, as my mind dwelt on the subject, I became inclined to a more realistic treatment.

Her mind's dwelling on the subject is certainly the result of Lewes's insisting that she should reconsider. He was half hearted about the whole idea, but on one point he was certain and positive: poetic drama wasn't her line – even though, a year or two later, when it came to *The Spanish Gypsy*, she was still sticking to the idea that perhaps it might be. In 1865 she became querulous with George – and this was very rare indeed with her – 'Ill with bilious headache, and very miserable about my soul as well as body. *George has taken my drama away from me.*'

And when they returned that summer from Italy, she to sudden vast fame, he to the simpler role of hard working man of letters which he'd been pursuing for years, there immediately arose another highly important matter about which she was prepared to be entirely submissive. They'd called at Hofwyl on their way back, and Charles Lewes, soon to be eighteen, came back with them – for good. Even today, when marriages are made and unmade without much fuss, without much forethought and without much afterthought either, the position of substitute mother and ersatz offspring presents considerable difficulties. And so: would Charles feel himself bound to Agnes and resent Marian? Would Marian, on her side, hesitate before shouldering the undoubted difficulties of taking on an adolescent to whom she was nothing except, perhaps, a name?

Lewes expected Marian to do her best with Charlie and obediently she did precisely that. She went through all the motions. Before she got back to Holly Lodge she wrote to Mrs Bell the housekeeper: 'Pray think of everything within reach that will make Charles's room look comfortable and, if possible, pretty.' But there are hints of distaste and displeasure. The richness and quietness of her communion with Lewes had been broken. He, being a man and a father, felt nothing at all of this – to begin with at any rate – and she did her utmost to conceal her disquiet at the arrival of a cuckoo in the nest. Charles was large and had a downy upper lip. He called her – it was his father's instruction – 'Mutter', and he seems to have been amiable and amenable, never given to obstreperousness and tantrums as boys of that age so often are. She wondered too, with all the width of perception of her subtle, creative mind, what exactly, beneath the politeness, Charles was thinking of her.

On the surface all was well. But did she detect a certain coldness? But was she wrong to be conscious of lurking disapproval? Didn't his presence renew and revitalise the wretched illegitimacy of her relationship with Lewes? Weren't these extra responsibilities perhaps being thrust too much upon her – 'We are quite uncertain about our plans at present. [July 18 1860] Our second boy Thornie, is going to leave Hofwyl and to be placed in some more expensive position in order to be carrying on his education in a more complete way, so that we are thinking of avoiding for the present any final establishment of ourselves, which would necessarily be attended with additional outlay. Besides, these material cares draw rather too severely on my strength and spirits . . .' But Charlie was tactful, and a good musician too, which was nice. 'We play Beethoven duets with increasing appetite every evening.' This was in mid-September – she was becoming reconciled. And in the meantime, Lewes, efficiently rushing around as always, had found a suitably furnished, suitably situated house on a six months' let, and Charlie, as well as being able to match her Beethoven, had, as she put it to Barbara Bodichon, 'won his place at the Post Office, having been at the head of the list in the examination. Magnificat anima mea! The dear lad is fairly launched in life now.' In this business too Lewes had had a considerable hand. He knew the value of the useful word in the useful quarter and had talked to Trollope about Charlie back in July. '. . . of him I only asked information [this would be the tactful, accepted approach] yet he most kindly interested himself and wrote to the Duke of Argyll [Postmaster General at the time – an odd billet, one might think, for MacCallum Mor] for a nomination to compete for a vacancy in the Post Office – which was granted on Friday last.'

Thornie, two years younger than Charlie, was another problem. On their way back from the Italian journey, and having collected Charlie, they paused to visit Marian's old Genevan friends, François D'Albert-Durade and his wife. She gave him the authorisation – something becoming swiftly valuable – to translate *The Mill* into French, and Lewes 'broached the subject of Thornie's residence in Geneva to him, and was glad to find that it seemed practicable, and that he would undertake the charge.' That seemed to be one difficulty cleared. Two of dear George's brood hanging about the house in London would really have been too much. But then D'Albert put too high a price on the job – more than Lewes could afford – and on September 11 he wrote – to Marian, be it noted, not to Lewes – to say:

Vous aurez compris quel chagrin c'était pour nous de ne pas pouvoir offrir à Monsieur Lewes des conditions plus faciles pour son fils, car c'eût été notre vif désir de faire quelque chose qui pût lui être agréable ainsi qu'à vous. Mais mon fils me coûte plus de trois mille francs par année en Allemagne et je suis obligé de chercher l'équivalent ici; si j'avais la place pour plusieurs personnes, la chose serait plus facile.*

So on Thursday night, September 27, Thornie arrived from Switzerland at 10 Harewood Place. He stayed there for three nights only. On Sunday night Lewes took him by mail train to Edinburgh where he'd arranged for him to attend the high school for ten months. He stayed in Edinburgh till

* 'You'll have gathered what regret it aroused in us not to be able to offer to M. Lewes more acceptable terms for his son, because our liveliest wish would have been to arrange terms which would have been acceptable to both of you. But my son is costing me more than 3,000 francs a year in Germany and I'm forced to look for an amount here which would set off that. If I had room for several pupils it would have been easier to arrange something.' 3,000 francs would have meant about £150 at that time.

the following Thursday, 'making all arrangements about Thornie's classes, and residence in Mr George Robertson's family – with the whole of which there is every reason to be satisfied, as far as one can judge beforehand . . .' He also talked over with Blackwood some proposed serialised articles on *Lives of the Elder Naturalists*, chatted with prominent Edinburgh scientists like the naturalist Darwin Rogers and John Gibson MacVicar who was looking into the structure of molecules. He also talked to Langford, Blackwood's man of business, about possible investments.

All this is astonishing. By now Lewes and Marian between them were doing very well indeed, so why couldn't they have afforded D'Albert's three thousand francs a year for the education and maintenance of Thornie? Come to that, Lewes, even though he was by much the smaller earner, could easily have afforded it on his own. But as the partnership between them was so close, so inseparable why should Marian have been reluctant to chip in? There's no discoverable whisper anywhere of division or disagreement between them over this. But it's difficult not to suppose that, somewhere along the line, there must have been a clash. The probability is that Lewes, with his close and sure understanding of women, was prepared in this instance to relinquish his normal role of master. Marian was maternal. She loved children. There can be no doubt about that. Whether the menopause came late or early for her we have no means of knowing, but in 1860 when she was forty-one it's unlikely that she couldn't have conceived a child. But they'd agreed between them that a child would have added immeasurably to their unavoidable difficulties, and for this reason the utmost precautions had been taken. But Marian, strong on logic and strong on intelligence, was at the same time a profoundly womanly woman and deep down, almost without being properly aware of it, she resented her enforced barrenness. To have two largish lads, one already with a downy upper lip, on her hands, and neither of them hers, was troubling to her – and probably all the more troubling because her brains kept shouting at her that she was being irrational.

Lewes with his quick perceptiveness – and this is a cru-

202

cial point in the whole matter of their strange as well as hugely successful relationship – would instantly see this central difficulty of hers, see it with his blood, as Lawrence would have put it, without the necessity to put any intellectual, analytical processes into motion. He gave in and Thornie had to come home. And he gave in because of this understanding. He knew also by now that with all her virtues and abilities and docilities there was in Marian a yeoman-Warwickshire-Robert-Evans-ineffaceable streak of meanness. That, beyond any doubt, he'd have overridden. The other was something vastly more important, and something to yield to. It's given to very few men to be as gifted in the difficult art of marriage as was Lewes. How many times in her long life must Agnes Lewes have lamented her inability to recognise an extremely rare bird when she held one in her hand.

About this time of their removal from Holly Lodge to Harewood Place came another instance of Marian's being given her head. On their way back from Naples in the early summer they'd stayed, not for long, in Florence, and Lewes had noted in his journal: 'This morning while reading about Savonarola it occurred to me that his life and times afford fine material for an historical romance. Polly at once caught at the idea with enthusiasm. It is a subject which will fall in with much of her studies and sympathies . . .' This was normal. Marian always caught at his ideas with enthusiasm. But this time something went wrong, though not immediately. On June 23 she told Blackwood, from Bern, 'I don't think I can venture to tell you what my great project is by letter, for I am anxious to keep it a secret. It will require a great deal of study and labour, and I am athirst to begin . . .' Why should she want to keep it a secret unless there were beginning to be doubts not admitted to herself? On August 10 came a hint of a warning from Lewes to Blackwood: 'We are looking forward to the Major's visit. [this was William Blackwood, John's brother] I wonder whether the "great secret" will be really a surprise or not.' And then, on the 28th, Marian wrote to John Blackwood.

I think I must tell you the secret, though I am distrusting my power to make it grow into a published fact. When we were in Florence I was rather fired with the idea of writing a historical romance – scene Florence – period, the close of the fifteenth century, which was marked by Savonarola's career and martyrdom. Mr Lewes has encouraged me to persevere in the project, saying that I should probably do something in historical romance rather different in character from what has been done before. But I want first to write another English story . . .

Here is evidence of another clash, unspoken, never clearly expressed on either side, but none the less a clash. Lewes, with his experienced, sensitive finger always laid on the pulse of the literary market, knew very well that historical novels were good for trade. Dickens was another who shared Lewes's journalistic impulses. Between April and November 1859, he'd been doling out *A Tale of Two Cities* for *All The Year Round*. With Carlyle's *French Revolution* open on the epistle side of his altar Dickens had pushed ahead. '. . . Heavens knows I have done my best,' he told Wilkie Collins that October. But he probably knew, even before the critics told him, that he was stumbling about in quite unDickensian country, labouring hard to give the public what it wanted. There can be no doubt that it was Lewes who pushed Savonarola, the fifteenth century Puritan-Catholic with the whiplash tongue, hard at Marian, assuring her that here was a Hero who could be made splendidly, upliftingly exciting, persuading her that here was a theme round which a Big Novel could be built.

For once Marian backed away and instead wrote quickly, beginning as soon as they were established at Harewood Place, a short novel she called *Silas Marner*, which one is tempted to call, in defiance of all the contemporary fuss about *Middlemarch*, the best single thing she ever did. Lewes said he was in love with it but he sounds perfunctory, and of all the books she wrote it's the one in which he had the least hand. He looked on it as a little something which would keep her in training, in trim, before she cantered up to the big black shadow of Savonarola lying just ahead. But

Silas Marner is essential Marian at her best: it's unlaboured, it's short, it gives expression, most movingly, to her central preoccupations. The child Eppie in the book quickens all that there was of the maternal in her – and there was much. Encompassed for the first time by Lewes's brood which was beginning to be loud and male, she dwelt with love upon the young female child she was condemned never to have herself. She was able also, through the weaver, Silas, to explore the anguish of ostracism which she had deliberately invited but none the less deeply suffered from. She had the opportunity, finally, to think about Treasure – about money. Suddenly, miraculously almost, money was flowing towards her in a spring tide. Did it demean? Did she recognise in herself a tendency to reach out and grab?

Lewes looked on perhaps for once a little impatiently. He was eager that she should get it over so that the shop floor could be stripped and cleared and the foundations of *Romola* laid. He was wonderfully sympathetic and sure footed on the whole in his relations with women, but the businesslike briskness of his approach to the matter of writing, which gave him the capacity to produce acceptable stuff about almost anything, here betrayed him into the biggest single blunder in the long and remarkable history of his relations with Marian. It was a blunder which neither of them ever acknowledged.

By December Lewes had found a house in Marylebone, 16 Blandford Square, which he took for three years.

The previous month he negotiated over another play, *Captain Bland*, with A. S. Wigan (1814–78), lessee and manager of the Olympic Theatre. In his journal entry for November 30 1860 Lewes wrote:

This afternoon went down to see Wigan about 'Captain Bland'. It seems as if I never should be free of bother and misunderstanding about this unfortunate piece which was written for him when we were at Worthing and Richmond, rehearsed, altered, rehearsed again and finally returned on my hands. This spring he again wanted to have it. I offered to sell him the piece to do what he liked with provided my name did not appear, and no application was made to me about alterations. He kept it some time and then returned it, not being able to make immediate use of it. About six weeks ago he again applied for it, accepted my terms; and now wants me once more to alter it and alter my terms. I agreed to do both. To alter it and get £50 down and £50 if he doesn't produce it before Easter, £2 a night if he does.

Lewes did get paid, but the play was never put on in England. It had five performances, however, in May 1864 at Wallack's Theatre in New York. This wasn't success on the George Eliot scale, but it does show George Lewes the professional writer disinclined to work for nothing.

In any event his falling so far behind as a breadwinner never seems to have worried him. This fact shouldn't be taken as showing that there was something of the sponger in him. There wasn't. He considered that what he was doing was important and useful; if the rewards from it were less than hers – well, that was simply the way it was. And in any case, wasn't he right in considering himself a partner in the Eliotian oeuvre? Of course he was. And Marian was always the first to say as much. 'In this respect,' she said once, 'I know *no* man so great as he – that difference of opinion rouses no egoistic irritation in him . . .' For 'opinion' she could have substituted 'aptitude' – and the remark would still have been wholly valid. In his summing-up of the year in his diary he admitted that there had been misgivings at the prospect of having Charles at home with them – son and stepson, 'but he has been a comfort and delight and never occasioned us any anxiety'. Charles was tactful. Making a plodding beginning at the Post Office after years abroad, and being at the same time an intruder at home into a very close, embattled alliance couldn't have been easy for a young man. Lewes, perhaps to celebrate in some sort his son's appointment, gave a lecture at the Post Office in January 1861. He called it 'Life from the Simple Cell to Man', and it went down well. Marian, he said, was 'relieved at having this one cause of anxiety the less – dear creature!' The other cause would have been *Silas Marner* which was going ahead rapidly.

When they went on their long walks they talked about the Italian romance which she had pushed to one side in favour of homely *Silas*, but to which Lewes was still keen that she should return. In February they were both ill again and took a break at Dorking. It was important for them both, Lewes, felt, never to resign themselves to too sedentary a life. On March 9 he noted: 'After lunch we took a cab and with net and jar drove to Hampstead Heath. There in the bright sunshine and glorious breeze we rambled, sniffing in the fresh air with delight, and finally I set to work to ransack the ponds for Frog spawn, insects, polypes, etc.' In mid March, with the last proofs of *Silas Marner* passed, they visited Anthony Trollope, substantially housed in Waltham. 'I like him very much,' Lewes said, 'so wholesome and straightforward a man.'

Returning home on the 16th, Lewes found himself having to cope with Captain Willim. Remote, cantankerous, mysterious, strongly hostile to his stepson, the captain makes only rare appearances in the Lewes story. He is a background presence, lurking and minatory, to be endured but not, except under strong necessity, mentioned. But now Mrs Lewes, his mother, was finding life with him very difficult. Age was beginning to nibble away at his wits. He refused company. Callers were not to be admitted to the house. Shut up alone with him all day, she was beginning to find his tantrums more than she could bear. She came to her son with this news – if George couldn't be admitted to see her, then she must come to him at Blandford Square. Whether Marian was present at the ensuing discussion we don't know, but probably she wasn't. Sordid domestic squabblings weren't an appropriate background for a woman preparing to sit down and write *Romola*. Lewes told his mother 'to tell him that unless he could treat her better she should come to live with us. She stayed all day and seemed to pick up wonderfully.' Another, and wholly regularised, Mrs Lewes coming to live at Blandford Square couldn't have been a prospect likely to cause Marian, dithering on the brink of a large literary undertaking, to leap for joy. But it never seems to have come to that. Captain Willim recedes into his shadowy retirement again – but lives on for a long while. He saw George Lewes and his concubine established in their full and final glory at The Priory, 21 North Bank, Regent's Park, and died very old indeed in February 1864.

On April 2 1861 *Silas* was published, and six days before Marian had written to Langford, Blackwood's London manager, to say, 'I don't wish for any presentation copies, except one for Mr Lewes's mother. Her address is: Mrs Willim, 51 Clifton Road East St John's Wood . . .' Her mother-in-law was being kept at bay, and being provided with a splendid read in compensation. From the same letter it's clear that she was already working and worrying over background detail for *Romola*. She can find so few pictures that give her the necessary details about Florentine costume around the 1490s, and – she adds mysteriously – 'unhappily, with my temperament, I fear it would be next to impossible for me to go to the British Museum . . .' This illustrates as forcefully as any remark could her neurotic shyness, her need for protection, for someone to go on ahead of her in order to ask questions, to buttonhole people, to find things out. A fortnight later she is writing to Barbara Bodichon, '. . . we are going to run away from London for two months . . . our departure has hitherto been dependent on unsettled matters, about our Edinburgh boy . . . Mr Lewes is gone to the Museum for me – else he would send his love with mine . . .'

They left for Florence on April 19. Charles stayed on at Blandford Square to work, take music lessons from Brindley Richards and look after Pug. They travelled in some style. They could afford it. Langford had told them on April 4 that the subscription for *Silas*, on the day of publication, amounted to 5,500. Lewes wrote to Charles from Avignon on the 21st to tell him that here the heat of summer was upon them and the lilac already disappearing. 'We got here at 12 and by paying 20 francs extra had a coupé all to ourselves so we had slept tolerably well . . .' Marian – 'the sweetest Mother' Lewes calls her in this same letter – added a postscript: 'Die Mutter thinks of her dear boy and loves him better than ever now she is at a distance from him.' Charles wasn't intended to take this seriously, but perhaps he did. She wrote to him herself from Nice four days later, a most loving and lively letter designed probably to make sure that he wouldn't misunderstand. Both of them had arrived at Nice with headaches – the recurrent malady – but now they were 'glad of the luxuries to be found in a great hotel' (how handy Blackwood's cheques were), and in a postscript she says: 'Best love to Grandmamma, of whom I hope you will have good news to tell us . . .' Lewes had clearly been worrying, and possibly also feeling a little guilty, about Captain Willim.

By the time they had reached Florence, travelling luxuriously in their own post-chaise, *Silas* had reached the 7,500 mark, and they were ready – or at any rate Lewes was ready – to get Florentine details right in preparation for *Romola*. Wonderfully tactful and sympathetic though Lewes was in his dealings with Marian, he was about to enter the least successful, most unhappy two years of all the time they spent in association. *Romola* wasn't finished until June 1863 – two years away. Marian hated both of them, said she began the book young and finished it old. She never wanted to write it. She knew deep down that her talent wouldn't kindle unless she stuck to Warwickshire and the old days. But her self-mistrust, her submissiveness, her utter dependence on him made her accept the idea that an historical novel – and a long and complicated one at that – would be well within her scope. The probability that it would be very good for business was one she was ready to accept more willingly still. Lewes was a journalising man, trained to write for a market, prompt and thoroughly competent in all his professional dealings. The notion of writing *Romola* had no terrors for him. He could do it himself. In the earlier stages he probably did do quite a lot of it himself. He couldn't understand the hesitancy on her part, all the postponements, all the urge to be forever researching and never writing the thing out fair and fast. They toiled away, and he was willing as always to toil; but he was uncomprehending and even disposed, at times, to feel impatient and irritated. 'Mr Lewes,' she wrote, 'is kept in continual distraction by having to attend to my wants – going with me to the Magliabecchian Library, and poking about everywhere on my behalf – I having very little self-help about me of the pushing and enquiring kind.'

By June 14 they were back in London, having collected Lewes's third son, Bertie, from Hofwyl on the way, and still she continued to research instead of write. In October she did make a start, but gave up almost immediately. In her journal in November she noted that she was 'so utterly dejected that, in walking with G. in the park, I almost resolved to give up my Italian novel'. Just before that Lewes had been complaining: 'Mrs Lewes is very well and buried in musty old antiquities, which she will have to vivify. I am a sort of Italian Jackal, hunting up rare books, and vellum-bound unreadabilities in all the second-hand bookstalls of London.' This doesn't sound at all like the buoyant Lewes. In December he wrote to Blackwood:

Polly is still deep in her researches. Your presence [Blackwood was in London] will I hope act like a stimulus to her to make her begin. At present she remains immovable in the conviction that she *can't* write the romance because she has not knowledge enough. Now as a matter of fact I know that she has immensely more knowledge of the particular period than any other writer who has touched it; but her distressing diffidence paralyses her. This is between ourselves. When you see her, mind your care is to discountenance the idea of a Romance being the product of an Encyclopaedia.

His word is diffidence. What he wouldn't or couldn't see was that here was a task which she knew inside herself was not one really for her. And Lewes had had enough of it. He wanted, moreover, to be getting on with his ambitious projected *History of Science*. He proposed to begin with Aristotle. They'd both been to Malvern to take the waters and clear their heads, and, as he said, 'I have made minute and extensive studies in Aristotle whose scientific works I am analyzing; and it is in contemplation to publish the chapters on Aristotle as a separate work by way of a forerunner.' As it turned out, he never got further than the forerunner, which he subtitled 'A chapter in the history of the sciences', and which didn't appear until 1864. The book is thoroughly informative – Lewes's work was never less than that – but there's nothing here that adds anything significant to what he had already said as a young man in his *Biographical History* which was still selling well, revised and much enlarged not only up to the time of his death but long after that.

Perhaps Aristotle suffered from the fact that 1862 was a difficult year for Lewes. For one thing he ailed a great deal – nothing disastrous but much that niggled and was enfeebling. '. . . livers and stomachs' Marian said in February; 'Mr Lewes has had much suffering of the usual headachy, indigestive kind.' Perhaps it was caused simply by the Victorian way of life, hot rooms, bad smells, rich and greasy food in too great quantity if you had the means to buy. In the same letter – it was to Barbara Bodichon – she said:

> George, in spite of ailments, has done a great deal of work since we said goodbye to you. He . . . has written so thorough an analysis and investigation of Aristotle's *Natural Science*, that he feels it will make an epoch for the men who are interested at once in the progress of modern science and in the question, how far Aristotle went both in the observation of facts, and in their theoretic combination . . . This work makes him very 'jolly', but his dear face looks very pale and narrow. Those only can thoroughly feel the meaning of death who know what is perfect love . . .

How deeply preoccupied the Victorians were with thoroughly feeling the meaning of death. Dire physical occurrences prompted them to it. Tait, at that time Bishop of London and in six years to be Archbishop of Canterbury, had, in 1856 when he was Dean of Carlisle, lost five young children from scarlet fever in the space of six weeks.

Romola offered difficulties as much to Lewes as to Marian. The book was to rough up, perhaps more thoroughly than any other single matter, the smooth path of the Lewes-Marian relationship. Someone very powerful, very persuasive and very pertinacious was about to surface like a killer whale.

Late in January George Smith came to Blandford Square. Smith, born in Elgin and so, like Blackwood, a Scot, had become by the 1860s a highly successful and highly resourceful publisher. He is remembered chiefly because he launched the *Dictionary of National Biography*, but he was an important general publisher as well and he was stronger financially than Blackwood. He wanted, he said, to talk to Lewes about the *Studies in Animal Life*. Smith's magazine, the *Cornhill*, had published six of these but had then ceased to go on with them though Lewes hadn't by any means said his say. Now, because the magazine wasn't prospering in quite the way he (Smith) expected and looked for, it was felt that Lewes should resume his contributions because these would give the paper the fillip it needed – this was the line of Smith's talk, a line which Lewes would be inclined to accept without asking questions. Lewes fought his inclination to accept, feeling that a man of his journalistic stature shouldn't show immediate eagerness. Besides, was the important George Smith calling personally at Blandford Square just for this? George Smith might have larger purposes in mind. And so it proved. The publisher was out to lay groundbait; he was out to hook an astonishingly successful and profitable novelist and to do John Blackwood in the eye. Lewes put it all down in a journal entry for February 27 1862.

George Smith called bringing with him the whole of the proofs of *Animal Studies*. In the course of our chat he made a proposal to purchase Polly's new work [Romola] for £10,000. This of course includes the entire copyright. It is the most magnificent offer ever yet made for a novel; and Polly, as usual, was disinclined to accept it, on the ground that her work would not be worth the sum. Moreover she felt it impossible to begin publication in April or May – the period when Smith wishes it to begin to appear in the 'Cornhill Mag'. Unless she sees her book nearly completed and such as she considers worthy of

212

publication she objects to begin printing it. I went down
to Smith to tell him of her difficulties . . .

So Marian was upstairs while all this was going on, the
queen bee leaving the workers to haggle.

In the same entry Lewes writes: 'Met Dickens in Regent
St. He turned back to walk some way with me, and I turned
back again with him. Pleasant talk. Bought Villani *Historie
Fiorentine* for Polly. In the evening Beethoven, singing; and
read my proofs . . .' He sounds elated. The London that
mattered was at last in a wholly accepting mood vis-à-vis
the Leweses. The right people were calling on them; big
publishers were eager to buy, at immense cost, what was
likely to be on offer at Blandford Square. He was sure he
could overcome Marian's diffidence and hesitation: she
recognised the importance of money as much as – perhaps
even more than – he did. After quiet talks with her, and
perhaps some modifications, the arrangement would
almost certainly go through. Moreover, George Smith
hadn't yet exhausted his stock of blandishments. On April
8 he called again,

. . . with a proposition to publish Polly's novel in weekly
numbers at 6d with one plate. He also spoke to me about
the editorship of the *Cornhill Magazine* which Thackeray
has resigned. I declined taking any responsible position,
but agreed that if he would edit it responsibly, get a
subeditor, and some other adviser of whom I approved, I
would act as *consulting* editor. He is to think over the
proposition.

They went to Dorking at the end of April. *Romola* was
advancing only very slowly and Lewes, despite the promise of huge prosperity and literary prestige, suffered, she
said, 'almost constant discomfort'. They returned after a
fortnight and Smith was soon at their door with his final
proposal. Lewes was to be chief literary adviser to the
Cornhill at a salary of £600 a year – '. . . very handsome,' he
thought, 'as the work promises to be light, and not disagreeable.' As for *Romola* and serialisation, Marian still

213

remained obstinate about chopping it up into sixteen parts. Finally it was agreed that it should come out in twelve instalments and that Smith, to compensate him for having to alter his plans, should pay her £7,000 instead of the £10,000 which had so dazzled Lewes a little earlier. Smith was still intent on keeping them sweet. On May 17 Lewes noted: '. . . I have been a good deal occupied reading proofs and arranging matters for the Magazine. On Wednesday we went to the New Philharmonic and tonight we go to the opera to see *Rigoletto*, G. Smith having given us his stalls.'

Family matters were taking a bit of the edge off all these successes and kind attentions, however. In the same entry he says:

> Another incident in the week has been a severely painful one to both of us. Anthony Trollope came to lunch, and heard with surprise that Charlie was back in his old office, [Charlie's holiday was in Geneva with the D'Albert-Durades and there were strong hopes of promotion when he got back] not having made any advancement. He [Trollope] inquired into the cause, and wrote me a kind, candid, but painful letter telling me that the boy was not doing well, was careless, slow, and inefficient. This completely upset me, and brought on a bilious attack.

He cheered himself up that same week by hiring a brougham for the day and taking Marian to see the fifteenth century Italian portraits at the British Museum. To be kept at a task distasteful to her, Marian needed constant urging and stimulation. He had to keep his mother cheerful as well, immured alone for long stretches with the Captain: 'Sent up for Mother, who came to lunch with us. Took her to the Zoological Gardens . . .'

But where did Blackwood stand in all this, Blackwood who had taken her on as an unknown beginner, as a wraithlike shadowy gentleman for ever hiding behind Lewes's not-so-broad shoulders? Blackwood knew nothing about it. Smith he knew, Smith was a competitor, but he knew nothing of the large sums that had been dangled before the noses of Lewes and Marian, he knew of no consultancy-editorship at the *Cornhill* which would carry with it the prestige left by the large, formidable, departing figure of Thackeray and also a very comfortable part time salary of £600 a year which would suit Lewes, with his uncertain health, so well. Marian wrote to tell him on May 19, a 'rather abrupt' letter, she admitted, but 'abruptness is unavoidable'. She concluded with an involved and wholly disingenuous paragraph which is wholly characteristic of Mary Ann Evans bent on doing the best she can for herself and, almost beyond doubt, urged to the sticking point by a prompting Lewes. 'I know quite well from the feeling you have invariably shewn, that if the matter were of more importance to you than it is likely to be, you would enter fully into the views of the case as it concerned my interests as well as your own.' Blackwood wrote back generously. Of course he quite understood. But with Langford, a few days later, his tone was very different. (Smith in the meantime had been boorish enough to send him an advertisement about his capture of *Romola*-of-ill-omen for insertion in *Maga*.) 'The conduct of our friends in Blandford Square is certainly not pleasing nor in the long run will they find it wise . . . I am sure she would do it against her inclination . . . In reality I do not care about the defection . . . From the voracity of Lewes I saw that there would be great difficulty in making the arrangement with them . . .'

Blackwood was right to recognise Lewes as the prime mover in the affair, but probably not so right to suppose that the deal had gone through against Marian's inclination. She liked money, and she was learning fast that money was the strongest weapon she had against the rejection which polite London had sought to force upon her. Blackwood also showed less than a full understanding of Lewes when he accused him of 'voracity'. Lewes was never an ungenerous man. He was simply a professional writer who tried, reasonably enough, to do as well for himself as he could, and as well also for the woman whom he loved in the deepest and fullest sense of that dodgy word. He knew that she was helpless and hopeless in a man's world, with none of the fighting spirit of (say) an

215

Eliza Lynn. To his brother William in June John Blackwood expressed his fury at the behind-his-back defection of the Leweses even more strongly than he had to Langford.

> Lewes was taken unwell while I was with them yesterday and she accompanied me downstairs to speak. She said that 'under all the circumstances she had felt that she must accept the enormous offer that had been made – that she could never feel to another publisher as she felt towards me – that pleasure to her was gone in the matter and she did not feel sure now whether she had acted right' – whether she meant this last as towards me or as wisely regarding herself I could not tell. She also said that she 'hoped another time would arise,' apparently meaning that she would then show how strong her feeling was. I did not wish any *confidences* nor in her peculiar circumstances to hit her, so merely looked her full in the face and shaking hands said, 'I'm fully satisfied that it must have been a very sharp pang to you' and came away.

Marian is here seen – and it's a touching as well as funny sight – labouring unhappily in rough seas alone, with the sturdy, reliable, protection-affording breakwater normally afforded by Lewes temporarily withdrawn because her cherished man is having one of his turns. (Indeed, Lewes, from the harrowing times of *Romola* right to his death sixteen years later, was never to enjoy any sustained period of good health.) She is flustered, ill-at-ease, innocent and guilty both at once, and totally unable to cope effectively with Blackwood, who walks out of the front door of Blandford Square with an immensely profitable asset lost but with colours flying.

Lewes himself, for the moment upstairs and out of it, was to feel the wash of his displeasure. A man swiftly brought low by seasickness, he was to find that Blackwood had the power, as well as the intention, to make him experience queasiness. A review by him – of a section of Victor Hugo's *Les Misérables* – lay on Blackwood's desk. In July Blackwood told him: '. . . The paper is a good one but I do not

216

much fancy it as Victor Hugo's theories inspire me with a stronger feeling of disgust than you express . . .' Blackwood did use the piece (in *Maga* for August 1862) but that was the last time Lewes appeared in the paper.

Lewes listened while Marian read to him the results of her labours on the novel, made amendments which she accepted, worried about Thornie who, still in Edinburgh, was studying Sanskrit (would he master enough of it to pass the examination for service in India?), went to Spa for a fortnight where he walked like a postman, ate like a German, and hobnobbed with Bulwer-Lytton, and returned in August to a Marian fretting for lack of him. Then he returned to the daily labour of priming the pump which would keep Marian's imaginative engine from faltering, took her off to Littlehampton for refreshment, and assured himself in the diary summing-up in December that it had been for him a year when he'd been 'serenely happy'.

11

1863 was the year of apotheosis. It was the year of The
Priory. It was the year when Lewes began in earnest to call
his Polly, his Marian, Madonna, and when all polite London (intellectual division) became prepared, without, or at
any rate with hardly a, dissentient, to kneel before a new
divinity. Yet it was at the same time a year full of pain and
harassment. Standing a little past the middle of it, looking
both backwards and ahead, Lewes made a journal entry on
August 22:

> Since the last entry [on April 18] many things have
> occurred, mostly painful, which deserved a record. Polly
> has finished *Romola* which has been flatly received by the
> general public though it has excited a deep enthusiasm in
> almost all the élite. Tennyson, Browning, Coleridge,
> [John Duke, not STC, long departed] Monckton Milnes,
> Trollope and others speak of it with unbounded admir-
> ation. The Rev. F. D. Maurice has written to her two
> letters which are among the most exquisite things I ever
> read. His sister, Archdeacon Hare's widow, has also
> written with great fervour, and asked Polly to go and see
> her . . .

So even the Church had by now come to heel. Maurice was
undoubtedly unorthodox in his churchmanship, but
Archdeacon Hare, though speaking only through the
mouth of his widow now, was solid and central. Lewes
went on:

> We spent 10 delicious days of quiet at the Isle of Wight
> . . . [this was immediately after she'd written the last
> word of *Romola* on June 9 – 'Put the last stroke to *Romola*.

Ebenezer! Went in the evening to hear *La Gazza Ladra'*] and a week at Worthing. Bertie and Thornie have come home. [Bertie from Hofwyl, Thornie from Edinburgh] Thornie has failed to pass his second Indian examination, and refused to go through the two years' ordeal again. Indeed he refused for a long while to choose any other career, having set his mind on going out to Poland to fight the Russians. The idea of his enlisting in a guerilla band, and in such a cause was too preposterous, and afflicted us greatly. But for some time we feared that he would set us at defiance and start. Finally, he consented to join Bertie in Algiers and learn farming. He then went to Switzerland for a holiday and is there now . . . The Algerine scheme has fallen through, and I must look out for a Scotch farm for Bertie. We have bought *The Priory*, at North Bank, for £2,000 for 49 years. But owing to the state of the funds [mysterious why the pound should have faltered during those opening years of British plunder and expansionism] we lost £90 on selling out. [Blandford Square] Today we went over our house with Harris the builder to see about alterations. I have finished *Aristotle* and the new edition of the *Life of Goethe*.

That the unbounded admiration of the élite was something genuine and general was beyond doubt true, and Browning's letter, received only three weeks before Lewes's journal entry, was a true reflection of what was being thought and said. 'I had hoped that the last thing I should do before going away would be, on shutting *Romola*'s last volume, to use pen and paper in at least an attempt to express my gratitude for the noblest and most heroic prose poem that I have ever read: but I go miserably away at the end of the chapter, "on San Miniato". . .' But Lewes himself is careful not to go on record as saying that he has been completely bowled over by it himself. And indeed he wasn't. There had been too much drudgery in it for him, too much pushing of his Madonna up a long rough hill which she didn't in her heart ever want to climb. He knew, too, where the book went wrong. The woman Romola was the first one in all Marian's novels so far who was treated bitchily and unsympathetically by her creator – Maggie Tulliver has faults in plenty, but they're always observed with sympathy. Lewes's insight into Marian's intricacies had failed him when he pressed *Romola* on to her, but now he could understand that this treatment on her part of her central character was her probably not wholly conscious method of self-rebuke for allowing herself to be persuaded (by him – her surest and truest mentor) to venture outside her range.

And so he's talking, in this August entry, of a 'mostly painful' year. He had failed her through lack of professional literary judgment – the quality he perhaps most prided himself on. George Smith's £7,000 would have been better foregone.

Something else, something more domestic, also accounted for his use of the word 'painful'. His three sons were all of them at that moment right on top of them. Marian was 'Mutter' but she wasn't 'Mother'. There were no obvious tensions. It was her Blackwood cheques, so much more sizeable than his, that paid for the expensive Hofwyl education which gave all three boys a fair start in life whilst at the same time putting a reassuringly safe distance between them and the nest. But now Hofwyl was over and the boys, in the way of boys at all times, weren't adapting themselves swiftly, easily and conformably to the battle of life. Lewes was full of genuine affection for them, but he always saw the stability of his relationship with Marian as coming first. It would be prudent therefore to have the boys well scattered. It would be enough to have the eldest and most amenable, Charlie, safe but not rapidly advancing at the Post Office, close at home. For the other two, if the Indian examinations were so dauntingly stiff, well, farming in Algeria, or failing that, in Scotland, might mean an initial outlay but would solve many immediate difficulties and turn out to be for the benefit of all. Full of good intentions, and aware of how pressing and complicated life's problems always continued to be, however prosperous you were, the couple discussed the options. By the end of November they had got safely through a very choppy stretch of water and Marian was able to tell her

Genevan friend and translator D'Albert-Durade of Thornie's

> . . . willing departure for Natal with a first rate rifle and revolver, excellent introductions to friends of our friends, and a very sanguine expectation of shooting lions . . . His father felt that it would be a sin to allow a boy of nineteen to incur the demoralisation of joining coarse men engaged in guerilla warfare [Poles against Russians – that story goes back a long way] . . . but for some time . . . he would take willingly to no other career . . . Our other boy Bertie is in Scotland, learning agriculture, so that at last we have regained our quiet domesticity with no interruption in our tête-à-tête beyond the occasional presence of our eldest boy. . .

That was the way she wanted it – quite understandably. And Lewes, with his lack of touchiness and his practical realism, recognised that no plans for the future of his progeny by Agnes that didn't provide for the widest possible separation between them and his Madonna could possibly be made to work, and was prepared to agree that that was the way he wanted it too. Bertie lingered on in Scotland for another three years; he was still too young for pioneering in Natal, but they persuaded themselves, or, more likely, Marian persuaded Lewes, that he was 'better fitted for colonial than for English life', and September 1866 found him safely on the mail steamer bound for South Africa and Thornie.

The other great event of 1863 wasn't painful at all. The buying of The Priory was splendid. It was a handsome house. It was the symbol of re-establishment, re-acceptance and visible success on a mighty scale. But the negotiations and the preparations meant plentiful work and plentiful bother for Lewes. The time he could give to his own work had to be restricted. *The History of Science* began to have the look of a task too vast and daunting to be contemplated. In his ailing late forties the energy which had cheerfully faced up to the *Biographical History of Philosophy* had, for the time at least, departed from him. Aristotle became *Aristotle tout court* – a volume on its own with no confident promise of successors. He had to talk to Harris the builder about alterations, and by September The Priory was all scaffolding and paint. Marian felt the lack of the old planning talks which she and Lewes used to engage in as they took their long quiet walks under the trees in Richmond Park. The grandeur required by success meant the sacrifice of much they valued. He called in Owen Jones, a notable architect and interior decorator then in his prime, to exercise his talents on the new house, and he 'made a very exquisite thing of it; only in the pursuit of artistic effect, he has drawn us into serious expense, sacrificing our drawing room furniture, and causing new furniture to be bought . . .' Like many another, Lewes found difficulty in adapting himself quickly to abundant cash flow. The move took a whole week. The piano tuner was sick over their elegant new drawing room wallpaper, and over the carpet as well. Perhaps he'd been drinking. Marian left a purse, quite full, in a dressing table drawer and a workman stole it. 'The idea of removal is too formidable,' Lewes noted; but by mid-November they were in.

On the 24th Charlie came of age, so they combined a party for him with a housewarming. The young man's friends came. So did Trollope and a reconciled Herbert Spencer. Edward Pigott, once the close associate of Lewes on the *Leader* and still the friend who had stood by him through the difficult years from 1854, was another who was there; Leopold Jansa the violinist came and played for them; Burton,* eager to paint Marian's portrait, came to represent a sister art: altogether the gathering represented a salon in the making.

And a salon was what The Priory ultimately became, although the climb upwards to top cultural status, when an invitation to one of the famous Sunday Afternoons was a certificate confirming your arrival amongst society's intellectual upper crust, was still to take a little time. There were little hiccups on the way. 1864 was for them both a year of travel, moderate ill health and relatively small creative

* Sir Frederick William Burton, Director of the National Gallery, 1874–94

activity. At the beginning of the year Lewes fiddled away, a bit listlessly, at the continuation of his *History of Science*. During a sleepless night he 'made out the skeleton' of a whole five act play. He thought it might do as a vehicle for the actress Helen Faucit; he thought Marian might flesh it out; but *Savello*, as he tentatively called it, dwindled away to nothing. Reassuringly, Thornie wrote to them from Natal full of high spirits. In May and June they went holidaying in Venice and Milan. Captain Willim, the old ogre, died, and Lewes had some sharp verbal battles with a Mr Evans of Hereford who threatened to dispute the Captain's will, alleging that he had evidence of the Captain's intention to leave him the reversion of his estate. Dead and buried, Willim went on rubbing his stepson in tender places.

Charles met them on their return from Italy with the news that he was engaged to Gertrude Hill. She was a niece of the Post Office's famous Rowland Hill, and in every way a most suitable bride. The news, Lewes said, 'made Polly happy, and me rather melancholy – the thought of marriage is always a solemn and melancholy thought to me.' There were indeed solid personal reasons why for him this should be so. Gertrude was handsome, had a splendid contralto voice, and was four years older than Charlie. Marian, looking forward now to a time when The Priory would be solely theirs, was delighted at the news and persuaded herself that Lewes was as satisfied as she. Samuel Williams, a Birmingham lime merchant, author of a book on euthanasia and a faithful friend since Weimar days, gave Marian a bull terrier called Ben to compensate for the long dead Pug. Marian was deeply attached to him. Lewes had his reservations. From Milan on June 5 he told Charlie: 'Ben seems to be enlarging the circle of his acquaintance: query? Will contact with dogs of an artistic society elevate and refine him? . . . Your feeble Pater.'

Altogether, feebleness seemed to be getting a hold on him. Back at The Priory in mid-July he made a private note: 'Horrible scepticism about all things. Shall I ever be good for anything again? – ever do anything again?' He got thinner and thinner and tried riding. In September they took the waters at Harrogate. These were nasty, but Lewes persuaded himself that they did him good. They visited Scarborough, where the sands were more magnificent even than those at Tenby – but there is no talk now of a microscope, and marine biology, and splashing about in rock pools for molluscs. Then they were off to Malvern for another water cure, and Marian kept reading him samples in successive stages of her drama *The Spanish Gypsy*, of which, though still listlessly, he seemed to approve.

Round about Christmas he gathered fresh strength, however. He gave up his consultancy at the *Cornhill*, but George Smith interested him in the launching of the *Pall Mall Gazette*, and on December 30 he 'went to dine with Danby Seymour to meet Trollope, Oliphant and Chapman, [this wasn't Chapman the ravisher of 120 Strand but Chapman the publisher, Meredith's Chapman, of the firm Chapman and Hall] with whom we were to discuss the *Fortnightly*. I have given a *provisional adhesion* to the proposal of my editing this, they offering me a subeditor and every facility.'

In the New Year the stresses became less tight, and he showed signs of recovering something of the tone and manner of the Vivian of earlier days. To have the promise of the editorship of the *Fortnightly* was to have reaffirmed in the strongest possible terms his position at the very top of London journalism. The *Fortnightly* was to be very grand and vey soundly and solidly backed. The intention was to seize for it in London the reputation of the *Revue des Deux Mondes* in Paris. He was to be allowed complete control of policy. He was to receive a salary of £600 a year and all financial responsibility, which could and can weigh so heavily on editors, was to be lifted off him. His task was to produce a strong, lively, authoritative paper and to choose contributors of sufficient calibre to ensure that this should come about. He had until mid-May to prepare for the first issue. In the middle of the month they went over to Paris for a brief stay, he to make plans, both of them to relax and enjoy themselves. They paid a pious visit to the apartment of Comte, their dead master, and were shown round by Comte's old servant. 'Such places, that knew the great dead, always move me deeply,' she said, and Lewes was doubtless similarly touched. In February they were back at The Priory; the splendid place backing on to the Regent's Park Canal (nothing of it is now left) had settled down, suitably remodelled to suit its new occupants. Robust youth in the persons of Thornie and Bertie were no longer there clumping around and unintentionally giving them headaches. Charlie would soon be married. 'We are very happy,' Marian said, 'having almost recovered our old tête-à-tête, of which I am so selfishly fond . . . But it is necessary to strive against this unsocial disposition, so we are going to have some open evenings . . .' Marian the reluctant salonière was beginning to be born.

Lewes himself was always happiest with relaxed Bohemian sociability. He didn't enjoy, was never at his best at, high society functions – even those laid on by others. His dislike grew stronger when he found himself in the role of host and author. Yet it was beyond doubt he who launched and organised the open evenings which were later to develop into the Sunday Afternoons. Why did he go to so much trouble to make himself uncomfortable? The explanation is a simple, human one. For Marian's sake – he himself had never been in any dire sense a sufferer – he wanted to get his own back. Simply because Marian was a woman and had thumbed her nose at the code, she had been made to suffer moral banishment. Now, against all the odds, she had triumphed. Even the Queen had been conquered by *Adam Bede* and was, some while on, to request her autograph. So Lewes wanted to make this triumph plain and public. After experiencing upwards of ten years of never being 'received' Marian was now, through his urgings and efforts, to be turned into a receiver herself – and on the grandest scale. The luminary in Regent's Park would attract all the gorgeous, high flying moths. Although not a vindictive man, Lewes would have, and would enjoy having, the chance to snub, the opportunity to exclude the exclusives. Furthermore, of course, a grand affair, or even a succession of grand affairs, would enable the prospective editor of the *Fortnightly* to widen his already extensive knowledge of eminent Victorians. The big night was fixed for mid-February.

225

It was a disaster. Lewes had hired an orchestra, splendid singers in splendid voice, carpenters to take down doors so that passage from room to room should be unimpeded as grandees sailed to greet fellow grandees in distant corners, waiters supervised the buffet. The two sat together in the preparatory days comparing and sifting lists of those to be invited. Marian decided on a velvet dress with lacy decorations; she arranged that flowers and greenery should arrive on the morning. They expected over a hundred guests. Lewes suggested she should take a central chair in the drawing room, and disposed the seating accommodation subserviently around it. He was determined to drive the lesson home. His friend Pigott would be there who was so clever and funny at charades. On the appointed evening in mid-February they sat and waited, orchestra at the ready, food prepared, full fig donned.

But, in Marian's words, 'the party was a mull' – a Victorian word for flop. For one thing the weather was bad – Lewes perhaps ought to have waited for more suitable campaigning weather. The charade misfired, probably because the attendance was so sparse. Only twelve turned up. Many were ill, many sent regrets – but were these anything more than trifling figments not seriously intended to disguise a harsher reality: that acceptance of the woman living openly in sin was still not to be vouchsafed? She confided her fears and her resentment in a letter to Mrs Congreve a few days later. '. . . so ill is merit rewarded in this world! If the severest sense of fulfilling a duty could make one's parties pleasant, who so deserving as I? I turn my inward shudders into outward smiles, and talk fast with a sense of lead on my tongue . . .' There is no mention of Lewes, no acknowledgment of a debt to him for his labours at promotion, no recognition of the undoubted fact that when it came to talking fast and spiritedly at a failed party he was much more resourceful and un-put-downable than ever she would be. *Romola*, thank God, was behind her – an endless, weary road down which Lewes had pushed her: now here he was – admittedly on a much smaller scale – at it again. For a moment there's a hint of discord in the quiet harmonious air of The Priory. What was more,

Lewes didn't like her play, *The Spanish Gypsy*, and said so. Was he, after this long while, contemplating a withdrawal of his support? And if that were to happen, wouldn't universal darkness immediately descend and cover the George Eliot myth once and for all? Again to Mrs Congreve a week after the fiasco she confided, 'I was ill last week, and had mental troubles besides.'

There can be little doubt that there was a muted crisis in their relationship about this time. There were no tantrums. There was nothing spectacular happening or threatening to happen. But the moodiness, the megrims, the (relative) lack of productivity on her part in the first half of 1865 are sufficient to underline the strange duality and contradictions of their relationship. The minor humiliation of the party that never was would soon be put right. The embarrassments of one evening would soon change, be forgotten, because they'd be overlaid by the confident, dignified splendours of the Sunday Afternoons. And it seemed to the visitors at those that Lewes always played, and enjoyed playing, the role of acolyte. He was like a court chamberlain conducting visitors up to royalty. So what had happened to her dependence on him? Had they exchanged roles? Had he given up being the directing male? Had she taken over as the initiator?

There can be no doubt at all of her passionate wish to have him always to lean on. Rather than lose that support she would have sacrificed anything, given up any project, however cherished, if she thought it might threaten the secure cosiness of their relations.

On Lewes's side it is possible to suggest, hesitantly, that there was the beginning of a cooling-off at about this time, the spring of 1865. He had had, and was continuing to have, his troubles. Agnes had been a constant anxiety until the money from Marian's novels started to flow in richly. It wasn't that Agnes made difficulties: she was a vessel of shallow draught who could dance through storms and come out of them undamaged. But Lewes's sense of responsibility was always keen. He accepted the role of guardian of Agnes just as much as of Marian. Wrangling with Marian over *Romola* had also taken a great deal out of him. By the end he knew, always a shrewd appraiser of literary worth, that the pressure he'd exerted had been misplaced, that *Romola* had turned out a failure because it was the sort of novel she wasn't equipped to write. This distressed him, somewhat quenched the zest and fizz which had always been so much part of him.

Then there was the *History of Science*. He was beginning to see that for the strict practicalities of science he wasn't sufficiently equipped; he had launched into theoretical super-structure without spending long enough over the hard slog of basic training. He was also beginning to see that any scientific writing of his would run the risk of being invalidated through lack of authority. John Morley,* the thin lipped careerist, was willing to talk of Lewes's 'vivacious intelligence', and to describe him as 'a source of incessant and varied stimulation'. But he stopped short of accepting him as a friend whom he liked. This was not so much because Lewes hadn't conformed to the moral code (Morley was perfectly ready to sustain a close friendship with Meredith, whose first marriage to Mary Ellen Peacock had proved to be such a distressful affair), but because Lewes's scientific dabblings were so distasteful. Morley spoke of Lewes's making vivisection experiments on the ground floor at home 'while George Eliot was at her novel upstairs', and Morley used to be horrified at 'meeting in the hall or on the stairs some animal limping about in a mutilated state'. Poor Lewes. Science was a hard taskmaster and his genuine enthusiasm for it could be so easily misunderstood and misinterpreted.

* 1838-1923. Able Radical politician and copious author. Succeeded Lewes as editor of the *Fortnightly* in 1867. Distinguished political career, one of Gladstone's strongest and most successful supporters and biographers. Held office for many years, various posts, but most notably Secretary for India 1905–10 and Lord President of the Council 1910–14. A founder member of the Order of Merit (1902). Formidable, serious minded, well intentioned, Morley belonged to those many in all generations who are happy to will the end but go shaky at the knees when it comes to willing the means. He resigned from the cabinet in 1914 when the war decision came to be made, though in fairness to Morley it should be said that nearly all of the cabinet – Asquith, Haldane, Grey – were also paralysed and dazed; in far from any sort of decisive mood.

Finally there was the persistent ill health. Nothing terminal or catastrophic had happened to him, but there were intervals – far too many – when work which he had promised to finish had to be put aside while he fled abroad, or to Malvern for the water cure, or to Harrogate, in an attempt at physical re-establishment. Altogether, forcefulness was beginning to leak out of him a little. He remained staunch; he remained cheerful on the whole; there were consolations, and indeed great successes, to come. But by 1865 he had ceased, to some extent, being the promoter, adviser and inspirer of novels in the *Adam Bede/Mill on the Floss* vein. Marian showed signs of venturing out into novelistic territory he didn't much like the look of. The cosy alliance none the less held through it all. By March the burden of Lewes's boys was completely shed. Charlie married Gertrude Hill in the Rosslyn Hill Unitarian Chapel in Hampstead, and, as Lewes noted, '. . . We went back to Church Row [Hampstead] and had a quiet and pleasant talk with them all. The young couple started at half past 1 for Folkestone on their way to Italy. Happier prospects never smiled upon a marriage. Polly and I then called on Mother. Drove home and were quiet and cosy together all day.'

At the end of the same week Marian also made a journal entry. 'During this week the commencement of the *Fortnightly Review*, of which George has been prevailed on to be the editor, has been finally decided on. I am full of vain regrets that we did not persist in original refusal, for I dread the worry and anxiety G. may have . . . Dear George is all activity, yet is in very frail health.' Five days later another entry went in, and it was underlined – a signal that she was asserting herself. *'I have begun a novel.'* Lewes didn't like it. *Felix Holt, the Radical* was the not overwhelmingly vote catching name finally chosen for it.

There was never any quarrel about it. They never quarrelled. But there's a feeling all through the time of its writing that Lewes is having to make an effort in order to appear enthusiastic, a feeling too that in some small measure he's been excluded. Financial complications figure prominently in the book and in order to handle them with authority she had to turn to someone better equipped – and perhaps better disposed – than Lewes. This was the passionate Comtist, Frederic Harrison, twelve years younger than she, who had had a legal training. They kept in close touch right through the writing of the novel until she finished it at the end of 1865. There aren't many signs of close concern on Lewes's part. In June he wrote: 'Sat with Polly two hours in the garden discussing her novel and psychological problems.' But there's no mention of how good it was or of how uplifted he felt. He was much occupied with his own concerns – the getting together of a strong team of contributors to the new magazine and pondering what form his own contributions should take. On June 20 she said: 'Read the opening of my novel to G. Yesterday we drove to Wandsworth. Walked together on Wimbledon Common, in outer and inner sunshine as of old.' Again there's no talk of Lewes being delighted with what he heard of the opening of the novel, but she treasures the memory of the walk – to her it didn't matter whether it was Richmond Park or Wimbledon Common so long as she could count on 'outer and inner sunshine as of old'.

It is in the opening numbers of the *Fortnightly* that summer that Lewes shows signs of a decision on his part to turn away from 'serious' experimental science. He was always a journalist first. In the serial articles he planned for the opening numbers of the *Fortnightly* he took up again his role of practising literary man. His first article appeared in the first (May 15) number and the series continued, not quite regularly, till November 1. Ultimately they were collected and published under the workaday title of *Principles of Success in Literature* and an additional, longer, feebler piece called *The Inner Life of Art* was added to them.

At the outset he seems to be principally concerned, as an editor, to set out for the benefit of his contributors the guidelines they should follow when writing for him. Writers should have a method and this method should bear carefully in mind the basic laws of psychology (Lewes the scientist is to the fore here). He insists also that you can't consider yourself to be any good unless you are 'successful', and success means that you must have the ability to

230

establish a relation between the work you do and the public mind.

The object of literature is to instruct, to animate, or to amuse. Any book which does one of these things succeeds; any book which does none of these things fails. Failure is the indication of an inability to perform what was attempted: the aim was misdirected, or the arm was too weak: in either case the mark has not been hit. 'The public taste is degraded.' Perhaps so; and perhaps not. But in granting a want of due preparation in the public, we only grant that the author has missed his aim . . .

This is hard headed businesslike stuff. The writer's business is to communicate, not to soliloquise. Once past the watershed of the First World War there has of course been a strong swing away from this attitude towards writing, and indeed towards art in general. All those at the receiving end are required now to be humble and to try to understand. The writer, in Lewes's view, must see to it that his whole personality is reflected in his work and he believes that that wholeness can be subdivided into a trinity: the intellectual faculty which enables you to 'see' things, the moral faculty which gives to your work the important, elusive quality of sincerity, and the aesthetic faculty which will give it beauty. It's all pretty confident, and pretty snipsnap. But good sound commonsense and an enormously wide range of reading lie behind the articles. He makes what he says both readable and persuasive.

Goethe is much in his thoughts as he writes:

We need not insist on the obvious fact of there being more irritability than mastery, more imitation than creation, more echoes than voices in the world of Literature. Good writers are of necessity rare. But the ranks would be less crowded with incompetent writers if men of real ability were less misdirected in their aims. My object is to define, if possible, the Principles of Success – not to

231

supply recipes for absent power, but to expound the laws through which power is efficient, and to explain the causes which determine success in exact proportion to the native power on the one hand, and to the state of public opinion on the other . . .

Lewes is following the master.

The whole book is shrewd, clear, plain and urgent. The manner in many ways anticipates that of Shaw in his prefaces – and Shaw was an admirer of Lewes, acknowledging him as a predecessor. The realist fiction of the 1890s and 1900s – Arnold Bennett's for example – owes much to Lewes and to the views he puts forward here. In its pages also we can see the result of lessons learnt from his long collaboration with Marian. This is most clearly evident in what he says about the uses and importance of memory in the work of the imaginative writer. He always believed that Goethe was right and that novelists should go into a sort of permanent confessional when they composed their books. In her later books – sometimes, not always, in *Felix Holt* particularly – he thought she missed her way. Novelists should follow their instincts, not Comte, not abstract theories of any kind, not over researched novels of any kind, not even *Romola* (he doesn't of course mention this last because this had been his own mistake, but it is implicit). He says:

> . . . those who have had ample opportunities of intimately knowing the growth of works in the minds of artists, will bear me out in saying that a vivid memory supplies the elements from a thousand different sources, most of which are quite beyond the power of localization – the experience of yesterday being strangely intermingled with the dim suggestions of early years, the tones heard a childhood sounding through the diapason of sorrowing maturity; and all these kaleidoscopic fragments are recomposed into images that seem to have a corresponding reality of their own . . .

The *Fortnightly* was expensive, sold only to the select few, and needed financial support. This had been foreseen and there were no serious worries about keeping it afloat. He abandoned the rule of unsigned, or at any rate simply initialled, articles which was so strong in Victorian journalism. Marian, who had clung to her pseudonym so tenaciously, approved of this. '. . . The principle of signature, never before thoroughly carried out in England, has given it [the *Fortnightly*] an exceptional dignity, and drawn valuable writers . . . It is still a question whether it will succeed commercially . . .' She was always worried about his health: would it carry the burdens he placed upon it? His own journal summary for the year 1865 is brief to the point of being dismissive. He sounds a hard pressed man.

Unusual literary activity, income £1300 – much beyond what it has ever been before – almost exclusively from the *Fortnightly* and *Pall Mall Gazette*. Gratifying success of the *Fortnightly*. 3rd edition of *History of Philosophy* which will be greatly altered. Charles's happy marriage. Thornie has been unfortunate in Natal. Polly has begun *Felix Holt* and written one volume of it. Burton's portrait. [of Marian] Paris in spring. Normandy and Brittany in Autumn.

That was it. If she wanted support for *Felix Holt* she would have to stick close to Frederic Harrison. Like all Victorians who were reasonably flush with money they were always eager to be across the channel and wandering in Europe where life was hard for some but the catering good for those who could afford it.

By June 1866 she had finished *Felix Holt*. '. . . Sense of relief,' Lewes put in his journal. 'Continued ill-health of the last month and her dreadful nervousness and depression made the writing a serious matter. Blackwood [who is overjoyed at her return to him and who pays £5,000 for the copyright for five years] thinks the book superior to *Adam Bede*. I cannot share that opinion. . . .' George Smith, like

Lewes, had been unenthusiastic about *Felix Holt* and had turned it down. There are signs here that Marian's glooms, her huge thirst for encouragement, were beginning to be hard to bear, but the needs of his indomitably sociable nature were being well satisfied.

The Priory was by now an address to be seen in the engagement books of London people who counted. On the first Sunday of June 1866 the pair called in the morning on 'Mother and Nursie', and before setting off Lewes had been busy with Kant, because he was hard at it revising and enlarging his *History of Philosophy*. Then in the afternoon there was the usual at home: Buxton Forman called. He was of Charlie's generation, set to become a very important Post Office man and to be recognised as a scholar with special interests in Keats. A German medical man of some distinction was there too, Emil Julius Baetcke, an MD of Göttingen who was practising privately in London after having been, till 1863, the Resident Physician to the German Hospital in Dalston. Emanuel Deutsch was there, a Semitic scholar working in the Department of Printed Books in the British Museum. Strenuous intellectualism did indeed spread its wings over them. In the evening Bain the philosopher called. The day before, amongst others, Doyle the caricaturist (uncle of Conan Doyle) and Greenwood, in charge successively of the *Cornhill* and the *Pall Mall Gazette* and through the mid-century one of the most distinguished of London editors, had dined with them.

The Monday following the At Home he was wrestling with Kant before going to the office, and there once more were Bain, and Dennis, another London editor, and Trollope too, who would be shortly deputising for Lewes at the *Fortnightly* because he and Marian would be off again on yet one more continental jaunt. Bain raised a few eyebrows with his anti-Christian talk, Trollope took the opposite line, and 'one bit [of Bain's diatribe] convulsed me with laughter', and then they swerved off to a discussion of Butler's *Analogy of Religion*, noting that the great Bishop of Durham took a poor view of the early Christian idea that converts to Christianity should accept the notion of sacrifice with enthusiasm. At some time, one must suppose, they got down to the practicalities of making up the paper, but clearly there was time always for high powered, rarefied conversation.

Then on Tuesday Lewes was at Kant again, before taking leave of mother – Marian and he would be away, in Holland, Belgium and Germany, until August 3 – and on his way back to Regent's Park after the day's work he ran into Dickens 'who walked home with me'. Dickens the summer before had been in the dire Staplehurst railway crash and was still full of the harrowing dreams he was having as a result, full of blood and mud and ooze and screams. Lewes heard all about it. Then, once home, 'Charles and Gertrude came to say goodbye; but I was suffering from a terrible sick headache and had to go to bed after dinner . . .' In a frail man, after so much high and melodramatic talk, this headache is understandable. But why did he delay going to bed till after dinner? Victorian man overworked his stomach as ruthlessly as his brain.

On Thursday, June 7, 'Head still very bad. Final preparation. Started at 8.30 for Dover. The train made my head worse. *Lord Warden*; comfortable room.'

Coming back, they hung about in Ostend for some days waiting for the wind to fall light, but it never did, and so Lewes was sick again, but none the less physically revived. The *Blackwood's* article on *Felix Holt* pleased him, and, as Marian said, he 'carried it off to his mother, a lively woman of eighty who thinks praise of anything related to her son as good as the best wine . . .' She doesn't sound particularly enthusiastic about her mother-in-law. How common this is. Bertie Lewes, transferred from Edinburgh to Warwickshire, came home in mid-August because '. . . Thornie . . . has a grant of 3000 acres of land on the Orange River, and wishes Bertie to join him as soon as possible.' So he had to be kitted out, and by September he was away. Marian said, 'We are feeling ourselves a comfortable old couple now our last boy has gone to take care of himself . . .' The relief seemed to do Lewes's health good too, but by November he 'had broken down again sadly', and he decided that December 1866 should be his last month as editor of the *Fortnightly*.

After Christmas they were off to Spain, pausing for a day or two in Paris where Lewes met the French philosopher Ernest Renan*. Madame Mohl†, Woolner‡ and a Swiss sculptress were present too, so it ought to have resulted in a good blend of philosophy and aesthetics. But Lewes brushed Renan off quite brusquely:

> . . . very much like a Belgian priest in aspect – broad, coarse, suave, agreeable, commonplace, he talked just as a thousand and one Frenchmen talk – inconsiderately, superficially . . . Of Comte he talked the usual nonsense. I could not help probing him when he was talking about Kant, and finding that, as I expected, he only knew Kant at second hand, and that inaccurately. He pressed me to go and see him – don't think I shall . . .

You always had to be circumspect when talking to Lewes: he had sharp insights and an astonishing width of philosophical knowledge. Here too we can see his journalist's love of quick, sharp generalisation. Had he seen Belgian priests in any such quantity as to bring them so unfavourably into the description? If Renan hadn't read Kant, had Lewes read Renan? All the same these snapshot remarks enable you to *see* Renan – and in a not by any means wholly misleading light. Woolner's savage attack of long ago was quite forgotten.

The Leweses were on their way to Spain. *The Spanish*

* 1823–92. One of the greatest masters of French prose. His best work is the *Origines du Christianisme* 1863–81 which is still, under its sober title, a fascinating and endlessly readable book. He can be tricky, but so dazzles you that you don't notice the sleight of hand.

† 1793–1883. Born Mary Clarke, she married Julius Mohl, the distinguished French orientalist, in 1847, and established thereafter, over long years, one of the most brilliant and famous of French salons in Paris. She was tiny and fascinating and on the whole a great despiser of women, but very close to Florence Nightingale. It was to Madame Mohl that Florence Nightingale addressed her great and famous declaration of love for Arthur Hugh Clough on hearing of his untimely death in 1861.

‡ Thomas Woolner (1826–92). Sculptor and poet. A notable pre-Raphaelite. He violently disapproved of the Lewes-Marian union at the beginning, but gradually, in company with so many, came round to acceptance.

Gypsy, which Lewes had taken away from Marian so cruelly, still stuck in her mind; like so many Victorian writers she longed to write a poetic drama, and no one could convince her – no one could convince Tennyson or Browning either – that she lacked the necessary knack. Lewes's work on the reissue of his *History of Philosophy* was reviving his slumbering Comtist enthusiasm. They lingered twelve days or so in Biarritz, and '. . . After breakfast we both read the *Politique* – George one volume and I another, interrupting each other continually with questions and remarks. That morning study keeps me in a state of enthusiasm through the day – a moral glow . . .' The solemnity of this doesn't surprise in the case of Marian. She could be immensely solemn in the morning. Lewes's is harder to understand, agile and jolly and sociable as he was and prepared to stick a sharp pin through Renan's pretentious amplitude. The answer must lie in the fact that the Victorians had experienced no shattering disillusionment of the kind that began to beat people about the head in 1914. They could believe in, become genuinely excited by, theories of oral betterment, without becoming uneasy, without feeling the need to laugh at themselves. Death and tragedy could stalk their personal lives more cruelly, more frequently, than our own, but for all that general theories could be canvassed with greater confidence, with no suspicion that perhaps they were absurd. H. G. Wells, forty-eight years younger than Lewes, still had that confidence till the atom bombs of 1945 brought his mind to the end of its tether.

While she completed her Spanish poetic drama, he was working on his Prolegomena to the new *History of Philosophy*. It accompanied him through Spain, back to business and socialising in London, and away again in August 1867 to Ilmenau and Dresden. On August 13 he noted: 'Stretched on barked pines. Meditating on problem. What is Thought? and what its physiological process? This at last I have solved.' A substantial body of Victorian high thinking speaks out loud in that last sentence. In October Herbert Spencer persuaded him to take a brief walking tour with him in Surrey, and they set off from Weybridge. 'Arrived at the inn we found friends of his – the Cross family . . . I was introduced to them and received like an old friend – they knowing my books well and worshipping Polly . . .' John Walter Cross, another, younger, but vastly more significant worshipper, was in New York at that time. But he would be back. It's odd how Spencer, so dangerously near to marriage with Marian himself at one time, should bring not one but both her eventual mates into her life.

Lewes was beginning to relapse into what was, for him, comparative idleness. Foreign travelling, which he so much liked and which gave him the opportunity to consult with academics about the big, final *Problems of Life and Mind* book which he was preparing himself for, occupied considerable stretches of time. After a lull, there was a return to more active scientific research, though not on the scale of earlier years. In December he looked back on the work and events of 1868:

A scattered year! Little work done and only £162 earned! This has been partly owing to absence from home and partly to ill-health . . . In point of work I have only published four articles on Darwin – which have been the means of making his personal acquaintance – an article on the 'Dangers and Delights of Tobacco', and two or three slight papers in the *Pall Mall*. But I have during working days advanced seriously with my *Problems of Life and Mind* and have grown into clearness on many important points: some of the conclusions are quite novel – may they prove true! – Dissection and preparation of nervous systems of mulluscs and crustaceans to a large extent . . . *The Spanish Gypsy* has reached its third edition. Its acceptance – as I foresaw – has been greatly biased by the difficulty people feel in readjusting their mental focus and learning that one who they classed as a novelist is *also* a poet. But on the whole there has been a greater effect than I reckoned on.

He still sounds as if he had reservations about Marian's Spanish drama. But no reservations about Marian as a money spinner. Life was becoming very comfortable indeed for both of them.

Much has been written about the Sunday Afternoons at The Priory through the late sixties and seventies – when they weren't gallivanting, which was often. Marian delighted in holding court. The hard streak in her took genuine pleasure in the fact that though she had flouted the code she could now choose whom she would invite and be certain of eager acceptance. She was a fighting woman as well as a clinging woman, and she enjoyed having her guests led up to her by Lewes, one by one – a queen giving audience. Oscar Browning, Eton master and then Cambridge don, who wrote a biography of her and admired her, carefully skirting mockery as he did so, described the procedures at The Priory in his *Memories of Sixty Years*: 'She usually conversed with only one person at a time; you were taken up to her when there was a vacancy, and then you made room for someone else . . .' Browning first came to know them through the *Fortnightly*. Pigott suggested to Lewes that Browning write a notice of Trollope's *History of Florence* for the paper. Browning accepted and was thereupon invited to The Priory for lunch – to be looked over. 'I shall not readily forget,' he says, 'my emotions at seeing George Eliot at the head of the table with her majestic arm carving a leg of mutton.' Here there's a hint of mockery, but anyone reading it, after having studied that odd Lewes-Marian relationship, might find the little detail puzzling too. Wasn't Lewes master of the house? Didn't Marian always want this to be so? And wasn't there impropriety in the sight of a feminine arm, however majestic, carving the luncheon joint? The matter is trivial enough, but it might none the less be taken as a symptom of something important in their relationship.

There was always a strong streak of the impresario in Lewes's character. He knew that in Marian he possessed a wonderful money making property; it was his business to coax, cajole and encourage this producer so that the goods she was capable of producing came home regularly and in a shape suitable for the market. He saw nothing ignoble in this role. He knew that her dependence was total. He knew

239

also – and he was much before his time in this – that it would help, help her, help him, if he could create for this person who was, in herself, the oddest imaginable mixture of strength and diffidence, a public image, an image of prophetess, sybil. He devoted himself to the projection of this image. Marian, with her powerful intelligence, could not have been unaware of what was going on, but she was always willing to accept the stage managing (part of the impresario role he so much enjoyed) because she believed that nothing that Lewes did on her – on their – behalf could be other than right and far seeing.

After Christmas, 1867, Lewes went off to Bonn on a brief visit alone. *Problems of Life and Mind* was preoccupying him and he wanted to 'get answers to some questions bearing on the functions of the nerves'. Maria Congreve proposed to call round for her whilst he was away so that they could attend some Sunday meeting together. On December 30 Marian replied to this suggestion. 'It is very good and sweet of you to propose to come round for me . . . But on reading your letter, Mr Lewes objected, on grounds which I think just, to my going to any public manifestation without him, since the reason for his absence could not be divined by outsiders. I am companioned by dyspepsia . . .' How biddable she was. How securely, even when in faraway Bonn talking to German academics about nerves, Lewes was able to keep his tabs on her.

1869 was a bad year for him.

As always when they were in London Marian stayed much at home. Those who wished to have sight of the great lady must come to her. *The Spanish Gypsy* was done and her mind ran much on poetry. There's no talk of the piecemeal beginning of *Middlemarch* till August. Was their decision that she should not herself go visiting taken because that was how they wanted it, or was it forced upon them? Was this so very grand alliance still being found unacceptable? At the end of January Lewes invited Charles Eliot Norton, professor of art at Harvard and a much Europeanised American, to one of the Sunday Afternoons at The Priory. He wrote an account of his visit which sheds light in all directions.

Lewes . . . asked us to come and see his wife, saying that she never made calls herself, but was always at home on Sunday Afternoons. She is an object of great interest and great curiosity here. She is not received in general society, and the women who visit her are either so émancipée as not to mind what the world says about them, or have no social position to maintain. Lewes dines out a good deal, and some of the men with whom he dines go without their wives to his house on Sundays . . . [It is as though Marian was still some kind of ogress, dangerous, breathing contagion, needing to be walled up, to be inspected, gingerly, only by strong males hardened by danger, ones who had charged with the Light Brigade not all that many years ago when they were younger.] . . . No one whom I have heard speak, speaks in other than terms of respect of Mrs Lewes, but the common feeling is that it will not do for society to condone so flagrant a breach as hers of a convention and a sentiment (to use no stronger terms) on which morality greatly relies for support. I suspect society is right in this . . . Lewes received us at the door with characteristic animation; he looks and moves like an old-fashioned French barber or dancing master, very ugly, very vivacious, very entertaining. You expect to see him take up his fiddle and begin to play. His talk is much more French than English in its liveliness and in the grimace and gesture . . . all the action of his mind is rapid, and it is so full that it seems to be running over. 'Oh, if you like to hear stories,' he said one day, 'I can tell you stories for twelve hours on end.' It is just the same if you like to hear science or philosophy. His acquirements are very wide, wider, perhaps, than deep, but the men who know most on special subjects speak with respect of his attainments. I have heard both Darwin and Sir Charles Lyell speak very highly of the thoroughness of his knowledge in their departments. In fact his talents seem equal to anything. But he is not a man who wins more than a moderate liking from you. He has the vanity of a Frenchman; his moral perceptions are not acute and he consequently fails often in social tact and taste. He has what it is hard to call a vulgar air, but at

241

least there is something in his air which reminds you of vulgarity . . .

There's much pomposity and cloudy wittedness in some of this. Lewes emerges from Norton's lofty scrutiny as a ruffianly little outsider who is too clever by half. Lewes lacked depth, Norton thinks, and depth was a quality much admired in the 1860s. He takes no account of Lewes's range, which was astonishing. He doesn't notice that Lewes in his fifties is a much altered man from the quickfire journalist of the *Leader* days. Something of Marian's concentrated (too concentrated?) seriousness had brushed off on to him. As Morley wrote in his 1885 review of Cross's *Life of George Eliot*: 'It is only a trifling illustration of the infection of her indefatigable quality of taking pains, that Lewes should have formed the important habit of rewriting every page of his work, even of short articles for Reviews, before letting it go to the press.'

As for his 'not winning more than a moderate liking from you' – well, this tells us more about Norton's grudging starchiness than anything else. Lewes enjoyed a bit of jocosity – a few days later he was writing to Mrs Norton and her daughter, inviting them also to a Priory lunch, and the letter was cheerful and joky. Perhaps the ladies enjoyed getting it; perhaps they were a bit apprehensive because Norton, in that earlier letter, had spoken of his own tête-à-tête with Marian.

. . . The head and face are hardly as noble as George Sand's, but the lines are almost as strong and masculine; the cheeks are almost as heavy, and the hair is dressed in similar style, but the eyes are not so deep, and there is less suggestion of possible beauty and possible sensuality in the general contour and in the expression. [What an innocent Norton must have been. Had he no idea, when he spoke of 'possible sensuality' in the case of George Sand, of that lady's rip-roaring sexuality?] . . . Indeed, one rarely sees a plainer woman; dull complexion, dull eye, heavy features. For the greater part of two or three hours she and I talked together with little intermission.

Her talk was by no means brilliant. She said not one
memorable thing, but it was the talk of a person of strong
mind who had thought much and felt deeply, and consequently it was more than commonly interesting. Her
manner was too intense, she leans over to you till her face
is close to yours, and speaks in very low and eager tones;
nor is her manner perfectly simple. It is a little that, or
suggests that, of a woman who feels herself to be of mark
and is accustomed, as she is, to the adoring flattery of a
coterie of not undistinguished admirers . . .

Norton would have had plenty of warnings for his wife – in
particular that habit of the sticking of the face close up to
one, so that the eager need is to back off. Norton's emphasis
on her being still shunned isn't very strongly borne out by
The Priory guest lists: Robert Browning, Frederic Harrison,
Palgrave, the Mark Pattisons, Stanley, Sidney Colvin, the
Alexander Bains – the list is long and could be made much
longer. But it has to be stressed that it was very much of a
one way passage. Lewes made sweeping and frequent
sorties abroad and came back with an impressive list of
prospective callers. Marian stayed at home and her complexion dulled.

The shunning was then, in some sense, still a reality. It
explains, almost beyond doubt, their incessant voyagings
abroad where the Victorian taboos didn't run. Lewes cosseted her, kept her enclosed when they were in London.
When they were there she was always crying for *not London*;
once he'd planned yet one more pilgrimage she was longing to be *home*. There was nothing of the true traveller about
her; the notes she made of her journeyings were perfunctory and lifeless. What roused the creative energy in her
was always Warwickshire and old days. When the poems
by which she set considerable store were received less than
enthusiastically, and her depressions deepened and became more frequent in consequence, his filtering and cen-
sorship of critical opinions became more stringent. He
treated her as if she were a sacred cow. Coming from a
companionable, worldly man they seem odd tactics. Did he
'love' her in the ordinary, everyday way? Was he sexually

faithful? Almost certainly he was, and there are two reasons in particular for this. Marian was sexually demanding, and once his health became shaky – which it did comparatively early – she was about as much as he could cope with. And also, more and more as the years of their partnership accumulate, he acts as if he were a hypnotised man. Where Norton saw a dull eye, others saw one that could cast a spell.

On May 8 1869 he noted the arrival of James Mill's *Analysis of the Phenomena of the Human Mind* in two volumes, and also visited as a first duty the Widow Willim, old now but still splendidly capable of mental fight.

They were just back from Verona, Munich and Paris. And on that same Saturday, May 8, Thornie arrived back from Natal. They had had complaints from him as long ago as January about what he took to be stones in the kidney. 'The vision of him haunts me incessantly,' Lewes had written in January, but the haunting hadn't put a stop to a foreign trip. Now, though, he was 'dreadfully shocked to see him so worn'. And the Sunday following turned out to be 'a dreadful day – Thornie rolling on the floor in agony. Paget came in the evening and examined him. Up 4 times in the night to give him morphia etc.' On Monday he went into town 'and got a prone couch for Thornie', came back and spent the day nursing him. In the evening, Tuesday, Thornie became excited – delirious perhaps – 'talking about his African experiences and singing Zulu songs'. Paget thought he was suffering from the results of an injury to the spine received four years earlier whilst he'd been wrestling. Paget seemed to be guessing. Victorian doctors did a lot of this. The forward strides the medical profession had made since Rabelais weren't all that large. At all events Thornie was in a very precarious state. Lewes was greatly concerned, and Marian also, although they'd both been discussing and meditating upon *Middlemarch* since the beginning of the year. She said firmly to Mrs Mark Pattison on May 22, 'Indulgence must be abolished from our lives for a long while – even the indulgence of applying ourselves with much concentration to . . . [the letter is torn away here, but she must be referring to *Middlemarch*]' Thornie was cheerful and buoyant by nature. He had much of his father in him. It was deeply painful to Lewes to see his son suffering much, declining steadily, and showing the clearest signs that, still only twenty-five though he was, he was going to die. He lasted until mid-October and during that half-year not much else was able to occupy Lewes's thoughts for long. At the end of the year he noted:

The past year a wasted and painful one. Thornie's terrible illness lasted six months during which little work was done by either Polly or me, and after his death went to Limpsfield to recover in the peace and beauty of that place some of the necessary strength to fit us for work. Our deepening love sustained us. It is something as the years pass on and one feels conscious of declining powers to know that love increases instead of diminishing . . .

Lewes had virtually ceased writing altogether. Marian told Blackwood in March that she was alarmed 'lest Mr Lewes's nervous system should break down, as is the case so often with men who at any time in their life have been overdone with work and anxiety. But he has had the wisdom to cease writing entirely on finding that it left him in a state of nervous exhaustion . . .' So, late in March they were in Berlin again. They could rely upon deference and universal admiration there, which could always uplift their spirits. Lewes, the author of the *Life of Goethe*, was a famous man to whom all doors were open; Marian had translated Strauss, she was a Germanophile and she was the queen of novelists. '. . . being lionised is very fatiguing' he told his mother. But it was very agreeable all the same to feed on universal praise. He was mercurial, as quickly up as down. But 'my cold has become worse,' said Marian, and '. . . the sick animal longs for quiet and darkness . . .' She could be trying.

In December 1870 Mrs Willim died, 'Quite peacefully as she sat in her chair.' She was eighty-three. She had loved her son staunchly throughout the long years of her marriage to the difficult Willim, had been proud of him, had

245

shown no shock at his breaking with Agnes and taking up with Marian and had indeed always striven for smooth and friendly relations with her. Mrs Willim belonged to a generation more accustomed than later ones to taking sexual irregularities in their stride. Lewes took it calmly, with none of the long anguish he suffered over Thornie's dying. His mother had 'wished to go to rest'. They bought in black edged writing paper, lamented the Franco-German storm which aroused in them divided loyalties, and Marian worked, as yet with no very comprehensive plan, at the beginnings of what would become *Middlemarch*.

In April 1871 Lewes told Charlie:

Society is oppressive – though pleasant. Last Sunday we had Tourgeneff, Bullock and Emily Cross to lunch – 17 people afterwards – including Lady Castletown (her *third* visit, Lady Colville, Mrs Clough, [Blanche Smith, Clough's widow, and cousin to Barbara Bodichon] Trollope, a broad church Mr Abbott, [headmaster of the City of London School] Rallston, [Russian scholar and British Museum man] Dr Payne, Barbara, Mr and Mrs Burne Jones, and Viardot [Michelle Viardot, operatic singer of great fame and wife of the journalist Louis Viardot] who sang divinely and entranced everyone, some of them to positive tears. This lasted till 6. At 9 I went to dinner at Mrs Orr's [sister of Lord Leighton who was President of the Royal Academy and painted 'Captive Andromache' together with much, much besides] to meet Tyndall, [an FRS, the sort of scientific achievement that Lewes would have liked for himself, he died from an overdose of chloral in 1893 – a not uncommon miscalculation amongst Victorians – Mrs Mark Pattison, later Lady Dilke, came to grief in the same way] Dr Budd, [a physician who did significant work on typhoid fever] Leighton and the Hardmands [Hardman was a close friend of Meredith and in the next year, 1872, was to become editor of the *Morning Post*] and got home at ¼ to 12. Imagine what a day of talk and excitement!

246

How Lewes enjoyed plunging into the social whirl, however dearly he might have to pay for it physically afterwards. Marian stayed at home, puzzling at *Middlemarch* and developing headaches – but Lewes never left her because he was neglectful but because this was how she wanted it.

After that came alterations to The Priory. The place was to be repainted. A bath was to be installed. From May till August Lewes rented a cottage near Haslemere from Anne Gilchrist, widow of the biographer of Blake. Marian wasn't very pleased with the place, and wrote Anne one of her heavily humorous, arch, somewhat bitchy letters. '. . . You will also infer that we have no great evils to complain of, since I make so much of the small . . .' Yes, she had made plenty of the small.

Meanwhile Lewes had been writing to Blackwood, setting out his ideas about how to make the maximum amount of money out of *Middlemarch*. It looked as though it was going to be a long book, so why not copy the plan Victor Hugo adopted with *Les Misérables*? '. . . publish it in *half-volume* parts either at intervals of one, or as I think better, two months . . . If in a stiff paper cover – attractive but not bookstallish – (I have one in my eye) this part ought to seduce purchasers . . . *Tristram Shandy* you may remember was published at irregular intervals; and great was the desire for the continuation . . .' It's characteristic, somehow, of Lewes that he should gaily run *Middlemarch* and *Tristram Shandy* in tandem, even though no two novelistic horses could conceivably ever be less alike.

He liked the Surrey cottage. She, perhaps because of the cottage's small evils, perhaps because the summer was an uncharacteristically fierce English one, did not. She wrote to Charlie in June: '. . . You would rejoice to see how well he [Lewes] looks and how thoroughly he enjoys his life here. He has a new vein of interest in Mathematics, and he no longer feels exhausted after brainwork as he had done for months, nay years, before we came down here. I too am gaining a little strength, I hope, and am more attached to the place in proportion as I am less ailing and weary . . .' So by now there had been another switch, and mathematics had become his passion; he was consulting, as usual, with

German pundits so that mentally he should be thoroughly equipped. By the 1870s it was much too late to set out to become a polymath, but he was not to be put off by that. Did Marian find her bouts of exhaustion increasing in frequency and intensity as she watched him endlessly darting about, poking his nose into this, into that? '. . . every evening,' she told Frau von Siebold, wife of a Munich professor, 'I read a German book of difficult science to my husband, so that, you perceive, I am used to much less charming styles than yours in that venerable language . . .' She sounds here as though there were moments when Lewes's capacity to bring a sort of genius to the art of amateurishness could become a trial to her. Early in August they exchanged Mrs Gilchrist's cottage for another one close by – to last them till the end of the month when The Priory should finally be painted over and the bath safely plumbed. Before they went she wrote another sharpish letter to the landlady: '. . . I trusted that we should leave it in all respects not worse, but perhaps even better than we found it; but after Mr Lewes had written to you, I was made aware that a small dessert or bread and butter dish had been broken . . . This note of course needs no answer . . .' The same day she wrote to someone else, '. . . I, having a talent for being cold, sit shivering, sometimes even a warm water-bottle at my feet . . .' But Lewes kept brisk. Mathematics was bracing.

Two people, both about twenty years younger than the Leweses, burst, or better perhaps insinuated themselves into their lives about this time: Alexander Main from Arbroath and Elma Stuart. Main wrote to Marian so adoringly in September 1871 that Lewes, sifting her correspondence, read it to her at luncheon when she was 'depressed in spirits and in liver'. 'I confess it made me cry,' she said. Tears always came to her easily, and almost always were a refreshment. Lewes, as usual, had judged well. By the end of September Main was suggesting that he compile an anthology of gems from her writing. Lewes approved this – 'a treasure for readers, and a good speculation for the publisher,' he thought, but told Main that at all costs the word 'beauties' shouldn't be allowed to creep into the title. Main was an earnest young man, and Lewes and Blackwood both laughed about him. Lewes's name for him, though not of course to his face, was 'the gusher', but he was ready to recognise that a collection of Marian's wisdom and wit might do a good deal to add to her already vast sales, and encouraged Main to go ahead. Blackwood told his nephew Willie on October 24 1871 that

The worshipper of Genius appeared soon after eleven today and has just left. [6 p.m.] This has destroyed my day's work . . . He is quite young . . . a little fellow . . . He does a little in teaching or rather in reading with lads. He evidently has some means and has a Mother who rather ties him to Arbroath . . . He used his knife in a dangerous manner at lunch but the ladies were all taken with him. He had confided to some young friends . . . his great anxiety to get a letter from me and they consoled him with the exclamation 'He'll be golfing and sometimes not look at his letters for days.'

Elvorinda Eliza Maria Fraser Stuart (usually called Elma which was surely a step in the right direction) was another Scot. She was a hard up widow with a son, and living in Dinan in Brittany. There she learnt wood carving from Paris tradesmen who had fled westward after the siege and the root-and-branch, short lived Commune of March 1871. Because she admired Marian's books so much she sent her, via Blackwood, some carved book ends of her own making. Lewes and Marian wrote separately in thanks at the beginning of February 1872. Why should Lewes have found it necessary to write? The answer here is simply that that was the nature of their relationship. 'She has long passed,' he informed her, 'that stage of authorship in which *praise* – public or private – is regarded as the desirable end; and indeed very little praise of the direct kind ever reaches her, for I rigidly exclude all public criticism from her sight, and when friends or acquaintances are disposed to be complimentary they are turned over to me, who have stomach

249

for any amount of eulogy on her (it can't hurt *me* you know!).' The question one wants to ask here is, did she pass these letters over unopened? And if she did, how did she know that they were letters, critical or adulatory, of herself as author? Might she not, for example, be handing over a note from some go-between appointed by her brother Isaac, whom she loved and whose forgiveness she longed for, announcing that at last he was braced for a rapprochement? The answer must be that in all things Lewes must decide for her, must do duty for the God she'd long lost faith in. *He* would sort everything out for the best. And indeed it was true that he usually did. He was careful for example to add a further, by no means discouraging, paragraph to his letter to Elma. A supporter, even perhaps, in however straitened circumstances, a book buyer wasn't someone to be put off. 'But while she is at once sceptical of praise and averse to be constantly "chewing the cud" by having her works talked about to her, she is proportionately affected by *sympathy* . . .' And herewith was Mr Main's little volume as earnest of their joint gratitude – something, he thought, that she mightn't easily be able to get hold of in Dinan.

'Sympathy'. Lewes couldn't have had the remotest idea of what he was letting her and himself in for. Elma went on and on, sprinkling offerings at the foot of the shrine in embarrassing profusion and accompanying these with letters even more embarrassing in their *schwärmerei*. In 1873 she visited them and immediately afterwards Marian sent her the 'shabby little lock of hair', but Lewes, in a note of the visit, sounds as if he'd already had enough. Elma Stuart clung on however. Until 1878 she was pinched for money but then her step-father's will left her comfortably off. She lies buried next to Marian in Highgate cemetery, '. . . whom for 8½ blessed years,' as the stone proclaims, 'George Eliot called by the sweet name of "daughter".' Lewes always refused to object openly to the vibrant passion which Elma showed, although not very long after the book ends he was to have Edith Simcox on his hands as well – and Edith was more tiresome because probably more intelligent. Early in 1875 he was at pains, after a visit from Elma and another gift, to reassure her that he derived nothing but pleasure from her oozy enthusiasm.

Dear Elma, It is not to thank you for the lovely *table* (and the thoughtful tenderness of the additions) because you said I was not to thank you – and because I can't properly express on paper in blue ink what is written on my heart in red ink. It is for another purpose I write – to beg you to dismiss from your mind the very preposterous anxiety lest your visits and letters should ever be other than a delight to us. Because we seclude ourselves from acquaintance that makes us only the more glad to have friends, and you are one of the *inner circle*. Therefore no more . . . of the old hesitation and reticence!

That mid-February she duly came to lunch, and he recorded the visit in his diary. 'Elma to lunch. She showed us the handkerchief with which she had wiped the tears from Polly's eyes, and henceforth has preserved as a *relic*.' The italicisation is the only comment he permits himself, but did he laugh about it? Did he tell the story at the Garrick? Probably he did. He was good always at getting the best out of a story.

Bertie married in far Natal in August 1871 and that November Lewes told Blackwood that *Middlemarch* (the first instalment) should be sent to him at Kalbasfontein, Wakkerstroom, Natal, but Lewes doesn't seem ever to have had the fondness for, and close relationship with, Herbert which he had, and showed for the two elder sons. There are few letters to him, and fewer still from him. He wrote to his father in May 1871 to say, 'Many thanks for the box of books, which I received in January. I have not been able to read many of them as yet, I've had too much to do . . .' Herbert's letter is one of his few long ones; he sounds bad tempered and hard pressed. Eliza Harrison, his bride, had parents of whom Herbert had nothing good to say. It's a rough sort of letter to burst upon the cosseted valetudinarianism of The Priory.

251

. . . He [Mr Harrison] is too stingy to part with anything
. . . For some months past Mr and Mrs Harrison have
been trying to make Eliza give me up . . . They want her
to give me up because I am poor. [Why should he have
been poor, with all those handsome, four-figure cheques
punctually arriving at The Priory?] In January in a fit of
rage he [Harrison] threatened to knock Eliza down and
would have done so, if Mrs H. had not been in the room
and prevented him. (Lucky for him he did not strike
Eliza, for I don't know what I would have done to the
Brute.)

He had sold his farm, Falls of Assegai, because it wasn't
safe for Eliza:

. . . too close to the timber Bushes and there are always a
lot of Bush workers passing, going to Wakkerstroom and
very often they are drunk. I could not have left Eliza alone
for a day . . . I often wish that I had learned some trade. A
man in a colony ought to have some trade, if he has not
got enough stock to live on a farm with. I have had hard
times of it since I lost my cattle with the lung sickness. I
have learnt some things I did not know before . . . The
next letter you get from me I shall be on my new Farm and
I hope married . . . Love to Mutter, and Gertrude,
Charles etc . . .

Herbert was a long way off and was to stay a long way off
until he died young in 1875. And that angry, frustrated
letter serves to emphasise for us what a vast distance
indeed it was that separated Herbert Lewes and Herbert
Spencer, what a fearfully uncouth and uncultivated place
Falls of Assegai must have been compared to The Priory.
Yet Lewes never shows signs of being particularly concerned about Herbert. He'd received a letter from Bertie's
fierce father-in-law six months earlier telling him that his
son's health wasn't good and his poverty considerable. In
August 1873 Bertie had written to his father, 'I had thought
you had quite forgotten me, it is so long since I last heard
from you. I have written to you and the little Mutter twice

252

and once to Charles and have not yet received any answer.' Lewes and Marian took the agricultural, non-Comtist South African Harrison's letter as amounting really to not much more than a begging letter, and a cheque for £100 was sent. *Middlemarch* was doing very well by then, even if not quite as well as the earlier books, so £100 caused not the slightest dent in their rock solid solvency. When Bertie died, still in his twenties, with a young baby, Lewes noted, 'Charles wanted to go to Natal to bring Eliza back, but we couldn't think it right.' Indeed the pair of them took the whole sad business with notable calm. Bertie after all had always been the farming one, the unintellectual one. And this colonial Eliza plus baby amongst the Herbert Spencers and the Frederic Harrisons, with Robert Browning and Ivan Sergeyevich Turgenev as well – no, certainly they couldn't think it right. Not, at any rate, for a while.

12

By July 1872 *Middlemarch* was almost done, though it was still being serialised. Marian wrote on the Ms. 'To my dear husband, George Henry Lewes, in this nineteenth year of our blessed union'. 'Blessed' is in a way an odd word to use. In this kind of context it usually refers to children – to the offspring you've begotten. Or else perhaps to God, implying gratitude for His approval of what's been going on for so long and a hope that He'll continue to keep a kindly eye, in this case, on the later stages of life's tandem pilgrimage. But the Leweses as a couple had no children – although Marian enjoyed greatly her ersatz-grandmother role vis-à-vis the three daughters, Blanche, Maud and Elinor, of Charles Lewes and Gertrude Hill (you could work off some of your motherly feelings without any of the toil and sweat which the real thing usually demands). And the Leweses believed in no god, unless in the social-justice god as proclaimed by Comte (though even here they came to insist on qualifications). So 'blessed' must be taken as her final defiance of the worldly *hochwohlgeborene* of Victorian England, of the tight inner circle which still stubbornly refused to part ranks and let her in, even as late on as this, when she was acclaimed England's premier novelist. When Arthur Helps died in 1875 Lewes wrote a note of condolence to Alice, his widow. By then Helps was a great establishment man, Clerk to the Privy Council and editor in 1868 of the Queen's *Leaves from a Journal of our Life in the Highlands*. Alice made a note on Lewes's letter paper. It reads: 'The double autograph of G. H. Lewes and G. Eliot asked for by the Queen on seeing the letter.' This marks the high point of their total acceptance. The Queen never got as far as to ask them to a garden party, but to ask them for both their autographs – even though she was at pains to make it clear she wanted no fake nonsense about 'Mr and Mrs

254

Lewes' – was an achievement. It did not, could not, signify acceptance, but it did signify Acknowledgment of Worth.

Thornton Hunt died in 1873 and although he and Lewes had long been estranged, this death could be taken as symbolic of Lewes's abandonment of active journalism. Such energy as he had left – and by fits and starts there was still enough of it left to labour at his long and ambitious *Problems of Life and Mind* – he preserved for private, long term ventures or for selective collecting into volume form of earlier journalistic work. *Selections from the Modern British Dramatists*, with introduction and biographical notes by himself, had come as early as 1867. In 1874 there was *Female Characters of Goethe*, from the original drawings by W. Kaulbach and with an explanatory text by Lewes. In 1875 there were more reprinted pieces, *On Actors and the Art of Acting*. The first two of these volumes have little value now, but the 1875 volume is first rate. Here, where Lewes is truly at home – in a way that he never really was after he'd strayed, insufficiently grounded, into the swiftly expanding territories of natural science and mathematics – he writes with a verse and insight which is as good to read today as it ever was. He knew about acting. He had been an actor himself. He knew how to write dialogue, how to make plays work on the stage, even if those plays were of shallow draught. Shaw's praise of him as a critic of the theatre has already been noted, and it is wholly justified. Here he was on ground where he was instinctively at home, and what he writes has value now as it had value then. Compared to the long hours, running on into weeks, months and years, which he spent in his labours on *Problems*, the time taken to write, and later to select, the book he called 'On Actors and Acting' represents only a few score hours spent scribbling between the fall of the curtain and bedtime, but there's still a little flame underneath these articles that keeps them warm, whereas the answers he proposed to his Problems have been superseded, and gone cold, long ago.

The self-confidence, which was never arrogant or affected but genuine and spontaneous, buoyed him up throughout his long researches. On the last day of October

255

1876 he noted: 'Discovered the psychological explanation of the relation of Body and Mind – the form of the function.' It sounds rather as though God had been keeping a diary through His six creative days, and then, at the end of the narrative of Day Six, had written: 'Finished the creative job satisfactorily. It looks good. Tomorrow I think I'll take a day off.' It was getting to be time, perhaps, for Lewes to take much more than a day off. Marian supported him as stoutly as he supported her. In the autumn of 1872, after she had got *Middlemarch* off her hands, they fled abroad in their usual way, this time by way of Trier to Bad Homburg where they took the waters and watched the gambling. *Daniel Deronda* was being talked about, a book which was to start with a casino scene, and Homburg might possibly supply them with dramatic *Stoff*.

In November, once they were back, Marian wrote to Alexander Main to say: '. . . I am going now to bathe my mind in deep waters – going to read Mr Lewes's manuscript which has been storing itself up for me, and to take up various studies which have been to sleep since I have found my strength hardly enough for *Middlemarch*.' Always, from the tone of her letters, it's quite clear that she considered Lewes's psycho-biological investigations wholly as important, wholly as valuable, as her fictions. There was the little difference of the money, but she made no allusion to that, took no notice of it. The cheques came to Lewes. All the same the midland hard headedness that was part of her even though overlaid by high thoughts and deep abstractions must have caused a tremulous little thrill of pleasure to run through her when the money came in. (In January 1869 she wrote to Barbara Bodichon from The Priory:

Do you remember borrowing a shilling from Grace [Grace Lee, The Priory cook] to pay for your cab, when you brought me the hamper of pretty things in the summer? She told me of it the other day and she is so accurate about money matters that I have no doubt she is right. I forget such things myself, and therefore feel sure that you, like me, will be glad to be reminded. Will you, when you come again, just give Amelia the shilling when she opens the door for you, and say what it is for?

It would never have occurred to the daughter of Robert Evans to give Grace the shilling she could probably well do with and say no more about it.

A cheque came for Lewes quite shortly after these resolutions of hers to give her whole mind to Lewes's *Problems*. It was only £125 for some foreign rights on *Middlemarch*, Blackwood explained, and then went on to talk of his labour troubles. '. . . I have gone over to the Printing Office. It looks melancholy to see the idle cases and machines and I am sorry for the men. They are most sorry for themselves, but they yield like slaves to the tyranny of the Union . . .' The little revolutionary of Red Lion Square would have sympathised with Blackwood over his troubles. Lewes had come far from those Red Lion Square days of revolutionary speculation. A year later, almost to the day, he was to buy a carriage: 1870s' symbol of having reached the serene uplands from which to look down on the toil and squalor of the urban sprawl below and applaud the efforts of the likes of Frederick Denison Maurice, the founder of Christian Socialism who died that same year, secure in the feeling that now you had done your bit at social reform and it was time to keep a closer eye on your investments.

For longer and longer periods The Priory was left untenanted except for the watchdog servants. Marian was getting good at writing careful, Olympian references for housemaids. Mary, she told Mrs Frederic Harrison in December 1872, had

> no other defect . . . than a want of cleverness . . . in some kinds of work required of her . . . I have grounds for thinking that there was a cabal against Mary in the kitchen as 'the proud housemaid'. Her underclothing was thought arrogantly good, and her bearing towards the men had a little too much dignity . . . her mother, who is our cook, is a worthy woman . . . I am sure that you and Mr Harrison are likely to feel, much more warmly than I do, that one must try to help any poor thing who is fairly blameless, in the general jostling . . .

257

Lewes, who saw to all business and literary correspondence, wouldn't have seen this note. If he had, one likes to think, and even faintly hope, that he would have told her not to be so bloody pompous. Had Lewes pumped away a little too hard at her so easily deflated self-confidence? Perhaps there were moments when he thought so.

On December 21 1872 Blackwood sent him 'tables of the sales and state of *Middlemarch* which make a very pretty show'. The cumulative sales of the eight separate parts amounted at that date to 41,000. Lewes sent him a shrewd and detailed reply. He thought business could still be kept brisk if ingenuity and resourcefulness were applied to sales promotion. He was an old campaigner by now and Blackwood could accept this sort of talk from him without offence – even gratefully.

On New Year's Day 1873 Marian had neuralgia; he read Delboeuf's *Prologomènes de la Géométrie* and went on with *Problems*. A fortnight before Marian had told Mrs Mark Pattison that she 'had come to a pause' and that it was 'a holiday to sit with one's feet at the fire reading one's husband's writing'. Perhaps it was that that had brought on the neuralgia.

Over Christmas, neuralgia and all, they stayed with the Crosses at Weybridge, but John wasn't there. The last paragraph of Lewes's bread-and-butter letter ran: 'Did nephew Johnnie forgive his uncle and aunt at lunch yesterday when he "found they were not"? Love to all.' Lewes and Marian were getting very close indeed to the Crosses. Johnnie Cross was indeed becoming a man to lean on. On January 17 Lewes noted in his diary that he 'went into City. Discussed shares (and a chop) with Johnnie Cross'. The money that was pouring in needed to be wisely spread out.

His social-politeness notes began to be very high flown indeed. On January 20 he wrote to Octavia Hill (Charlie's sister-in-law): 'Saturday at 6.30 is the day fixed for our synthesis of the two Philanthropists [that is, Octavia herself, and Hall, who married into the Crosses] through the copula of a chop . . .' It sounds a terrible way to fix up a little do-gooding dinner party but Lewes wasn't doing more than following the idiom of the time.

December 13 1872 was also the date when there began for him the incubus of Edith Simcox. This was when she was first invited to call. When Blackwood had applied the description 'worshipper of genius' to Main the year before, he could hardly have imagined – and neither could Lewes – that Edith Simcox was already lurking just over the horizon demanding a phrase much more exalted, much more ecstatic. Between Alexander and Elma and Edith, Lewes, especially as he grew frailer and more ailing in the late 1870s, must have found the buzzing around of the three of them burdensome in the extreme. And the enveloping advances of Edith Simcox are in particular terrifying to contemplate.

In October 1874 Lewes and Marian went off briefly for a tour of the Salisbury area. She – and he – were working on local colour for *Daniel Deronda*. Edith was punctually at The Priory on the first Sunday after their return. Elma, Edith informed them, was in a highly worked-up and tense state. Lewes wrote Elma a warning letter as soon as Edith had departed.

> For the sake of others, if not your own, do bring a little of your energy and intellect to bear on the question of keeping yourself in a normal condition of health and do not play tricks with Valerian, Opium etc! You will perhaps retort on me that I have not practised my own precepts – but it is not so – I damaged my body by overwork and over-confidence, till it was too late to do more than patch and patch the old carcass . . . We enjoyed our stay in Paris very much . . . we went every night to the theatre and saw *nobody*!

Indomitably sociable though he was, he would have been glad to see nobody by then. It rained on Sunday November 11 1877, but wrote Edith,

> I thought if I didn't come there would be nobody to ask after Mr Lewes's headache . . . and they said, well, I should have the afternoon to myself and we had better sit down, which I proceeded to do on the rug at her feet,

259

which I kissed [the feet, not the rug] . . . she said . . . that she suffered much when worthy men were unfortunate in their choice of trouserings. Herbert Spencer had improved in that particular – but improvement had been needed. This led to the mention of his having been one of the visitors the Sunday before, his companion was an American admirer. Everyone, Mr Lewes observed, had an American admirer . . . Mr Lewes spoke of the unreasonableness of people who ask your advice when the last thing they would think of would be to take it . . .

Edith had not long before written a book called *Natural Law*, and 'she [Marian] . . . said that Charles Lewes had read some of the book with interest, and appealed to Mr Lewes if he himself had not sympathised with its spirit – to which he, in a somewhat uninviting tone – oh yes, what I read of it . . .' This isn't the Lewes we're used to, not the cheerful, tactful, sociable smoother of exits and entrances, the dedicated producer and presenter of his Madonna to a select company eager to snatch up and treasure crumbs of wit and wisdom as they dropped from the arms of the easy chair. Madonna or no Madonna, he is grumpy and offhand. You imagine that behind that bushiest of moustaches he is muttering to himself something about that recent stay in Paris where he could show off his not far from impeccable French and where, Comte's god be thanked, they saw *nobody*.

After Thornton Hunt's death and the settling of the initial difficulties which Agnes experienced over the will, there's little mention of Lewes's easy going, vigorous little legal spouse. But all the time, all through everything, she's there in the background, the insurmountable, not consciously unrelenting bar to Marian's entry into the safe harbour of legalised married womanhood. There is no doubt that this irregularity of status was a source of deep torment to Marian. She was a woman of outstanding intellectual power; she was also a woman of genius which is something different and something more. You would have expected to find her a leader in the ranks of the female emancipators – the Harriet Martineaus, the Frances Power Cobbes – but at no period of her life did she ever find, or want, a place there. Marian Evans was a bundle of contradictions. She could do Chapman's work for him far better than he could do it for himself; she could easily fulfil the intellectual requirements of Herbert Spencer; Oscar Browning, admittedly not the least fallible of men, 'regarded her as a prophetess, her will to me was law, I enquired of her as of an oracle'.

She can of course envisage a defiant role for women in society: in *Daniel Deronda* there's the character of the Princess Halm-Eberstein, the mother of Daniel. When she is dying she tells her son

> . . . I have not felt exactly what other women feel – or say they feel, for fear of being thought unlike others. When you reproach me . . . for sending you away from me, you mean, that I ought to say I felt about you as other women say they feel about their children. I did *not* feel that. I was glad to be freed from you.

All of this Marian Evans did, or caused others to say on her behalf, or caused characters in her books to say about themselves. When she was thirty-three she visited Harriet Martineau at Ambleside where Harriet was busy getting up a cooperative scheme out of which might come the erection of necessary workmen's cottages. '. . . we have all been trudging about looking at cottages,' she tells Mrs Bray, and without doubt Marian would have had incisive and constructive things to say, but there's little in the letter about the business, 'man's world' side of the visit. For the most part it's a 'feminine' letter. '. . . She [Harriet] came behind me, put her hands round me and kissed me in the prettiest way this evening, telling me she was glad she had got me here . . .'

In fact, accompanying this most muscular intelligence, this confident creative imagination which by the 1870s had promoted her to the undisputed first position amongst the prose writers of her time, there was a submissive, clinging, tremulous, 'feminine' creature who wanted to be a properly documented wife, supervising her kitchen and her children, having all ready for when the man came back from manly duties – in the City, in legal chambers, in a counting house, did it really matter where? – to restore and fortify himself in the evening and be fed and perhaps sung to. Lewes saw this, and understood this as nobody else did. The range of his writing is extraordinarily wide: lives of philosophers, commentary on philosophy, literary and dramatic criticism, plays, novels, biology, zoology, problems of life and mind – no one could fault him on versatility, and no one could fault him on fake and easy superficiality either. How odd it is therefore that he never wrote a book about sex. How adroitly, after all, he managed his own sexual affairs. When one considers the unhappy mess which so many Victorians made of their sexual lives – Carlyle and Jane Welsh, Ruskin and Effie Gray, Meredith and Mary Ellen Peacock, Dickens and Kate Hogarth, Mark Pattison and Emilia Frances Strong – it seems extraordinarily strange that Lewes didn't find time to sit down and write a book telling them how the sexes should set about the business of getting along together. Immediately it will be said that he parted from Agnes Jervis. But this isn't to call in question his tact and dexterity in the handling of sexual affairs. Agnes had been promiscuous in youth. Very well. So had Lewes. But marriage and the coming of children ought to have put a stop to dalliance in his view. It wasn't for him a matter of absolute law. It was simply that, other things being equal, it was better that children should grow up in a united family. If Thornton Hunt, or the idea of Phalansteries, or Fourierism, or something else, cast doubt on, or even shattered, the idea of a united family, why then he would stand by the children of any wrecked marriage he found himself faced with as well as he possibly could. And this indeed was what he did – even if, when it came to Bertie, who was a bit sullen and who didn't bear the manner, or intellectual stamp of the Leweses, he was perhaps a bit quick to let him go out of mind as well as out of sight.

But he understood perfectly well that this wasn't at all the way Marian viewed marriage. In principle she viewed marriage much as Lewes did. She denied and rejected orthodoxy. But at the same time, in the depths of her nature, she longed for banns and a white veil, and a ring, and a blessing, and Isaac Evans close at hand to give her away. 'If there is one attitude more odious to me than any other of the many attitudes of "knowingness", it is that air of lofty superiority to the vulgar . . .' Anyone who thought they detected that attitude in her 'will soon find out that I am a very commonplace woman'. She bore with Elma Stuart, she bore with Alexander Main, she bore even with Edith Simcox; she could give Herbert Spencer as good as he gave or better, but all the while you have the impression that with one part of her capacious mind she must see how it stands with George's shirts, must ensure that enough for the coming week are ready and laundered. The long conversation she had with Emily Davies in August 1869 – the summer of Thornie's illness – shows Marian in all her complications. Emily reported:

. . . she is afraid, she inherits from her father, longevity. The anxiety about Mr Lewes's son upsets her a good deal, but 'one hates oneself for being perturbed'. Then she remarked how easily one fell both into any little vice that belongs to us, after being disturbed in it, and spoke of the state of perturbation as entirely caused by not being sufficiently occupied with large interests. I referred to something in *Felix Holt* about Mr Lyon's preoccupation which set him above small cares, and said what an enviable state it must be. She said Yes, one only knew it by contrast, by the sense of the want of it. Somehow we got to talk of *The Mill on the Floss*. She said her sole purpose in writing it was to show the conflict which is going on everywhere when the younger generation with its higher culture comes into collision with the older . . . I asked if she had known actual people like the Dodsons, and she said 'Oh, so much worse.' She thought those Dodsons very nice people and that we owe much to them for keeping up the sense of respectability, which was the only religion possible to the mass of the English people. Their want of education made a theoretic or dogmatic religion impossible, and since the Reformation, an im-

263

aginative religion had not been possible. It had all been drained away. She considers that in *The Mill on the Floss*, everything is softened, as compared with real life. Her own experience, she said, was worse . . . She spoke of having come into collision with her father and being on the brink of being turned out of his house. And she dwelt a little on how much fault there is on the side of the young in such cases, of their ignorance of life, and the narrowness of their intellectual superiority.

Ah, what a subtle, brilliant and tragic lady comes most movingly near to us here out of her *querencia*: a non-bluestocking talking to a bluestocking. She hates herself for being perturbed about Thornie. Why after all – at this point the hard intellectual in her surfaces – should she, except in the conventional, verbal sense, why should she be perturbed about a son she hadn't borne? And the anguish of hating herself is the genuine anguish of a maternal woman denied motherhood. And her sticking up for the Dodsons and respectability is irremovably part of her nature also because she recognised the Dodson element in herself, even though in one sense she'd turned her back on it for ever when she took the cab down to the docks to set sail with Lewes for Germany. So is her rueful acceptance of the fact that the young will always be cocksure as she had been, yet on shaky grounds because their 'intellectual superiority' is a narrow, narrow thing owed entirely to the steady accumulation of knowledge as each generation in turn adds its tiny contribution to the common stock . . . Self-revealing stuff, even though it wasn't probably in the nature of that very clever woman, Emily Davies, to seize upon the intricacies and the self-torture underlying it.

Yet Lewes did seize upon them. This is unexpected, because he was a very masculine man even though a bit dandified. He understood her wholly – the depressions, the psychosomatic ailments, the restlessness, the longing to be away followed almost immediately by a longing to be back, the holding out of her hands towards a rustic childhood world which was solid and certain and limited, untouched by Comte or Mill or Herbert Spencer, the constant

264

need to be reassured, the immensely powerful intelligence looking sourly on, as it were, and telling her what a contemptibly feeble figure she was cutting – all of this – all these contradictions which beset her he took into account. He struggled endlessly to pluck out the weeds threatening to choke the frail plant of genius. Quite early on, just after *Adam Bede* had come out, he told Sara Hennell of the special measures he knew he'd have to take.

We [always the imperial, undivided 'we'] resolved to exclude [talk about her writing] as far as we could. No one speaks about her books to her, but me . . . Besides . . . there is a special reason in her case – it is that excessive diffidence which prevented her writing at all, for so many years, and would prevent her now, if I were not beside her to encourage her. A thousand eulogies would not give her the slightest confidence, but one objection would increase her doubts . . .

Did he enjoy being a flunkey? – so the grand folks thronging The Priory on Sunday afternoons must often have asked themselves. Was being a mercurial little show-man all he was fit for, as Meredith thought? The questions simply served to emphasise the total lack of comprehension displayed by these smart, successful, mensa-minded people. Lewes was never, in the remotest sense, her flunkey; he was her creator. Without him she would have struggled to the small eminence of (say) a Frances Power Cobbe; she would never have made anything like the mark of (say) Eliza Lynn – because Mrs Linton had a thrust-ful self-confidence which she could generate for herself. In Marian's case the self-confidence had to be worked up by someone outside herself and then transmitted. Lewes was her dynamo. It was a difficult, exhausting job, a full time one, many might say, once the heavy wheels had started to turn and the products had started to flow, and more and more products out of line with her basic inspiration – *Middlemarch*, *Felix Holt* and *Daniel Deronda* – came to be worked on. These were books which came from insistent public demand more than anything else. Lewes never thought she was at her best in them. But when he was with her he was all enthusiasm, all encouragement. '. . . it is difficult,' he told Elma Stuart in 1876, 'to get Madonna away from her own home . . . we have both been much gratified at the fervent admiration [of *David Deronda*] of the Chief Rabbi . . . This is all the more welcome because the Christian public – at least a large part of it – is decidedly unsympathetic towards that part of DD . . .' He was maintaining the strong alliance, eager for her success, getting more doubtful about it. And how insistently she relied on him, even right at the end when it was hard indeed for him to blow away her gloom, mortally sick as he was. Edith Simcox spent Wednesday April 10 1878 with her. '. . . Mr Lewes was dining out and I prayed to be allowed to stay without talking till he came in. She said she couldn't read with me there. I complained a little at such evidence that one did not belong to her and she spoke of her complete dependence on his society and unreasonable anxiety when he was away . . .'

By then Marian was nearing sixty. She was famous, lionised, wealthy. For the benefit of the public at large, of those who didn't know her well – and only the tiniest handful of people did know her well – she'd learnt how to put on an appearance of majestic calm. Young Edmund Gosse, seeing her out driving in the park, could make his little joke about how like the horse she looked, but all the same he was impressed. She was England's greatest living novelist and he'd have been surprised indeed to discover how quickly she became anxious and fretful when Lewes got home late.

The closest of the ties made between the Leweses and anyone in the later stages of their life was the one with the Crosses. This began as far back as 1867. Lewes and Herbert Spencer were breathing health into themselves by tramping through the Surrey hills. They put up at The Hand and Spear inn near Weybridge, where Anne Cross was taking refuge whilst her house in Weybridge nearby was being set to rights after a fire. Spencer knew the widow, now in her middle fifties, and introduced her to Lewes. Her daughter Elizabeth was with her and she had published some poems

266

not long before – so here was a literary connection all forged and ready. Elizabeth visited Madonna.

Then in Rome, in 1869, Elizabeth, now Mrs Bullock, was on her honeymoon and they met again and dined together. Not long after that, still in Rome, the Widow Cross and her twenty-nine year old son John somewhat oddly arrived as well – one says 'oddly', but perhaps Mr Bullock was one of those rare beings prepared to have honeymoon privacy knocked on the head. At all events from then on Lewes, Marian and the Cross family gradually became very close. All through the first half of the 1870s, when, turn and turn about Lewes and Marian were struggling to keep themselves well, they took numerous houses – at Limpsfield, Shottermill, Elversley House in Redhill, Blackbrook House at Bickley in Kent, the cottage at Earlswood Common – and from all of them a pony chaise could manage to take them to Weybridge on a visit. John Cross was soon being frequently written to, and by August 1872 he was 'Nephew John', or 'Nephew Johnnie'. Being a banker he was useful on the financial side. Lewes dealt with the money coming in from publishers, Nephew Johnnie dealt with the investments.

That same month Lewes wrote to Main from Redhill: '. . . her translator [says] that *Middlemarch* is more difficult in style than *Felix Holt*, and *Felix* more so than *Silas* or *Adam* . . . is it the fact that there is any appreciable change? *We* of course cannot see – we do not see the changes in our person so obvious to others. . .' Again, as constantly, the identification of himself with Marian. But isn't there here perhaps a slight backing away from total identification? It's tempting to guess that he was seeing something that was so obvious to others – that late-Marian was laborious-Marian, that research was winning the day over the spontaneous overflow of powerful feelings which was what he had admired in the earlier books, that he felt guilt in himself for switching her on to the wrong rails when he'd pressed the idea of *Romola* on her, that spending days in synagogues so that no detail in *Daniel Deronda* should strike the wrong note – this was still a year or so ahead – wasn't the most fruitful way for a Warwickshire lass, daughter of an estates bailiff, to be spending her time.

Indeed, there must have been times in the glorious seventies when she was a great trial to him. In May 1873, for example, they visited Cambridge and stayed with F. W. H. Myers and mingled with the first class brains, apostolic and other – Myers himself, Henry Sidgwick, Jebb, the Balfours, Maitland, Henry Jackson and others. Myers's account of his conversation with her in the Fellows' Garden at Trinity on that occasion has often been quoted, but it needs to go in here, bearing in mind that Lewes the companionable, the convivial, the often suffering, was probably drinking port in some senior common room near at hand at the time, and bearing in mind also that having to live with a prophetess was beginning to impose upon him the necessity for sacrifices. Myers remembers:

> . . . how at Cambridge, I walked with her once in the Fellows' Garden at Trinity, on an evening of rainy May; and she, stirred somewhat beyond her wont, and taking as her text the three words which have been used so often as the inspired trumpet calls of men, – the words *God*, *Immortality*, *Duty*, – pronounced, with terrible earnestness, how inconceivable was the *first*, how unbelievable the *second*, and yet how peremptory and absolute the *third*. Never, perhaps, had sterner accents affirmed the sovereignty of impersonal and unrecompensing law. I listened, and night fell; her grave, majestic countenance turned towards me like a Sibyl's in the gloom; it was as though she withdrew from my grasp, one by one, the two scrolls of promise, and left me the third scroll only, awful with inevitable fates.

It's a fine passage, and Myers must have had fun writing it. Perhaps, telling the story to Lewes afterwards – if he got the chance to have a private word – they might well have had fun together over it. It was a time when Lewes had need of all the fun he could get. His health was frail. 'Trinity Library and music in the chapel,' he notes. 'Tea. Then to the *boat race*. Brilliant day but very cold. Dr Phelps and his wife. At supper several of the fellows. Home at 12 knocked up.' He was having trouble with *Problems* too. When he got back to The Priory on May 24 there was a letter waiting for him from Blackwood. '. . . I am sorry to say your book grates upon me more than I expected and I have been hesitating for some time whether to say anything to you on the subject but the more I think of it the less I am reconciled to it . . .' Lewes took this like the old pro he was – 'Let us therefore consider the whole project at an end . . .'* It wasn't a case of abandoning the whole huge opus, the publishing of which began in 1874 and wasn't finished when he died. Blackwood was objecting to bits.

The ready acceptance of Blackwood's criticism is particularly characteristic of Lewes in his last decade. He was working and writing to suit himself, to please himself. Marian's novels were bringing in cheques enough and to spare. There was no need now to be scribbling away at an article and to be waiting anxiously for the fee. He and Marian were a partnership; they were 'we'; he considered himself part author of Marian's novels and he was perfectly justified in so considering himself. And so, now that the weight of years were beginning – prematurely but none the less certainly – to count, why shouldn't he write about what genuinely interested him? As a scientist he was an amateur; but Lewes lived in an age when academic compartmentalisation hadn't properly begun. In a very real sense all the Victorian scientists were 'amateurs'.

Between 1857 and 1861 Henry Thomas Buckle published his *Introduction to the History of Civilisation in England*. This very odd, undeservedly neglected book is an assertion of Buckle's belief that, in the second half of the nineteenth century, it was still possible to be a polymath in the sense that Milton had been a polymath. Lewes and Buckle tugged at opposite ends of the same rope. Lewes thought that

---

* It's interesting to note, by the way, what an intensely personal business Victorian publishing tended to be. Whether it was Lewes, or Marian, or anyone else, John Blackwood himself read, criticised, approved, declined, suggested amendments, and fellow publishers in the main followed the same rule. They backed their fancy without much, or event any, recourse to editors. It is true, however, that Fred Chapman relied very heavily on Meredith over a great number of years.

science could be integrated with history; Buckle thought that history could be integrated with science. Basically it was a Comtist attitude – for Comte, sociology was his own invented bridge allowing you to pass freely without frontier between history and science. (Lewes remained, with just a few reservations, a loyal Comtist to the end.) Predictably, Macaulay brushed Buckle aside. Buckle 'wants to make a system before he has got the materials; and he has not the excuse that Aristotle had, of having an eminently system-atising mind'. This is typical Macaulayan cheek and we love him for it. How much, in the way of non-Whig materials, had Macaulay got? Lewes yearned to make a system, and knew perfectly well that he was short on materials, but that was no reason why he shouldn't work away at *Problems*. Could it not be said that Huxley was short on materials too? And even Darwin himself? And hadn't Darwin written to someone about Buckle – 'Have you read Buckle's second volume? It has interested me greatly; I do not care whether his views are right or wrong, but I should think they contain much truth . . .' Darwin expresses here the very essence of the Victorian scientific spirit. Lewes, had he seen the words, would have applauded them. Rightness or wrong-ness of view? What you had to do was plug unweariedly away and take stock of progress at the end of each day's labour. Marian, Comtist, rationalist, 'scientific' just as he was – though perhaps she never succeeded in quite quen-ching the evangelicalism of her childhood – stood behind him and admired. There's no suggestion anywhere, in her books, in her correspondence, that she thought Lewes's work less 'important', less 'significant' than her own.

They were both, but Lewes more particularly, moving around unabashed in the uppermost tiers of society by the middle of the 1870s. In July 1875 he wrote a letter to John Cross's sister Maria – she was his 'Dearest Niece' – about a garden party he'd attended given by Lady Airlie (she was the second daughter of Lord Stanley of Alderley and so quite impeccably bred). There's a studied lack of awe in his account.

270

I arrayed myself in my 'war-paint', and presented myself at Airlie Lodge. To my surprise I found that the Queen [Queen Sophie of Holland who had met him as long ago as 1867] had expressed a special wish that I should be presented to her, so immediately on her arrival that ceremony took place. You must imagine a pale plain elderly woman of somewhat feeble and certainly unenchanting aspect – and opposite her stands – The Matchless! Then this dialogue ensues. *Queen*. Very glad to see you, Mr Lewes. I saw you in 1871 at Florence. *The M*. I was, your Majesty. *Q*. You were pointed out to me at the theatre, you and your wife. *Lady Airlie* (not having caught the word Florence or because Weimar was running in her head, we having been talking of it when the Q arrived) 'Mr Lewes says they were so very kind to him at Weimar'. *Q (with something like fretful impatience)* I don't want to hear about Weimar (loftily) I have done with them (*family quarrel*) – So you like Weimar, Mr Lewes? (*a touch of sarcasm in the tone*). *The M*. Well, your Majesty, I was very happy there and much interested in everything. *Q*. It's a very ugly place. You can't say it's beautiful. *The M*. No, not beautiful – certainly not like Florence. *Q*. Oh! Florence is charmimg. (*a pause*) I admire your writings – as to your wife's, all the world admires them. Here The Matchless bows, and begins to think, 'when will this come to an end'. Lady Dillon and Jenny Lind were brought up to be presented, and this seemed an opening for escape, so I whispered to Mrs Howard [a sister of Lady Airlie's] 'May I consider the audience over?' 'Yes, if you are bored.' 'I am.' 'Then come and talk with me'. . . . It was a brilliant sight that garden dotted with lovely women and lovely dresses (with some *not* so lovely!) and celebrated men and 'nobs'. I enjoyed an hour and a half of it; and came away wondering whether I had produced anything like the same impression on Royalty that Royalty had produced on me . . .

This is Lewes in his Slingsby Lawrence mood, writing to amuse a young girl and unaffectedly unimpressed as always by high ranking pomp. He sounds young and

271

sprightly – the sparkish married man that Thackeray had drawn long ago singing away while Agnes accompanied him at the piano with Thornton chiming in behind. But now he was fifty-eight, still busy, still hurrying about, still working at his big book, still supporting and shielding Marian, still finding himself 'knocked up' far too often, still hunting for the country house that would exactly suit, still looking after Agnes (£200 went to her in 1874), still traipsing the continent of Europe because Marian was so restless . . .

In December 1875 he noted: 'Polly upstairs with bad cold. I read aloud to her George Sand's *Le Marquis de Villemer*. After dinner while dozing in my chair felt a strange pressure inside the ears accompanied by inability to move or speak. Thought paralysis had come on or Death. But it passed away, leaving only a sense of Indigestion behind . . .' He was used to indigestion; he could cope with indigestion, and the day after he appeared before the Royal Commission on Vivisection (this might have been Morley's doing) and was grilled, and stood up to it well, and the very same evening enjoyed music and singing. Marian was long accustomed to his alarming bouts of this and that and made no mention of this latest business in a letter she wrote the day after to Blackwood. She was in the middle of *Daniel Deronda*. She told him, surprisingly, that she couldn't 'risk the reading of other English fiction', and had been obliged to tell Anthony Trollope so. She added at the end: '. . . It is wonderful how *Middlemarch* keeps afloat in people's minds. Somebody told me that Mr Henry Sidgwick said it was a bold thing to write another book after *Middlemarch*, and we must prepare ourselves for the incalculableness of the public reception in the first instance . . .' But she seems in no way troubled by Lewes's nasty turn the night before.

In 1876 he met, with others, to form the Physiological Society and was elected to its founding council. Physiology is a very Victorian word and a very Victorian science. It concerned itself with the functions of living organisms. For the close scientific specialisms of today it's altogether too vague and all embracing a word and has more or less ceased to be part of a living scientific vocabulary. It suited Lewes's amateurism well, however, and he was soon busy taking the chair at committee meetings, attending dinners, proposing toasts, playing host to foreign investigators and listening to lectures on 'Measurement of Thought and on the Movement of the Eye'. In November he was reading Otto Liebmann, a youngster of thirty-six, who had just brought out *Zur Analysis der Wirklichkeit*, so physiology hadn't been able to elbow out his old metaphysical loves.

Then, on November 29, 'We went with Johnnie to Witley to see a house. Met him at Waterloo at 11.30 and reached Witley at 12.40. Enchanted with the house and grounds. The day transcendently beautiful made everything look glorious . . .' At last after years of hunting it looked as if the perfect second residence had presented itself. Lewes immediately had the place surveyed and then instructed Hutchins, Johnnie Cross's solicitor, to go as high as £5,000 for the property. He got to this stage in just a little over a week. Dickens could complain of dawdling lawyers and of the Circumlocution Office, yet how swiftly the Victorians could put through a large business transaction once their minds were made up. It's probably the secret of their vast prosperity.

On New Year's Day 1877 Marian wrote to Elma Stuart – she was signing herself 'Mother' now – that they rather trembled to take another view of what they'd bought – for £50 under the asking price. '. . . we both of us like to live undisturbedly in our ideal world, where furniture and tradespeople are an inexpensive comedy – rather than to see about our own wants and give orders. In fact, we don't like our own business, in the external sense. But these are the grievances of people who have more than their share in the world . . .' It's possible to dislike quite sharply the tone of this. It has the Eliotian, not the Lewesian, ring. Living undisturbedly in their ideal world sounds prophetess-ish and Madonna-ish. But she was perfectly prepared to go gallivanting endlessly provided Lewes's arm was there to cling to.

In the summer of 1873 they went to the Vosges and paused briefly in Paris on the way. 'Walked to the Elysées,' noted Lewes, 'and sat awhile, then went to the Café Chantant. Six over and *under*-dressed women, ugly and impu-

dent (except one fat, pretty and bonne) singing comic songs
in a thin nasal manner, a robust tenor, a feeble tenor, and a
comic. Came away marvelling at what the crowd finds
"Pleasure".' Lewes has found Marian's displeasure catching, but at any rate they went, and she went under no sort
of compulsion.

Witley Heights was spacious, looked grand indeed, but
the surveyor, as is often the way, had been much too quick
to give the nod. Lewes's quick deal, with fifty pounds off,
proved for once to be a bad one. There was plenty wrong
with Witley Heights, and it was only after many months of
labouring and rehabilitating that they were able to use it
and nurse their renal troubles (Marian's) and gout troubles
(Lewes's) in reasonable comfort. Lewes started calling the
place 'Witley Cross'. This was one of his little jokes but it's
likely that he wasn't quite such a devotee of the Cross
family as she, so that his quip may have had a sharpish edge
to it.

Marian's wholehearted adoption of them is best explained by emphasising the fact that the Crosses were
outstandingly pious, outstandingly strait-laced. By now
she had achieved recognition almost everywhere – even by
a foreign queen – but there were still some circles, rich,
influential, orthodox and prim who wouldn't open their
doors to the author of *Middlemarch* and the translator of
Strauss's most unsuitable life of Jesus. The Crosses, amply
provided for, were accepted by and at home in groups of
this sort. To be welcomed, and indeed revered, by such a
family represented a kind of final breakthrough for Marian.
She valued the relationship highly on this account. For
Lewes there was no symbolic triumph in the relationship;
he liked Johnnie Cross well enough. He was someone to
talk to, someone to go on strolls with. And anyway he'd
trained himself to bear with people. Even Edith Simcox, for
whom his role must have been, in her eyes, that of frustrat-
ing, impassable guardian of the fortress, had to admit that
he possessed this gift.

Long after the event Edith was talking to Madonna's
great friend Mrs Richard Congreve who told her how
unhappy and irritable Marian had been at the time of the

great success of *Adam Bede*. Lewes had had to cope with depressive melancholy – try to explode it out of her – even at moments of great triumph. 'The fact,' says Edith, 'that She needed in some ways as much forbearance as she showed is a point to be remembered on Mr Lewes's side – he was not a mere recipient.' This is grudging, but the fact that she was prepared to concede anything at all to Lewes is a sign that here was a man who suffered long, bore much and grumbled little.

They were in by June 1877. Mr Hoole, an architect, had been busy, Lewes had been busy, Johnnie Cross had been helpful, and now they were there for the summer, and reasonably comfortable. There were visits from Tennyson over on his hill at Aldworth. He was fond of reading to them from *Maud*. He also read *The Northern Farmer* to them, and this must have been even more agreeable because Tennyson was very good at reading *The Northern Farmer*. Sometimes Tennyson's sister Matilda came along too, and annoyed him because she held what he felt to be foolish, sentimental, non-scientific views about vivisection. Johnnie Cross laid out a tennis lawn for them, and then a badminton court. He seems determined to keep them young in spirit – not that Lewes's frisky youthfulness ever failed him for long: he could be down and low one day and up ready to sing comic songs the next. By November 1877, when it was time to return to The Priory for the winter, Marian was able to say that they were at last 'in love with our Surrey house, and mean to keep it'. In the same note she said that the third volume of *Problems* had had a good reception and had 'sold satisfactorily for a book so little in the popular taste'. George was still having his headaches, but she doesn't sound in any way apprehensive about him; headaches after all had been nagging at him for twenty-five years.

Then, quite soon in 1878, he began to be troubled more seriously than usual by what Sir James Paget diagnosed as gout. But still they visited, were visited, and Lewes worked on at *Problems*, with the end in sight. In July, when they were back at Witley, Lewes described his way of life to Philip Hamerton. '. . . five weeks in our Paradise *without*

275

the serpent (symbol of visitors!) . . .' He vegetated mostly, so he said, but it was far from what most would care to call a vegetable existence. He was up at six and out for a stroll 'leaving Madonna in bed with Dante or Homer'. Then he smoked a cigar and did some reading. He also wrote a little. Marian kept at it till nearly lunchtime upstairs, satisfying her craving for knowledge, but she was down in time for them to play some tennis before luncheon. Then came the drive which lasted two or three hours. Then music and reading till dinner followed by a cigar and a nap. Then Marian read to him till ten, and after that, before bed, he did another hour's work. It hasn't the sound of a day in the life of a man seriously ill.

Sometimes he did the afternoon drive alone. He drove over to the Tennysons, for example, in a fierce summer storm. And there Tennyson read him parts of *Becket*, a drama not yet finished but one on which Tennyson wanted an experienced critical opinion – and what commentator more seasoned than Lewes? 'Greatly interested by many scenes of it,' Lewes noted afterwards, 'though I had some serious doubts which I did *not* express and some doubts which I did.' Lewes knew about plays like *Becket*. Sometimes Cross accompanied him on his drives and became aware that for all his perkiness, there might be something badly amiss with Lewes. He 'used sometimes to be suddenly seized with severe cramping pains . . . but the moment the pain ceased the extraordinary buoyancy of his spirits returned.' By October even Sir James Paget had given up being reassuring – except when faced with Marian. The consequences of not being reassuring in the company of Marian might have been dire indeed.

On November 22 Edith Simcox called. '. . . the first thing I saw was Lewes stretched upon a sofa, and in concern for him I lost something of the sight of her. He was affectionate, and when I said I wanted to kiss her feet he said he would let me do it as much as I liked – or – correcting himself – as much as she liked.' He could still be joky, still find some means of coping with this terrible woman. Turgenev, much concerned, had sent him some gout pills all the way from France ('Les capsules de François-Joseph'), but it was too late for capsules, too late for Sir James Paget. On November 30 Lewes died.

Marian was numb, suicidal.

On January 1 1879 she wrote one sentence in her diary: 'Here I and sorrow sit.' There was much of the parasite in her. She was like mistletoe. She needed a sturdy tree to grow and flower on.

AFTERMATH

After Lewes's death it looked for a while as though Marian would simply sit quietly down and will herself to join him. She refused to see people. One of the maids, Brett, reported to an excluded Edith Simcox that she had heard screaming coming from her mistress's bedroom. Sir James Paget, the Leweses' faithful, friendly though fallible physician, became much concerned at the way things were going, and then, for once, found a remedy that worked. Had not Mr Lewes died with his crowning masterpiece, *Problems of Life and Mind*, still unfinished? And was not she herself uniquely qualified to put the finishing touches to the toil of years and give his work to the world?

Immediately she was roused. Here was a task for which it was right that she should preserve herself, and her energies, to carry through. George would have wished it; furthermore, in that work she could take genuine pleasure, and immerse herself. Another accompanying idea sprang into her reactivated mind. George must be commemorated. It would be appropriate to found a George Henry Lewes Studentship in Physiology at Cambridge; and for this capital from the estate should be set aside. But here immediately was a problem. Lewes himself was comparatively poor. He had left a mere £2,000. The money, the real money, was Marian's, a fact which that calculating factor's daughter knew very well. But Lewes had always seen to everything. Marian's harvest of cheques, from Blackwood, from George Smith, had swelled his own account – and to say this isn't in any way to accuse him of anything fraudulent. It was how Marian had always wanted it to be. But now, with no Lewes at hand to write a signature, there would have to be much legal disentangling. This was a wearisome business, and indeed altogether too much for her. So how convenient in every way it was to have banker Johnnie Cross at call . . .

Altogether, in fact, there was much unfinished business to see to, and it was deplorable that a principled and strong minded woman should have so allowed personal grief to deflect her from it.

She was ill in February, but kept on, seeing very few people. Charles Lewes, her favourite proxy-son and always agreeable and biddable, was probably her strongest support at this time. In her autobiography, Edith Simcox says:

On Friday as I was going there [to The Priory on March 23 1879] I met Charles coming away and turned and went with him to the station. She has sent to the printer the first 'Problem' – about 200 pages, and is going to publish them in that way singly, not in large volumes. He rather negatived her being discouraged, but said it was well that it should be out of her hands, otherwise she only read it through and through, wondering if it was yet complete. He said she was always much exhausted after seeing anyone and never went himself the day anyone else did . . .

This last part of Charles's reported speech would have been warningly said. Knowing what Mutter would have wanted, he would have been disposed to hold Edith off by any tactful means at his disposal. But he doled out a few bits more of information to comfort her hunger. '. . . she had been much interested in arranging for a memorial endowment at Cambridge, about which she had been seeing two or three people – Sidgwick, Foster etc., besides Johnnie Cross about changing investments . . . She is going to try living at Witley this summer . . .' So perhaps Johnnie Cross was already beginning to take over the Lewesian role of guardianship – one which Charles, with his wife and young family, not to speak of his by now considerable responsibilities at the Post Office, would have been glad to be relieved of.

On April 29 Edith did manage to slip in, and Marian at last seemed ready to talk. She had clearly been going over and over her life with Lewes. She referred to the step they had taken, which, without injuring, perhaps favouring the work they could do best for other people, forced them to live for each other and in such complete independence of the outer world that the world could do nothing for them. She said it seemed a sort of dual egoism: but then again that it must surely be best to make the nearest relation perfect . . .

There were other meetings with Edith after this, distressful ones, punctuated by sobs, but all the same Marian had clearly by now overcome her despair. She had also been going through Lewes's papers and on May 16 1879 she wrote the one word 'Crisis' in her diary. Three days later, going through the fourth part of Lewes's *Problems* – the part where he is considering the question of remorse – she added lines from Wordsworth's 'Excursion' which speak of a man's marital infidelity. There are those who have been disposed to brood pretty intensely over these two Maytime moves of Marian's and to come up with a strong deduction. They support their suspicions with vinegary remarks made about Lewes, and Marian too, by Eliza Lynn Linton, that intelligent woman and good novelist who hated Lewes's bounce and envied Marian her huge success and her happy union with Lewes whilst her marriage to the journalist Linton, Lewes's old colleague, had gone wrong. They remember also Oscar Browning's mischief making hints in his *Life of George Eliot*, especially where, in commenting on *Romola*, he talks of Romola's passionate love for Tito turning suddenly to hate once she finds out that Tito has been unfaithful. This, Browning suggests, might well correspond 'to something which George Eliot probably found in her own nature . . .'

So what the deduction amounts to is that Lewes was a lustful little man who was unfaithful to his Madonna; this was her discovery as she went through his papers; this was what prompted her to put down the single, bitten off word 'Crisis' in her diary. The critic John Bayley writes*:

---

* In a review of two books on George Eliot in the *Times Literary Supplement* for July 23 1982.

. . . Great novelists must make use of their lives and those of other people on their own terms. Lawrence was well aware of Frieda's infidelities; George Eliot possibly only discovered about Lewes's after he died . . . George Eliot's revenges on the Rosamunds and Lydgates [in *Middlemarch*] show her up as much as does the fantasy life with Ladislaw, the perfect physical and intellectual helpmate; but, for a great novelist to be shown up in this way is a positive asset, and in George Eliot's case in particular it corrects the retributive majesty of the biographical approach . . .

Here, John Bayley is taking the unfaithful-lecherous-Lewes view as something to be regarded as a matter of fact. But the reaction to this must be: impossible to prove and virtually impossible to believe. Of course, Lewes, like most, had his lusty youth with affairs short rather than long. Marian would have known about these, as would Agnes. Would any note of them have appeared in his papers? This is possible though unlikely. Would Marian have been surprised, dismayed, if she had come upon any reference? Certainly not. She was a married woman with twenty-five years of experience; her own sexuality was strong and demanding; her 'liberated' views told her that the fleshly imperatives ought to be attended to – even though her strict and narrow upbringing might have given rise to distressful tensions in her. Was Lewes the first man she ever went to bed with? Or had Bray or Chapman, or Brabant even – all experienced Tarquins as they were – noticed that look in her eye? Impossible to say. But however it was, it's most unlikely that anything she may have discovered in Lewes's papers should have prompted her to that word 'Crisis'. The word is probably a private signal to herself that some time – not now, but in a little while – she would have to get finally and properly married and that she had a candidate in mind. That decision in no way diminished Lewes. Their alliance had been long, fruitful, faithful and loving: people are wonderfully complicated and surprising of course – the dead ones as well as the living – but this can stand as a certainty with far less shakiness than most. When she was writing *Middlemarch* she had Lewes very much in mind, especially when she was writing about Lydgate, the frustrated researcher. She says of him:

. . . All his faults . . . were those of a man who had a fine baritone, whose clothes hung well upon him, and who even in his ordinary gestures had an inbred air of distinction. Where then lay the spots of commonness? . . . How could there be any commonness in a man so well bred, so ambitious of social distinction, so generous in his views of social duty? . . . Lydgate's spots of commonness lay in the complexion of his prejudices . . .

She gets lovingly near to Lewes here – lovingly because there were 'spots of commonness' in Marian too. That was why they got on so snugly together all those years.

At the end of May 1879 she escaped to Witley, dodging Edith who planned to lie in wait and see her off at Waterloo. At Witley she had the comfort of Johnnie Cross close at hand, but it was the winding-up of Lewes's affairs which still pre-occupied her. James Sully (1842–1923), the philosopher and psychologist, was writing an obituary article on Lewes for the *New Quarterly Magazine*, and submitted his manuscript to her for approval. She made small criticisms, thinking particularly that Sully had underrated the commercial success which had greeted the *Life of Goethe* on its first appearance in Germany, and the large and genuine enthusiasm felt for it there.

Edith Simcox got down to Witley in late November, and by then Madonna was talking much of the 'wearisomeness of business and letters'. She had been aware for a very long time of all that Lewes had done for her, but now that awareness was being painfully rubbed in. She had been working at her own problems though, as well as Lewes's, and was coming close to decisions on how her life should go. Paget had prescribed a pint of champagne a day for her, a neck-or-nothing prescription perhaps but she'd profited from it. Herbert's widow Eliza had arrived from Natal the previous April and had been surprised by her cool reception at The Priory. At frequent intervals through the summer she read Dante with Cross in the Witley summer house and by October was able to tell Elma Stuart: '. . . My health is wonderfully better, and by dint of being better taken note of *medically*, I am really stronger . . .'

Did she owe this to Dante and Cross or to Paget and champagne? Whichever it was, two days later she wrote (October 16) a letter to Cross which was full of *vibrato*. It's also funny and sad, written perhaps when she'd exceeded Paget's prescribed champagne dosage, but at the end Warwickshire prudence and hard headedness do at least renew a partial grip on her. By the time she starts her second paragraph she has reached a cruising altitude.

> . . . Through everything else, dear tender one, there is the blessing of trusting in thy goodness. Thou dost not know anything of verbs in Hiphil and Hophal or the history of metaphysics or the position of Kepler in science, but thou knowest best things of another sort, such as belong to the manly heart – secrets of lovingness and rectitude. O I am flattering. Consider what thou wast a little time ago in pantaloons and back hair . . .

Is there a hint of Lewes-mockery here? If there is then beyond question she was drunk when she wrote it. She goes on:

> I shall think of thee this afternoon getting health at Lawn Tennis, and I shall reckon on having a letter by tomorrow's post.
> Why should I compliment myself at the end of my letter and say that I am faithful, loving, more anxious for thy life than mine? I will run no risks of being 'inexact' – so I will only say 'varium et mutabile semper' but at this moment thy tender Beatrice.

What would a normal, prosperous, thirty-nine year old banking man (unmarried) do on receiving such a letter from a woman of sixty-one? He would seek three months' leave of absence from his employers and make immediate enquiries about sailings to the Cape.

But by the following March Johnnie Cross was still in attendance, and it was becoming urgent that somehow she should find means to defend herself if not against the world in general, at any rate against Edith Simcox who was forceful and persistent as well as highly intelligent. On March 9 1880 there was a long tête-à-tête between the two.

> . . . I kissed her again and again, [says Edith] and murmured broken words of love. She bade me not exaggerate. I said I didn't, nor could, and then scolded her for being satisfied with letting me love her as I did . . . she said – expressly what she has often before implied to my distress – that the love of men and women for each other must always be more and better than any other . . . I hung over her caressingly and she bade me not to think too much of her . . . Then she said – Perhaps it would shock me – she had never all her life cared much for women . . . friendship and intimacy with men was more to her . . .

This was getting steamy, and Marian was determined to get out of the bathhouse. On April 9 1880 she wrote in her journal: 'Sir James Paget came to see me. My Marriage decided.' Sir James was sure her health would benefit from marriage, and couldn't see what harm might come to her literary standing from being legally married for the first time at the age of sixty-one.

Poor Sir James. How good he was at being wrong. Her literary reputation did start to slump. Edmund Gosse, for example, who had reached a position of considerable eminence as a literary pundit and arbitrator by the mid-1890s, could write at that time:

> George Eliot is a very curious example of the danger of self-cultivation. No writer was ever more anxious to improve herself and conquer an absolute mastery over her material. But she did not observe, as she entertained the laborious process, that she was losing those natural accomplishments which infinitely outshone the philosophy and science which she so painfully acquired. She

was born to please, but unhappily she persuaded herself, or was persuaded, that her mission was to teach the world, to lift its moral tone, and, in consequence, an agreeable rustic writer, with charming humour and very fine sympathetic nature, found herself gradually uplifted until, about 1875, she sat enthroned on an educational tripod, an almost ludicrous pythoness . . .

Plenty of people shook their heads quite vigorously over the decision. Close women friends like Maria Congreve, Elma Stuart and Lady Georgiana Burne-Jones were much upset. Henry James's sister Alice thought it was a betrayal of 'the much-mentioned "perfect love" of the past'.

But the ever faithful Barbara Bodichon backed her, and, in any event, Marian's very strong mind was made up. This was going to be not a betrayal but a continuation. She was always earthy and unflinching as well as feminine and clinging. Johnnie Cross would do.

There can be no doubt that it was she who made the running – though it was only seemly that he, as a man, should do the actual asking. He was tactful, reverent and scared out of his mind. In June, in Venice, on their honeymoon, he tried to commit suicide by jumping out of their hotel bedroom into the Grand Canal. They fished him out and after that he seemed to settle, and all apparently went well, though as a writer George Eliot was finished.

She found abundant consolation for this drying up because she got a brief note – through his solicitor – from Brother Isaac, congratulating her upon her renunciation of impropriety. She answered at length, though she was never to be reunited with him. That didn't matter; she had once again become part of the old days at Griff. She would put his note somewhere safe and then be ready – quite soon, indeed after only seven months, in December 1880 – to be hauled in the hearse through the winter slush up the hill to Highgate, there to rejoin George Lewes.

INDEX

288

Stuart, Elma, 248–51, 266
Syme, James, 8

Tennyson, Alfred, 275–6
Trollope, Anthony, 3, 9, 207, 214

Vivian (GHL), 2, 73ff, 76, 93, 96

Westminster Review, 34, 57, 87, 88, 91, 94
Willemer, Marianne, 139
Willim, Captain, 10, 11, 192, 207, 223
Witley Heights, 274–5

Young Germany, 23

LEE COUNTY LIBRARY
107 HAWKINS AVE.
SANFORD, N. C. 27330

LEE COUNTY LIBRARY SYSTEM

3 3262 00018 3589

B
Lewes
Williams
Williams, David
    Mr. George Eliot

DATE DUE			
OCT 11 '84			
NOV 12 '84			
Feb Ke 84			
JAN 8 1988			

828
W
Williams

Mr. George Eliot

LEE COUNTY LIBRARY
107 HAWKINS AVE.
SANFORD, N. C. 27330